THE OXFORD INTERNATIONAL RELATIONS IN SOUTH ASIA SERIES

SERIES EDITORS
Sumit Ganguly and E. Sridharan

After a long period of relative isolation during the Cold War years, contemporary South Asia has grown immensely in its significance in the global political and economic order. This ascendancy has two key dimensions. First, the emergence of India as a potential economic and political power that follows its acquisition of nuclear weapons and its fitful embrace of economic liberalization. Second, the persistent instability along India's borders continues to undermine any attempts at achieving political harmony in the region: fellow nuclear-armed state Pakistan is beset with chronic domestic political upheavals; Afghanistan is paralysed and trapped with internecine warfare and weak political institutions; Sri Lanka is confronted by an uncertain future with a disenchanted Tamil minority; Nepal is caught in a vortex of political and legal uncertainty as it forges a new constitution; and Bangladesh is overwhelmed by a tumultuous political climate.

India's rising position as an important player in global economic and political affairs warrants extra-regional and international attention. The rapidly evolving strategic role and importance of South Asia in the world demands focused analyses of foreign and security policies within and towards the region. The present series addresses these concerns. It consists of original, theoretically grounded, empirically rich, timely, and topical volumes oriented towards contemporary and future developments in one of the most populous and diverse corners of the world.

Sumit Ganguly is Professor of Political Science and holds the Rabindranath Tagore Chair in Indian Cultures and Civilizations, Indiana University, Bloomington, USA.

E. Sridharan is Academic Director, University of Pennsylvania Institute for the Advanced Study of India, New Delhi.

irsa

THE OXFORD INTERNATIONAL RELATIONS IN SOUTH ASIA SERIES

Heading East

Security, Trade, and Environment between India and Southeast Asia

edited by

Karen Stoll Farrell
Sumit Ganguly

OXFORD
UNIVERSITY PRESS

Oxford University Press is a department of the University of Oxford.
It furthers the University's objective of excellence in research, scholarship,
and education by publishing worldwide. Oxford is a registered trademark of
Oxford University Press in the UK and in certain other countries

Published in India by
Oxford University Press
22 Workspace, 2nd Floor, 1/22 Asaf Ali Road, New Delhi 110002, India

ISBN-13: 978-0-19-946724-2
ISBN-10: 0-19-946724-2

Typeset in Adobe Garamond Pro 11/13
by The Graphics Solution, New Delhi 110 092
Printed in India by Manipal Technologies Limited, Manipal

To Justin, without whom the Farrells would truly be feral
—Karen Stoll Farrell

To my mother, Nandini Ganguly
—Sumit Ganguly

Contents

List of Figures   vii

Acknowledgements   ix

List of Abbreviations   xi

Introduction: India and Southeast Asia   1
Karen Stoll Farrell and *Sumit Ganguly*

I Security

1. India and the East: Connectivity Begins at Home   11
   David J. Karl

2. ASEAN–India Cooperation in Counterterrorism:
   Evolution and Future   53
   Julio S. Amador III

3. India's Engagement with Myanmar: Regional Security
   Implications of Acting East Slowly   69
   Jonah Blank

4. The Indo-Myanmar Border and India's Security
   Problems in the East   90
   Bertil Lintner

5. Making People's Voices Count: Northeast India
   and Its Neighbourhood   108
   Sanjoy Hazarika

II Trade

6. India and the Potential of Trade East   127
   Rani D. Mullen

7. India and RCEP: Challenges and Opportunities of
   Opening Up the Farm/Food Sector   148
   Surupa Gupta

8. Motor Vehicle Movement and Standards between
   Bangladesh and India: Regional Connectivity and Trade   170
   Bipul Chatterjee and *Prithviraj Nath*

III Environment

9. Regional Integration and Its Discontents: The Case of
   Transboundary Water Sharing   195
   Douglas P. Hill

10. Governance, Connectivity, and Knowledge Transparency
    in the Brahmaputra Basin   216
    Kelly D. Alley

11. Pulses against Volumes: Transboundary Rivers
    and Pan-Asian Connectivity   240
    Rohan D'Souza

Index   254
Notes on Editors and Contributors   271

Figures

3.1 Myanmar's Bilateral Trade with India and China   76

3.2 Myanmar Arms Purchases from Top 7 Suppliers, 1990–2014   80

3.3 Arms Sales to Myanmar by Year   84

6.1 Map of India and the 15 Trade East Countries   130

6.2 India's Top 12 Trading Partners, 1997–8 versus 2014–15 (April–February)   131

6.3 India's Trade East (with ASEAN–BIMSTEC–China) in U.S.$ million between 1997–8 and 2014–15   132

10.1 Status of Hydropower Projects in the Northeastern Brahmaputra Basin as of 2013   222

10.2 Constructed, Under Construction, and Proposed Dams in Lower Tibet, Arunachal Pradesh, and Assam as of January 2015   223

10.3 Map of Road Projects in Arunachal Pradesh and Assam   226

10.4 Sediment in the Brahmaputra River near Dibrugarh   227

10.5 Bridge Destroyed by Flooding in a Tributary of the Siang River   228

10.6 A Ferry Boat Crossing the Brahmaputra River   229

10.7 The Staff of Brahmaputra Radio in Dibrugarh   230

Acknowledgements

A T THE OUTSET, we wish to thank the U.S. Department of State which provided support for this project through the underwriting of an author's conference held in Kolkata in March 2015. Several individuals at the U.S. Consulate General in Kolkata were especially helpful in organizing the conference. To that end we acknowledge the sterling efforts of Helen LaFave, the then Consul General; Craig Hall, the present Consul General; Gaurav Bansal, the Political and Economic Affairs Officer; Joanne Joria and Andrew Posner, Public Affairs Officers; Greg Pardo, the Assistant Public Affairs Officer; Diya Erica Basu, the Chief of the Media Section; and Sameek Ghosh, the Public Affairs Specialist, respectively, at the Consulate. We would be remiss if we did not acknowledge the generosity of the Honorable Richard Verma, the United States Ambassador to India, who, despite myriad and pressing commitments, chose to give the keynote address at this conference. We would also like to thank Walter Douglas, the then Minister Counsellor for Public Affairs at U.S. Embassy New Delhi, for his vision and constant support.

Separately, we wish to thank Samir Saran and Abhijit Mitra-Iyer of the Observer Research Foundation, New Delhi, for their excellent partnership which made the conference possible. Dr Rakhahari Chatterjee, an Advisor to ORF- Calcutta, also proved to be of immense assistance in organizing the conference. We also wish to thank the management and staff of the Oberoi Grand Hotel for their excellent service during the conference.

Finally, a special thanks to Hannah Carter and Brandon Miliate for their editing assistance.

Abbreviations

ACCT	ASEAN Convention on Counter-Terrorism
ADB	Asian Development Bank
ADDs	Abu Dhabi Dialogues
ADMM+8	ASEAN Defence Ministers' Meeting+8
APLAC	Asia Pacific Laboratory Accreditation Cooperation
ATTF	All Tripura Tigers Force
ACFTA	ASEAN–China Free Trade Area
ARF	ASEAN Regional Forum
ASBM	anti-ship ballistic missiles
ASEAN	Association of Southeast Asian Nations
AFSPA	Armed Forces (Special Powers) Act
AMPC	ASEAN Master Plan for Connectivity
BBIN	Bangladesh, Bhutan, India, and Nepal
BCIM	Bangladesh, China, India, and Myanmar
BIB	Bhutan–India–Bangladesh
BIMSTEC	Bay of Bengal Initiative for Multi-Sectoral Technical and Economic Cooperation
BJP	Bharatiya Janata Party
CEA	Central Electricity Authority
CECA	Comprehensive Economic Cooperation Agreement
CISMHE	Centre for Inter-Disciplinary Studies of Mountain and Hill Environment
CWC	Central Water Commission
DGFI	Directorate General of Field Intelligence
DPR	detailed project report
EAC	Expert Appraisal Committee
EAS	East Asia Summit
EU	European Union
EIA	environmental impact assessment

FAC	Forest Advisory Committee
FDI	foreign direct investment
FSSAI	Food Safety and Standards Authority of India
FTA	free trade agreement
GIS	Geographic Informations Systems
GMS CBTA	Greater Mekong Subregional Cross-Border Transport Agreement
GNLA	Garo National Liberation Army
GTAP	Global Trade Analysis Project
HS	Harmonized System
ICD	Inland Container Depot
ICP	integrated check post
ILAC	International Laboratory Accreditation Cooperation
IMG	Inter-Ministerial Group
IPPC	International Plant Protection Convention
ISI	Inter Services Intelligence
JICA	Japan International Cooperation Agency
JWGs	joint working groups
KIA	Kachin Independence Army
KLO	Kamatapur Liberation Organization
ICIMOD	International Centre for Integrated Mountain Development
IUCN	International Union for Conservation of Nature
LoC	line of credit
LPDR	Lao People's Democratic Republic
LSHPP	Lower Subansiri Hydroelectric Power Project
MoEFCC	Ministry of Environment, Forests, and Climate Change
MPAC	Master Plan on ASEAN Connectivity
MRA	Mutual Recognition Arrangement
MRC	Mekong River Commission
NABCB	National Accreditation Board for Certification Bodies
NABL	National Accreditation Board for Testing and Calibration Laboratories
NCA	Nationwide Ceasefire Agreement
NDA	National Democratic Alliance
NDFB	National Democratic Front of Bodoland
NEMA	National Environmental Management Agency
NGO	non-governmental organization
NHPC	National Hydroelectric Power Corporation

NIB	Nepal–India–Bangladesh
NIIF	National Investment and Infrastructure Fund
NLFT	National Liberation Front of Tripura
NPG	Naga Political Groups
NSCN	Nationalist Socialist Council of Nagaland
NSCN-IM	Nationalist Socialist Council of Nagalim-Isaac and Muivah
NTB	non-tariff barrier
OIE	World Organization for Animal Health (translated to English)
OECD	Organisation for Economic Co-operation and Development
PPA	Power Purchasing Agreement
PPP	public–private partnership
PRC	People's Republic of China
PSI	pre-shipment inspection
QCI	Quality Council of India
RCEP	Regional Comprehensive Economic Partnership
SAARC	South Asian Association for Regional Cooperation
SADC	Southern African Development Community
SAGQ	South Asian Growth Quadrangle
SARSO	South Asian Regional Standards Organization
SASEC	South Asia Subregional Economic Cooperation
SAWI	South Asia Water Initiative
SEATO	Southeast Asia Treaty Organization
SEMA	State Environmental Management Agency
SIA	Social Impact Assessments
SIPRI	Stockholm International Peace Research Institute
SLORC	State Law and Order Restoration Council
SPS	sanitary and phyto-sanitary
TEC	Techno-Economic Clearance
TPP	Trans Pacific Partnership
TTIP	Transatlantic Trade and Investment Partnership
ULFA	United Liberation Front of Asom
UNFCCC	United Nations Framework Convention on Climate Change
UNLF	United National Liberation Front
UWSA	United Wa State Army
WTO	World Trade Organization

Introduction

India and Southeast Asia

Karen Stoll Farrell and Sumit Ganguly

During much of the cold war India's policymakers chose to ignore the bulk of the states of Southeast Asia. The reasons for this neglect were relatively straightforward. Prime Minister Nehru's initial hopes of Asian solidarity in the wake of the collapse of European colonialism failed to materialize after the famous Bandung Conference of 1955, around when the Cold War entered the region as a consequence of the US–Pakistan military alliance of 1954. The vast majority of the states of Southeast Asia who feared Communist penetration chose to cast their lot with the United States. The US promotion of various military alliances, most notably the Southeast Asia Treaty Organization (which its implacable adversary Pakistan joined), further alienated India from the region.

India, which under Nehru's tutelage had self-consciously chosen to pursue a foreign policy based on the principle of nonalignment, thereby failed to make common cause with the US-aligned states. Not surprisingly, diplomatic relations with most of these states remained largely perfunctory.

Apart from the adoption of nonalignment, India's foreign economic policies also isolated it from Southeast Asia. It embraced an autarchic economic development strategy based upon import-substituting industrialization and thereby cut itself off from the global market.

Finally, the US involvement in the Vietnam War and India's staunch opposition to the conflict placed it even further at odds with the bulk of the states of Southeast Asia. Later, India's forthright support for the Vietnamese invasion of Cambodia, which led to the overthrow of the genocidal Pol Pot regime, brought it into further conflict with the Association of Southeast Asian Nations (ASEAN). The ASEAN member states, fearful of the possibilities of the expansion of Soviet-backed Vietnamese power, chose to simply uphold the principle of sovereignty and overlook the untold brutality of the Pol Pot regime.

Indeed it was not until the Cold War's end that India did finally turn to the region in any meaningful fashion. This shift came about as a consequence of India's gradual termination of its state-led strategy of economic development in the wake of an unprecedented fiscal crisis. Along with fitful attempts at ending the state's stranglehold of the economy, India's policymakers, most notably prime minister Narasimha Rao and the then finance minister, Manmohan Singh, also sought to reduce tariff barriers and attract foreign investment.

It was in this context that Rao launched his well-known 'Look East' policy designed to court the vibrant economies of the region. The crux of this policy was designed to attract investment from the states of Southeast Asia, to obtain access to their markets, and to boost trade. Subsequent to the announcement of this policy in 1995 India was made a full 'dialogue partner' of ASEAN.

Apart from its enhanced status within ASEAN, India also launched a series of other multilateral initiatives designed to foster trade, travel, and other connections with the region. This is not the place to provide an exhaustive account of all the efforts that have been undertaken; however, a few salient endeavours should be highlighted. Prominent amongst these were the Bay of Bengal Initiative for Multi-Sectoral Technical and Economic Cooperation (BIMSTEC), the Mekong–Ganga Cooperation Initiative, and the India–ASEAN Free Trade Agreement. All of these, while worthwhile endeavours, have yet to deliver fully on their promise. At the moment they all remain in an incipient stage. These particular efforts at outreach towards Southeast Asia, along with others, are discussed in more detail in the various substantive chapters of this volume.

Since assuming office in May 2014, Prime Minister Narendra Modi has sought to build upon the erstwhile 'Look East' policy, changing the nomenclature to an 'Act East' policy. Two factors seem to be motivating the new regime as it seeks to bolster ties to the region. The first is simply a continuation of past policies. India seeks markets in the region and wishes to attract capital and investment from it. The second, though mostly unstated, has to do with its concerns about China's rise. To that end Prime Minister Modi has sought to strengthen existing ties with Vietnam, where India has significant offshore investments in hydrocarbons. He has also sought to expand India's infrastructural investments in Myanmar, and has attempted to strengthen both business and defence ties with Singapore.

The chapters in this volume examine the overarching trajectory of India's expanding ties to Southeast Asia, but also focus on more specific elements of this developing relationship. To that end the chapters deal with questions of security ties, trade expansion, and physical connectivity.

Part One of this volume contains five chapters relevant to security concerns for India and its eastern neighbours. The first two describe India's relationship with the Southeast Asian nations that make up ASEAN. Following this, two additional chapters focus specifically on the history and difficulties regarding India's relationship with Myanmar. Finally, the last chapter in the security section focuses more directly on India's northeast region as it relates to security concerns and India's relationships with closely neighbouring countries.

In Chapter One, entitled 'India and the East: Connectivity Begins at Home,' David J. Karl provides a trove of detail on the history of India's relationship, as an independent nation, with the ASEAN region. From Nehru to Modi, Karl paints a clear picture of the points at which India's promises have far outreached their implementation. The author describes a history of policymaking in India that has created this issue by making vague, sweeping statements that fail to become strategic goals.

Karl gives detailed historical and contemporary examples of India's lack of implementation as they specifically relate to its northeastern region and to ASEAN. The author looks at the recent history of trade and infrastructure problems as evidence for the challenges that India will continue to have in the security arena. India must find a way to move beyond its implementation difficulties within its own domestic political sphere if it is to successfully reach its potential for greater engagement with ASEAN.

In Chapter Two, Julio S. Amador continues the discussion of India's relationship with ASEAN in terms of counterterrorism efforts, taking into account the limitations of the ASEAN model. In this chapter, Amador provides an overview of ASEAN's counterterrorism efforts and recent policy developments. While the author sees limitations to the ASEAN policy in terms of regional level action, there are a number of bilateral agreements that India has taken up which can be built into regional cooperation. In other words, the ASEAN counterterrorism policy essentially places the onus of action back onto its member-states. There can be a way forward, however, if India is able to build its separate bilateral counterterrorism ties with ASEAN nations into a regional group. Ultimately, Amador sees a long road but also reason for optimism in building cooperative counterterrorism efforts between India and the ASEAN nations.

The third chapter, by Jonah Blank, moves to a consideration of India's relationship with Myanmar and its security implications. In the independent histories of India and Myanmar, Blank describes the disparities in perceptions about the nations' relationship from each side of the border. While the Indian view calls up long-standing cultural similarities and early support for Burmese democracy, the Myanmar view of India remembers India's later support for the military junta, and a general lack of engagement.

Despite the differing viewpoints, the author sees strong potential for deepening ties between the two countries moving forward, provided that India is able to make some changes domestically. Once again, India's lack of strategic goal-setting and implementation is a major challenge. While Blank asserts that there are some recent changes in place that make engagement less difficult, it is clear that India still has to overcome a history of inaction in order to Act East.

In Chapter Four, Bertil Lintner takes a closer look at security issues along the border between India and Myanmar. The author outlines four critical motivations for India to build its relationship with Myanmar, from its interest in trade development in Southeast Asia and with Myanmar specifically, to rebel security issues that cross the border, to the challenges of China's role in the region.

Rather than focus on India's domestic political problems, Lintner explores the past difficulties faced by India's Look East initiatives because of Myanmar's troubled recent history. In addition, the author highlights the role that China has played, and Myanmar's own changing relationship with the superpower. Lintner finds a critical need for India to actively engage with Myanmar to promote peace in the area if India is to build a long-standing, successful relationship with its eastern neighbours.

Finally, Sanjoy Hazarika considers the unrest and insurgencies along the border of India and Myanmar from the perspective of India's northeastern region. He first reviews the history of divisions along ethnic lines, and the ways in which the violent history of Partition has led to the region's current problems. Hazarika highlights some of the various insurgencies and current parties involved in the unrest, as well as central government activities that have exacerbated issues rather than resolve them. In the end, the author looks to the need for local connectivity and peace-processes that must occur before India can move beyond to broader relationships with its neighbours in ASEAN.

Part Two is focused on India's trade with the East, and includes three chapters that discuss multiple levels of the issue. From Mullen's broad overview, to Gupta's examination of the agricultural sector, to Chatterjee and Nath's detailed explanation of overland border points, each chapter ultimately circles around three major challenges that India faces in trying to develop trade with its eastern neighbours. Rani Mullen highlights these barriers succinctly as 'non-tariff barriers, lack of infrastructure, and the need for political resolutions to lingering border issues'.

In Chapter Six, Rani D. Mullen provides a background of recent developments in India's trade with its eastern neighbours, and lays out the potential challenges and critical needs in order for India to move forward with an Act East Policy relevant to trade. Although changes have occurred since the creation of India's Look East policy in 1991, it is also clear that in many ways this policy has not led to an overall blossoming of trade with the East and that trade with neighbouring Southeast Asian countries continues to represent only a small percentage of India's total trade. However, because of the Look East Policy, India has engaged in a number of free trade agreements (FTAs) with its eastern neighbours over the last two decades through both regional associations and bilateral agreements. Mullen highlights four regional and two bilateral agreements that have been critical in some way, and in each case explains the significant potential that the agreement offers to both India and the partnering countries as a foundation for future development and growth.

As Mullen points out, each of these agreements, and any potential future trade arrangements that India seeks with its eastern neighbours, will ultimately come upon three significant hurdles: non-tariff barriers, a lack of infrastructure, and political border issues. It will be critical for India to seek solutions to these issues at the national level in order to successfully implement trade through the Act East policy.

In Chapter Seven, India's possibilities for trade are examined more closely within one particular sector. Surupa Gupta explores India's agricultural trade potential within the Regional Comprehensive Economic Partnership (RCEP) which, once fully implemented, will become the largest FTA worldwide. After providing some background to the creation of the RCEP, Gupta calls attention to a number of broad-based opportunities that it can offer to India.

Of course, India will have to contend with a number of challenges as well. Historically, India has avoided bilateral trade with China, which this agreement ostensibly creates. In addition to the regional political issues, these challenges are expressly connected to India's defensive response to international trade within the agricultural sector in particular, as it has a vested interest, both politically and economically, to stabilize the many players within this large sector.

As Gupta asserts, India's protectionist stance, coupled with a lack of economic transformation in manufacturing or other sectors that could provide job growth, has led to an 'insufficient transformation' of the agricultural sector. In a theme that continues to arise regarding India's trade, Gupta looks to the lack of technology and infrastructure within the sector, along with a hodge-podge of reforms across the country that have created barriers to trade. Ultimately, Gupta calls for further liberalization of India's agricultural sector in order to boost its role in international trade.

In the final chapter on India's trade with Southeast Asia, the themes of infrastructural and policy reform challenges continue to arise. Bipul Chatterjee and Prithviraj Nath closely examine India's overland bilateral trade with Bangladesh which is dominated by agricultural and textile exports from India. Once again, this trade is plagued by infrastructural barriers, and a conglomeration of reforms and policies that create additional barriers to India's trade with its neighbours to the east.

The authors provide detailed examples of the current problems that plague the border points along trade routes, citing a number of commonly traded goods between the two countries that require additional certifications and safety testing standards that add to the complications at the ground level. The protectionist bent of agricultural trade in India is in full evidence here.

Finally, Chatterjee and Nath put forth the now familiar calls to action: a harmonization of standards and policies, work on infrastructure and a few related technologies, and political cooperation at multiple levels to streamline processes.

Part Three of the volume revolves around issues pertaining broadly to the environment, and more specifically to water issues. The question of what ought to drive the development of hydropower projects in the transboundary rivers of northeast India and its eastern neighbours defines much of the discussion taken up by the three authors writing on critical water issues. Each of them comes to the question from a different angle, but ultimately reaches a similar place: namely that current methods of infrastructure development in these rivers must be modified to address regulatory issues, and that there must be greater participation in the development process granted to both local and regional stakeholders.

In Chapter Nine, Douglas P. Hill offers a framework for the difficulties associated with transboundary water sharing in the region, pointing out that water issues are increasingly viewed from a security standpoint. As this viewpoint overtakes all other concerns, a multitude of environmental, social, and economic challenges that must be considered are left out of the conversation. Additionally, Hill emphasizes that traditional top-down infrastructure development that has been used by the government of India in the past in order to complete these projects, coupled with singularly focused security concerns, has created problematic hydropower development that negatively affects local populations and erodes not only their trust, but also the trust of neighbouring nations.

The author, however, also indicates examples in the region where the beginnings of change may be seen. These are arrangements where a few mechanisms have been put in place, and where some dialogue has begun that could increase the transparency of the development process, building trust with local populations and neighbouring countries. These examples also point to the possibilities for inclusion of local stakeholders, allowing them to reap some of the benefits that arise from hydropower development. Hill is aware of the many benefits that may be derived from building such infrastructure, but ultimately cautions that future developments must change course, in terms of both transparency and stakeholder participation, in order to accommodate the multiple challenges of transboundary water sharing.

In the following chapter, Kelly D. Alley examines closely related issues of transboundary water development as it relates specifically to the Brahmaputra river basin in northeastern India. Alley expands on issues of governance, transparency, and local stakeholder participation through an examination of water and related infrastructure development projects in this region.

First, the author explains the recent government changes to project approvals and planning that have had significant effects on development in the Brahmaputra region. While these processes are often changed ostensibly to streamline projects in public interest, Alley explores the ways in which this top-down style of governance has ignored the needs and interests of local populations. From agriculture to communication to roadways, local needs are not a consideration of larger developmental projects. She also points to massively scaled projects in the northeast that involve India and China, in which lack of transparency on both sides of the border will continue to hinder these water projects.

Alley indicates a number of considerations that ought to be brought to bear on large-scale water development, including specific considerations for local practices and ways of life. However, the interests of local stakeholders can only be met through increased governmental transparency and participation from the local stakeholders themselves.

The final chapter of this volume continues the theme of addressing the problems of social, political, and economic concerns. Rohan D'Souza further explores the problems inherent in top-down style developmental projects. Rather than point to security-focused development or to governance issues, however, D'Souza problematizes infrastructural development as a financial investment scheme. Here, profit-making becomes the driving force for these projects, to the detriment of environmental and other interests.

D'Souza's conclusions, however, ultimately align clearly with Hill's and Alley's: in order to successfully achieve pan-Asian connectivity through transboundary water development projects, local stakeholders' worldviews, ways of life, and local knowledge must be taken into account. Their participation and points of view will offer further insight into the social, political, and economic issues, so that the benefits of development are shared amongst not only multiple nations, but by the multiple local populations as well.

I

Security

1   India and the East

Connectivity Begins at Home

David J. Karl

Undoubtedly in the future [India] will have to play a very great part in security problems of Asia and the Indian Ocean, more especially of the Middle East and South-East Asia. Indeed, India is the pivot around which these problems will have to be considered...India is the centre of security in Asia.

—Jawaharlal Nehru, Ministry of External Affairs memorandum,
5 September 1946

It is fitting that India should play her part in this new phase of Asian development. Apart from the fact that India herself is emerging into freedom and independence, she is the natural center and focal point of the many forces at work in Asia. Geography is a compelling factor, and geographically she is so situated as to be the meeting point of western and northern and eastern and southeast Asia.

—Jawaharlal Nehru, remarks to the Asian Relations Conference,
23 March 1947

I do not pretend to say that India, as she is, can make a vital difference to world affairs. So long as we have not solved most of our own problems, our voice cannot carry the weight that it normally will and should.

—Jawaharlal Nehru, remarks to the Indian Parliament,
17 March 1950[1]

NEHRU'S REMARKS ABOVE ILLUSTRATE a central contradiction regarding India's role in Asia—grand ambitions and high-minded sentiments are frequently hobbled by internal deficiencies and the lack of credible follow-through. This condition once again came into view in December 2012 as the top leaders from all of the 10 member states of the Association of Southeast Asian Nations (ASEAN) gathered in New Delhi. The special two-day event, hailed as a 'Commemorative Summit' to mark the 20th anniversary of New Delhi's formal engagement with the regional grouping, effectively served as a review session for India's so-called 'Look East' policy, its long-term effort beginning in the early 1990s to expand ties with its eastern neighbours. Indian officials at the event had good reason to take pride in their accomplishments over the previous two decades. Since 1993, when India began interacting in the fields of trade, investment, tourism, and science and technology, the extent of its dealings with ASEAN had increasingly broadened and deepened, first in the economic domain and then in the security realm. It graduated to across-the-board dialogue partner status in 1995 (a few months ahead of China being accorded this status); joined the ASEAN Regional Forum the following year; was elevated to a summit-level partner (on the same level as China, Japan, and South Korea) in 2002; was part of the founding membership of the East Asia Summit in 2005; joined the Asia–Europe Meeting (ASEM) mechanism in 2006; and two years later participated in the inaugural meeting of the ASEAN Defence Ministers' Meeting + 8 forum (ADMM+8), which involves all ASEAN member states and eight extra-regional powers.

Singapore's elder statesmen had long been vocal enthusiasts for India assuming a larger regional role. The legendary Lee Kuan Yew affirmed the need for New Delhi to be 'part of the Southeast Asia balance of forces', and Goh Chok Tong, the city-state's Prime Minister from 1990 to 2004, routinely referred to ASEAN as a jumbo jet, with China and India comprising its wings (Suryanarayana 2011). The presence of both, Goh said, was necessary to give the region lift and stability. ASEAN countries had also rebuffed Beijing's efforts to build exclusivist institutions designed to box out New Delhi from regional decision-making. Indeed, when China succeeded in keeping New Delhi out of the ASEAN + 3 grouping, Singapore and Indonesia backed the creation of the annual series of summit meetings between India and ASEAN (Brewster 2011: 231).

This trajectory illustrated India's success in overcoming the initial doubts within ASEAN over its relevance to East Asia and whether it even deserved a seat at the region's high tables, a point that was underscored at the Commemorative Summit when the Southeast Asian leaders called for a greater Indian profile in the region in order to offset China's growing economic clout and military capabilities. The run-up to the meeting featured mounting regional concern about Beijing's assertiveness in the South China Sea, which had erupted into the open at an ASEAN leadership meeting just a month earlier in Phnom Penh (Bland 2012; *South China Morning Post* 2012; and Szep and Pomfret 2012). Indian Prime Minister Manmohan Singh was responsive to these anxieties when he stated at the Commemorative Summit that 'the India-ASEAN engagement began with a strong economic emphasis, but it is also becoming increasingly strategic'. Referring obliquely to Chinese behaviour, he added that 'India and ASEAN nations should intensify their engagement for maritime security and safety, for freedom of navigation and for peaceful settlement of maritime disputes in accordance with international law' (Colvin 2012; Mallet 2012). Indeed, a few weeks before the session, the chief of the Indian navy proclaimed New Delhi's readiness to use military force to defend the freedom of navigation and protect its oil-exploration interests in an area off the coast of Vietnam that China claims as its own (Pandit 2012; *Reuters* 2012).[2] Significantly, at the summit Singh invoked the geopolitical portmanteau of 'Indo-Pacific', a nomenclature signifying the tight security and economic connections between the Indian Ocean and Asia–Pacific theatres (Bagchi 2012).[3] The term had been given currency by Japanese Prime Minister Shinzo Abe five years earlier when he was courting India as a strategic partner, and has since been picked up by U.S. policymakers and strategists focused on New Delhi's participation in Washington's 'strategic rebalance' in Asia.[4]

The Commemorative Summit's concluding statement announced plans for a new 'strategic partnership' aimed at enhanced diplomatic, economic, and security cooperation between India and ASEAN, and hailed the conclusion of a new trade in services and investment accord that complemented a trade agreement on goods that took effect three years earlier. It endorsed the Trilateral Highway, an ambitious project to develop a modern road system linking India's northeastern region to Myanmar and Thailand, as well as its extension to Laos and Cambodia. It further called for a new highway project connecting India–Myanmar–Laos–Vietnam–Cambodia, as well as developing the Mekong–India Economic Corridor ('Vision Statement ASEAN–India Commemorative Summit' 2012). As a way of emphasizing the growing physical connectivity between India and the ASEAN states, the summit even featured the ceremonial closing of an 8,000-kilometre car rally that began a month earlier in Indonesia.

But if the summit served as an endorsement of the 'Look East' policy's aims, it also took place against the backdrop of regional doubts about the calibre of India's engagement with Southeast Asia. New Delhi's approach had long been plagued by complaints within ASEAN about its policy constancy and resource commitments. In mid-2007, a senior Vietnamese foreign ministry official cautioned that China was stealing a march on India, warning that 'the dragon is scratching away and the elephant must move fast' (PTI 2007). This view surfaced more explicitly during a September 2009 conversation in which a top Singaporean diplomat, who was then co-chairing the India–Singapore strategic dialogue, described New Delhi to U.S. officials as 'half in, half out' of ASEAN institutions, contrasted India's 'stupid' diplomacy in the region with China's 'intelligent' course, and noted that the country failed to match its rhetoric about looking eastward with corresponding actions (Suryanarayana 2010). A former Indian foreign secretary who had served in the area more tactfully conceded this point when he wrote that the sentiment in most of Southeast Asia was 'that India was not doing enough to establish a much stronger presence in the region'.[5]

Nor were these doubts confined to Southeast Asia. Seeking to firm up Washington's own strategic partnership with New Delhi, President Barack Obama, during his November 2010 visit to India, encouraged the country's leaders not only to 'look east' but also 'to engage east' for the sake of enhanced security and prosperity throughout Asia (Obama 2010). Secretary of State Hillary Rodham Clinton underscored this theme in her visit to India in July 2011. Speaking in Chennai, a port city that has significant economic ties with Southeast Asia, she urged India to take on a larger role in shaping the regional architecture for the Asia–Pacific. Reiterating Obama's formulation, Clinton stated that 'we encourage India not just to look East, but to engage East and act East as well' (Clinton 2011).[6]

Although the ASEAN leaders assembled in New Delhi hailed the free trade agreements (FTAs) reached with India, they no doubt were mindful of the arduous process entailed in their creation as well as other instances in which Indian action failed to measure up to its rhetoric. The trade in goods agreement originated in a bold proposal by the then prime minister A.B. Vajpayee, issued at the inaugural ASEAN–India summit in

November 2002. Six years of difficult negotiations ensued, mainly due to the recalcitrance of the Indian commerce ministry. An Indian diplomat involved in the process recalls that New Delhi's stance in the talks in large measure 'focused on the damage that the FTA would cause to the Indian business community...' He added that the 'positions taken by the Ministry of Commerce appeared as if they (and the Indian business community) were being taken to the slaughter and how India had little to gain from the FTA' (Ravi 2012: 181).[7]

Given India's difficulties in building robust connectivity inside the country or even with its immediate neighbours, doubts must similarly have occurred to the ASEAN leaders in New Delhi about the prospects for developing strong transport linkages to states farther afield. The Trilateral Highway mentioned in the summit's concluding statement was a case in point. The project began work nearly nine years earlier and progress had been (and still is) disappointingly slow. As one knowledgeable Indian observer notes, 'It is the typical project that figures in the records of ministerial and summit meetings that India holds with Southeast Asia, but sees no real activity thereafter' (Tripathi 2012: 152).[8] Likewise, the confidence of the ASEAN leaders in New Delhi's proclamations about 'Indo-Pacific' security ties must have been tempered by the knowledge of India's limited power projection capabilities, especially east of the Strait of Malacca. Indeed, Mr Singh's foreign minister quickly insisted at the meeting that New Delhi would not insinuate itself into the South China Sea's maritime disputes, cryptically adding that 'doing something about it includes not doing something about it' (*South China Morning Post* 2012). And the Indian navy chief's assured words about deploying military force to the area were offset by the earlier warnings of his immediate predecessors about the dangers of sustaining a naval presence in such a distant location (IANS 2012b; Prakash 2011). Other branches of the Indian government were also quick in diluting the impact of the chief's comments (Dasgupta 2012; Express News Service 2012).[9]

New Delhi's approach to Southeast Asia has long been undermined by a yawning gap between promise and performance which has become a trademark of modern India. Prime Minister Narendra Modi's government has vowed to remedy this deficiency through its newly unveiled 'Act East' initiative (*Economic Times* 2014). But to avoid the fate of its predecessor—that is, finding welcome within the ASEAN region but regularly falling short of expectations—this effort will need to be underpinned by major policy changes within India and a greater exertion of political will than has been evident over the past two decades. This argument is advanced as follows: the next section provides a brief overview of New Delhi's relationship vis-à-vis Southeast Asia during the Cold War era, when an early Indian attempt at regional leadership soon collapsed into prolonged mutual indifference between New Delhi and the area. A subsequent and more detailed section focuses on the economic dynamics inside India since the early 1990s that have enabled a new era of engagement with Southeast Asia but also hindered its potential reach. This is followed by two shorter sections, one dealing with the challenges of using India's isolated northeastern region to foster overland connectivity with the ASEAN region, while the other examines New Delhi's growing involvement in Southeast Asian security affairs along with the constraints it faces in this realm. A closing section offers some concluding thoughts relevant to the new 'Act East' initiative.

Affinity and Then Estrangement

The Indian subcontinent has left a deep civilizational imprint on what is now the ASEAN region. As Prime Minister Singh told the 2012 Commemorative Summit, 'India and Southeast Asia have centuries-old links. People, ideas, trade, art, and religions have long criss-crossed this region. A timeless thread of civilizations runs through all our countries' (M. Singh 2012). Notions about this common cultural past inspired modern India's early attempts at regional leadership. Beginning in the 1920s, the Greater India Society, a Calcutta-based group of scholars, popularized ideas about ancient India's leading role in the cultural development of Asia as well as the existence of Indian 'cultural colonies' in Southeast Asia long ago. As a result, many Indians in the closing decades of the British Raj 'came to believe that the entire South and Southeast Asian region formed the cultural progeny of India; now that the subcontinent was reawakening, they felt, India would once again assert its non-political ascendancy over the area.... While the idea of reviving the ancient Greater India was never officially endorsed by the Indian National Congress, it enjoyed considerable popularity in nationalist Indian circles' (Keenleyside 1982: 214).[10] At the same time, notions about pan-Asian regional solidarity and the need for a federation of Asian nations circulated widely within the Indian nationalist movement.[11] Both currents resonated with Jawaharlal Nehru, who admitted in his memoirs to boyhood fantasies about liberating Asia from European dominion (Nehru 1941: 30). Writing later on in *The Discovery of India*, his celebrated 1946 work on the country's history and role in the world, he depicted Southeast Asia as 'Greater India'. He also took the initiative in organizing the Asian Relations Conference, attended by over 200 delegates from 28 countries and colonies in early 1947, for the purpose of laying the basis of 'some kind of Asian organization'.[12]

Nehru invested much energy in exerting political leadership in Asia during the first years following Indian independence. In August 1950, a *New York Times* (1950) editorial asserted that the emerging Cold War struggle in the region 'conceivably could be won or lost in the mind of one man—Jawaharlal Nehru', while the *New York Herald Tribune* (1950) opined six weeks later that 'India's title to leadership in the new Asia is unquestioned'. Nehru provided considerable economic and military assistance to Burma from its independence in early 1948 and convened a regional forum (often called the second Asian Relations Conference) in January 1949 that championed Dutch de-colonization in Indonesia. He played an active part in the diplomacy of the Korean War and New Delhi chaired the Neutral Nations Repatriation Commission that oversaw prisoner exchanges at the conflict's end. In early 1954, New Delhi took the lead in bringing together the so-called Colombo Powers focused on the escalating French effort to extend its colonial rule in Indochina, and headed up the International Control Commission that supervized the July 1954 Geneva Accords, bringing that conflict to a close. India had a large hand in convening the April 1955 conference of 29 African and Asian states in Bandung, Indonesia, that paved the way for the founding of the Non-Aligned Movement. Indeed, a member of the Indian delegation even drafted the address with which Indonesian leader Sukarno inaugurated the conference. Sukarno used the gathering, which was presided over by Nehru, to pay tribute to India, calling it his country's 'window on the world' (D. Das 1969). Beyond the ideals of anti-colonial solidarity and Asian unity, Nehru was also mindful of the need for active diplomacy to contest Chinese influence in the region. In 1952, he confided that 'the basic challenge in Southeast Asia is between India and China. That challenge runs across the spine of Asia ...' (Moraes 1973).

But India's engagement with Southeast Asia began to flag from the mid-1950s. The formation of the U.S.-backed Southeast Asia Treaty

Organization (with its inclusion of Thailand and the Philippines) in September 1954 offended Nehru's sentiments about the bloc politics of the Cold War, as did the growing inclination of the area's nations to seek America's security protection as the Indo-China conflict heated up once again. In 1957, the Thai prime minister reportedly expressed a desire for his country to be more associated with India in the security realm 'since Thai culture was predominately Indian', but came away frustrated by Nehru's lack of interest (D. Das 1969). The Indian leader dismissingly referred to the region as 'Coca Cola countries' before a 1963 conclave of Indian envoys (Malik 2012: 28). His successors were no better, not even bothering to reply to a 1965 invitation by Singapore for assistance in training its newly formed army (Brewster 2013: 159). The military coup in Burma in early 1962 put the freeze on New Delhi's relations with the country for the next three decades. New Delhi and Jakarta fell out in the early 1960s over Indian support for the creation of an independent Malaysia, with Indonesia retaliating by providing armaments to Pakistan during the 1965 conflict with India and even briefly threatening to attack the Andaman and Nicobar Islands, the Indian archipelago overlooking the western approaches of the Malacca Strait.[13]

Contributing to New Delhi's estrangement with the region was the discord between the export-oriented, high-growth economic systems that were widely adopted by Southeast Asian countries in the 1960s and 1970s, and Nehruvian socialism's inward-looking policies and 'Hindu rate of growth'. As one commentator observes, 'If India's economic footprint spread across the Indian Ocean under the British Raj, it steadily diminished thanks to the policies of self-reliance and import substitution in the first decades after Independence' (Raja Mohan 2015). The result was that trade and investment flows between India and Southeast Asia remained quite modest until well into the 1990s, even as the industrialization and economic development of previously backward countries in the region took off. A further factor was that India's defeat in its 1962 border war with China, along with the wars with Pakistan in 1965 and 1971, caused leaders in New Delhi to recast their focus closer to home. In his memoirs, Lee Kuan Yew notes that during a 1970 trip to India he asked Prime Minister Indira Gandhi whether New Delhi intended to extend its naval interests into Southeast Asia, only to have her foreign minister jump in to say that the defence of India's western sea lanes was a greater focus. Lee writes, 'I sensed that India's primary defense concern was Pakistan, fearing a U.S.–China–Pakistan line-up' (Yew 2000: 406).

Indian leaders interpreted ASEAN's establishment in mid-1967, in reaction to the threat of North Vietnamese aggression, as the Southeast Asia Treaty Organization's (SEATO) second incarnation and rebuffed Singaporean and Thai entreaties to become an active partner of the new grouping. This suspicion, combined with regional concerns over India's quasi-alliance with the Soviet Union and the strong support New Delhi extended to Hanoi during the Vietnam conflict and beyond, ensured that India had little substantive interaction with Southeast Asia during the first quarter-century of ASEAN's existence.[14] Indira Gandhi, for example, displayed little interest in the region during her long reign in New Delhi. The one major exception occurred in 1980, when India attempted to negotiate a cooperative arrangement in the run-up to an ASEAN summit meeting in Malaysia that was to decide on which regional powers the organization would engage as dialogue partners. The whole effort was subverted when Gandhi recognized the regime that had been installed in Phnom Penh during the Vietnamese occupation of Cambodia. Gandhi's act elicited such strong negative reaction from the ASEAN states that India's foreign minister, Narasimha Rao, felt it prudent to decline an invitation to attend the summit in Kuala Lumpur.[15] As it was, the summit ended in a condemnation of the Indian move.

New Delhi's continued support of Hanoi soured the equation with ASEAN throughout the 1980s. An additional factor was the regional security concerns raised by a bout of muscle-flexing behaviour by the Rajiv Gandhi government, including the build-up of naval and air power in the Andaman islands; the 1987–90 intervention in the Sri Lankan civil war; the November 1988 military action beating back a coup attempt in the Maldives; and the 1989–90 economic coercion of Nepal, which undermined that country's political stability. As late as 1992, Singapore's Goh was expressing alarm about India's 'capability to project its navy way beyond its shore' and wishing that 'India will also appreciate the security concerns of its neighbours' (Datta-Ray 2015).

'Look East' and Economic Policy Dysfunctions

Since the early 1990s, the 'Look East' policy has emerged as one of India's most fruitful international initiatives, recovering much of the standing New

Delhi lost in Southeast Asia during the previous era. ASEAN has now become a key trading partner for India. Total trade levels currently stand at about U.S.$80 billion, up from U.S.$30 billion in 2008, and have been expanding at a compound annual growth rate of 23 per cent over the past decade. Exports to ASEAN countries have doubled in the same period and the ASEAN area's share in India's export profile is now at about the same level as that of the United States and northeast Asia. Indeed, export growth to ASEAN eclipses India's overall export growth by a wide margin. According to one new estimate, exports to ASEAN will climb to the U.S.$280 billion mark within a decade, at which point ASEAN would have a 15 per cent share in India's export portfolio (Kak 2014). New Delhi has signed two broad trade accords with ASEAN—the 2009 agreement covering goods and one dealing with services and investments that will come on line in July 2015. It is participating in the negotiations for the sixteen-country Regional Comprehensive Economic Partnership (RCEP), which aims to establish the world's largest free-trade bloc among the ASEAN nations and the six other countries with which it has free trade agreements. It also has bilateral economic arrangements in place with several ASEAN countries, though as an Indian government document acknowledges, these contain 'relatively few obligations, generous exemptions, and lenient timetables for implementation' (*Economic Survey* 2014–15: 37). In 2005, it entered into a comprehensive economic cooperation agreement with Singapore, the first such accord that India has signed with any country. As a result, the number of Indian companies operating in Singapore jumped from 1,100 in 2001 to 4,000 in 2011, and to 6,450 by the end of 2013 (See *et al.* 2015: 124). Singapore has further emerged as the largest single source of foreign investment into India, though much of this is pass-through funds. Bilateral trade accords also exist with Indonesia, Malaysia, and Thailand.

The solid trade gains racked up by the 'Look East' policy pale, however, in comparison with the advances made over the same period by China, whose overall economic profile was similar to India's in the early 1990s. For all of the expansion in India–ASEAN trade relations, India still comprised just 2.7 per cent of ASEAN's total merchandise trade profile in 2013, a figure that is half what South Korea—a country with a miniscule population compared to India—has been able to achieve. China's portion, in contrast, stands at 14 per cent. While China ranks as ASEAN's premier partner in merchandise trade, India occupies the ninth spot, just ahead of the United Arab Emirates (ASEAN 2014b: Tables 19, 24).

Much like the country's overall economic performance over the past two decades, India's foreign economic engagement continues to fall distinctly short of its potential. Indeed, it is important to note that the Look East policy shares the same provenance with the domestic economic reforms launched in the early 1990s. Both are products of the severe economic and diplomatic dislocations India experienced at the end of the Cold War and both originated in the same departure point—the need to rejuvenate Indian economic growth. Far from New Delhi's previous lack of interest toward the region, key officials in Narasimha Rao's government that came to power in mid-1991 drew inspiration from East Asia's fast-growing markets and sought to emulate their success at home as well as draw benefits from interacting more deeply with them. Several of these officials had earlier served in foreign postings providing vantage points for the economic dynamism the region had enjoyed over the past 25 years. Manmohan Singh, the new finance minister, was Secretary General of the South Commission, a Geneva-based panel focused on global development issues, from 1987 to 1990. And Rao's principal secretary, Amar Nath Verma, had spent nearly seven years at the Bangkok secretariat of the United Nations Economic and Social Commission for Asia-Pacific.

The domestic reforms unveiled back then and the Look East policy share another similarity: both were never articulated in a comprehensive and compelling manner for either policy elites or the general public.[16] Indeed, Prime Minister Rao later emphasized the political importance of concealing the full details of the economic reform process started in 1991, stating that 'you cannot afford [policy] U-turns in this country' (NDTV 2004). One expert who played a key role in economic policymaking over the past two decades has argued that the reform process cannot even be described as gradualist in nature:

> [G]radualism implies a clear definition of the goal and a deliberate choice of extending the time taken to reach it, in order to ease the pain of transition. This is not what happened in all areas. The goals were often indicated only as a broad direction, with the precise end point and the pace of transition left unstated to minimize opposition—and possibly also to allow room to retreat if necessary. This reduced politically divisive controversy, and enabled a consensus of sorts to evolve, but it also meant that the consensus at each point represented a compromise, with many interested groups joining only because they

believed that reforms would not go 'too far'. The result was a process of change that was not so much gradualist as fitful and opportunistic. Progress was made as and when politically feasible, but since the end point was not always clearly indicated, many participants were unclear about how much change would have to be accepted, and this may have led to less adjustment than was otherwise feasible. (Ahluwalia 2002: 86–7)

As a consequence of this policymaking environment, the disjuncture in the domestic and foreign realms between official rhetoric and practical implementation is often painfully visible, with foreign audiences uncertain whether the necessary political will exists in the country to push through or if it is worth their while to seriously engage Indian interlocutors. Consider the difficulties in advancing major economic reforms since 1991, which are ultimately due to the lack of a home-grown intellectual tradition that can underpin them, or what one expert refers to as 'a strong consensus for weak reforms' (Ahluwalia 2002: 87). Prime Minister Singh acknowledged as much in a 2012 interview, lamenting that

the logic of an open economy and its benefits are still not widely understood among the general public. Public discourse still sees markets as anti-public welfare. The instinctive reactions of many, both in the political class and in the public at large, is[sic] to revert to a state controlled system. There is no realisation that a reversal to an earlier era is neither possible nor desirable. Even a neighbour like China has understood the logic of an open economy and is developing the institutional framework which is required for this.[17]

In far too many quarters, the steps enacted during the 1991 economic calamity are regarded as the modern equivalent of the East India Company, something imposed on the country by overwhelming external forces.[18] Thus, reform has crept along at a leisurely pace for the past 25 years and its advancement is too frequently the result of technocratic subterfuge that is subject to humiliating rollbacks in the event of political backlashes.[19] A prime example is the Singh government's ignominious retreat in December 2011 on liberalizing the country's huge retail sector, even though it originally hailed the step as a landmark action.[20] The glaring silence in New Delhi at the twentieth anniversary of the 1991 reforms—even Singh himself remained mute—is also instructive.

Nor is the phenomenon limited to the Indian political left. For Mr Modi's Bharatiya Janata Party (BJP), the credo of swadeshi (national self-reliance) runs up against the ideals of free markets. As one expert observes, 'the BJP still contains constituencies committed to economic nationalism. They view globalization as a recipe for deindustrialization, for dominance over key economic sectors, and impoverishment for small businesses and farmers' (Menon 2014: 57). Yashwant Sinha, who served as finance minister in A.B. Vaypayee's cabinet, reportedly drafted a 'rollback announcement' before presenting his annual budgets to the Parliament (Jenkins 2004: 257). And at the BJP's leadership conclave in January 2014, Rajnath Singh, then the party's president and currently Modi's home minister, offered up *kisan bazars* (farmer's markets) as an alternative to retail-sector liberalization, proclaiming that 'modernization and vested business interests have sounded the death knell for vegetable markets and weekend markets' (S.R. Singh 2014).

The shallow consensus on the domestic reform agenda has important implications for foreign economic interaction, including the trade and commercial dimensions of the outreach to East Asia. One is a marked defensiveness in international trade negotiations, including a tendency to default to zero-sum calculations.[21] This posture was exemplified by the obdurate approach India pursued during the Doha Round talks of the World Trade Organization (WTO). The declaration by Commerce Minister Kamal Nath—'I reject everything'—as the negotiations collapsed in July 2008, is revealing. This line met with wide acclaim at home, though most developing nations blamed New Delhi for derailing an agreement they were ultimately willing to accept.[22] Indian actions were repeated six years later when it delayed the WTO's trade facilitation agreement that was thought to represent 'low-hanging-fruit' measures to which every country could easily agree (Bellman and Kenny 2014).[23]

This defensiveness spills over into New Delhi's dealings with Southeast Asia, as evidenced by the lengthy and difficult negotiations over the 2009 India–ASEAN trade accord covering merchandise goods.[24] Despite the 2012 Commemorative Summit hailing the conclusion of talks for the follow-on agreement on services and investments, a final deal was held up for nearly two more years, due, in part, to inter-ministerial disputes in New Delhi over concessions for foreign companies.[25] The debate prompted the governor of India's central bank to express concern that 'we seem to be reverting to a dialogue of protection and subsidies that we left behind long ago' (Fe Bureau 2013).[26] New Delhi's support for the RCEP negotiations has also been highly qualified due to concerns that the

Indian economy will be further disadvantaged by any trade concessions involving China.

The domestic reform course impacts the calibre of India's engagement with East Asia in a second major way. The highly fragmented structure of the internal market is a large impediment to deeper regional economic integration. As one foreign business leader recently put it, 'outsiders are amazed that much of India resembles pre-revolutionary France with many internal barriers standing in the way of economic efficiency and growth' (Forbes 2015).[27] A recent World Bank report found, for instance, that regulatory barriers to the efficient movement of goods within the country put manufacturing firms at a significant disadvantage vis-à-vis foreign competitors and push 'logistics costs in India to two-three times international benchmarks' (World Bank Group 2014: iii). Another obstacle is the country's pronounced inability to build up an export-oriented manufacturing sector or construct modern infrastructure connections that can plug into global production networks (*Economic Times* 2013). According to the blunt assessment of one commentator, 'right now, it is not obvious that India can show a competitive advantage in the manufacturing of anything' (Sender 2015).[28] A prime illustration here is India's lack of success in capitalizing on the migration of labour-intensive light manufacturing capacity out of China to countries with lower wage structures, like Bangladesh, Cambodia, Indonesia, and Vietnam. This should be a point of India's comparative advantage given its vast reservoir of low-skilled workers, especially in the apparel and footwear industries. As one analyst notes,

> If any Indian industrial sector were well positioned to benefit from the nation's growing low-cost advantage, cotton fabrics and garments would seem a likely candidate. India is the world's second-leading exporter of raw cotton and has an immense, growing workforce. What's more, the cost of Indian labor has remained virtually flat over the past decade when adjusted for productivity gains. That should give India a big advantage in apparel, a sector for which labor accounts for nearly 30 percent of the total cost. By contrast, labor costs in China's coastal provinces have nearly tripled.
>
> Yet India accounts for only 3 percent of the global apparel trade—and there has been no big rush to build cotton textile or apparel plants in India. Instead, much of the country's raw cotton and yarn is still shipped to China, where it is woven into fabrics and converted into apparel at factories that are primarily located in China, Bangladesh, Cambodia, and Vietnam. (Bruce 2014)[29]

Moreover, seaport infrastructure in India falls well short of East Asian standards and does not even measure particularly well compared to ports in other South Asian countries.[30] Indian port facilities are renowned for inefficiency, with turnaround times far longer than in Colombo on the other side of the Palk Strait.[31] Indeed, much of the recent handwringing in New Delhi over Chinese involvement in Colombo's port expansion is that the facility has become an important transshipment hub for India. The lack of modern infrastructure forces large container ships with cargo bound for India to unload in Sri Lanka and use feeder ships for the rest of the journey to India.[32] As a result, upwards of 70 per cent of shipping to and from Indian ports is handled by Colombo.[33]

A third point linking the domestic sphere and New Delhi's eastward engagement is that both the economic reforms and the 'Look East' policy were rolled out two decades ago in a way that lacked clear policy articulation and bureaucratic follow-through. As a result, the uneven progress and occasional rollbacks evident in domestic economic policy are mirrored by long delays and missed opportunities in 'Look East' endeavours. One former Indian official concedes that the 'Look East' approach was 'neither an ad hoc reaction to India's geo-strategic and economic vulnerabilities of the early 1990s ... [nor] a deeply thought out foreign policy response to the challenges confronting the country in the early post-Cold War years' (Ram 2012: 63).[34] No official statement heralded its launch or spelled out its tenets in a detailed way. Indeed, its exact genesis is a bit murky, as demonstrated by the difficulty in attaching a precise date to its starting point. A number of accounts put it in 1991, while others in 1992, and still others fudge the issue by saying 'the early 1990s'. According to Salman Haider, who served as foreign secretary in the mid-1990s, the 'Look East' appellation was 'a rather off-the-cuff slogan' devised to garner media attention for Prime Minister Rao's September 1993 trip to South Korea (Haider 2012: 53).[35] A year later, Rao interjected some substance into the approach when he delivered a major address in Singapore. Although he did not mention the 'Look East' phrase, he declared his intention of turning the page in India's relations with Southeast Asia in the hope that 'the Asia–Pacific could be the springboard for our leap into the global marketplace' (Rao 1994).[36]

Even before his address, Rao had reached out to Singapore, which had reacted to the new eastward orientation with the most alacrity among the ASEAN states. Singaporean Prime Minister Goh Chok Tong, a self-described Indophile, was invited as the chief guest at the January 1994

Republic Day celebration, a gesture laden with even more diplomatic significance than usual since Czech president Vaclav Havel had put out word that he desired the invitation.[37] Goh brought along a large business delegation to the country, hoping to spark what he called 'India fever' within the city-state (Reuters 1994). His call for a 'long-lasting strategic alliance between India's and Singapore's private sectors' quickly found expression in a proposed joint venture between the Tata conglomerate and Singapore Airlines (SIA) to establish a new airline within India, a project which the Singaporean government came to view as an important test of India's economic liberalizations. Despite the support of the Indian foreign and finance ministries, civil aviation officials within both the Rao and the subsequent Deve Gowda governments blocked the project due to discomfort over foreign equity participation in the domestic aviation sector.[38] The combo teamed up again in 2001 in an abortive bid to acquire a 40 per cent stake of Air India, which was founded as Tata Airlines in the 1930s before it was nationalized in 1953. But this attempt was also thwarted by political opposition despite reports that the Vajpayee government was mulling the airline's privatization.[39] In the end, the Tata–SIA joint venture did not take flight until January 2015.

A similar scenario played out with plans to construct a private airport in Bangalore, an idea endorsed during Prime Minister Rao's 1994 visit to Singapore. The Tata conglomerate teamed up with Singapore Changi Airport and Raytheon, but the project foundered when the civil aviation minister declared that private ownership of airports was contrary to the 'national interest'. As one of its last acts, the Deve Gowda government adopted a policy barring any foreign equity involvement in the domestic aviation sector (Kripalani 1997). In the end, airport construction was delayed until mid-2005, when a consortium of German and Indian entities broke ground. A number of joint infrastructure projects involving Singaporean, Thai, and Malaysian companies were likewise stalled or delayed in the late 1990s.

India's Northeast and the Challenges of Connectivity

The tandem of leadership indifference and bureaucratic lethargy is also evident in the two sub-regional arrangements that are part of the 'Look East' approach and which feature efforts to use India's northeastern region to foster cross-border linkages with Southeast Asia. In 1997, India became a founding member of what is now known as the Bay of Bengal Initiative for Multi-Sectoral Technical and Economic Cooperation (BIMSTEC), a Thai effort bringing together Bangladesh, India, Sri Lanka, and Thailand to work on trade, investment, and cross-border connectivity projects. Myanmar joined soon thereafter, and Bhutan and Nepal came aboard in 2003. But this effort quickly lost steam and little has come of it so far, including the ballyhooed Trilateral Highway project and a proposed free trade accord whose initial framework agreement was inked more than a decade ago. In the nearly two decades since its existence, the grouping has managed to hold just three summit meetings.

Another grouping, the Mekong–Ganga Cooperation forum involving six countries—Cambodia, India, Laos, Myanmar, Thailand, and Vietnam—was likewise launched in 2000 as a result of a Thai initiative. This effort has been marking time, too. The lack of progress is partially due to Bangkok's loss of interest in both groups in favour of the higher-profile Greater Mekong Subregion initiative linking Thailand and the Indochinese countries with China (but excluding India), as well the Ayeyawady–Chao Phraya–Mekong Economic Cooperation Strategy effort comprising Thailand, Myanmar, and Indochina (but again excluding India). The BIMSTEC effort is also undermined by the vagaries of the India–Bangladesh and Bangladesh–Myanmar bilateral relationships, as well as the growing focus on the competing Bangladesh–China–India–Myanmar (BCIM) forum for economic cooperation that is being driven by Beijing.[40] In 2005, for instance, tensions between New Delhi and Dhaka derailed a 900 kilometre-long pipeline project that would have brought natural gas from Myanmar into India via Bangladesh, which in turn prompted Myanmar to shift its focus to a Chinese-sponsored pipeline initiative to deliver gas supplies from the Bay of Bengal to China's southwestern Yunnan province. The project's collapse has forced New Delhi to turn to less viable alternatives like the proposed Iran–Pakistan–India and the Turkemistan–Afghanistan–Pakistan–India pipelines to fill the country's energy security needs.[41] It is also worth noting that despite the Modi government's major commitment to upgrade and expand the Indian rail system, its spring 2015 budget failed to allocate funds for completing an important project connecting the Northeast to Bangladesh (PTI 2015).

Another significant factor behind BIMSTEC's stalling is that, despite the high-minded rhetoric from New Delhi, 'there was never much enthusiasm from the Indian side' for the initiative, as a former Indian ambassador to Thailand noted recently (Gupta 2014). This attitude is part of New Delhi's relative indifference to the country's much neglected northeastern region, a geographic and economic *cul de sac* that is tenuously connected to the rest of India by the narrow Siliguri corridor and cut off from traditional commercial links with what is now Bangladesh by the effects of the subcontinent's partition in 1947. Ever since India gained a land border with ASEAN when Myanmar joined the organization in 1997, New Delhi's leaders have rolled out ambitious plans to transform the northeastern region into an economic hub via cross-border linkages with Myanmar, similar in rhetoric if not actual implementation to China's development of landlocked Yunnan Province as a regional centre connecting with Southeast Asia's markets.[42] In 2008, the Indian government released a planning document vowing to put the northeastern region 'in the vanguard of the country's Look East Policy' (North Eastern Council 2008). During a trip to the area in late 2013, Indian president, Pranab Mukherjee, called it 'a core stakeholder in India's Look East foreign policy.... The north east of India provides a natural bridge between us and South East Asia. The essential philosophy of our "Look East Policy" is that India must find its destiny by linking itself more and more with its Asian partners and the rest of the world'. A year later, Prime Minister Modi declared the northeast a 'natural economic zone' and pledged that it 'would be a gateway of Southeast Asia in future' (IANS 2014b; PTI 2013; Talukdar 2014).

But New Delhi's performance with regard to the region has so far failed to correspond with its pronouncements. In 2002, a special incentives programme meant to spur investment in the Northeast was extended to other states, which had the effect of diverting a number of prospective investors away from the area. Similarly, an ambitious programme designed to foster industrial development in the region was unveiled in 2007, only to be suspended recently due to lack of funding (B. Singh 2014; PTI 2014b). This 'on the map, off the mind' attitude has knock-on implications for policy towards Myanmar.[43] As a former senior Indian official explains:

> Among all of India's neighbors, Myanmar is the most disadvantaged in getting the serious and sustained attention of decision-makers in New Delhi since the bordering Northeastern Region states of India are political lightweights that are often themselves ignored and their complexities little understood by an indifferent political class and

bureaucracy ensconced in geographically distant New Delhi. This is in sharp contrast to the attention that, for example, Afghanistan gets, even though India's stakes in Myanmar are equally high. (Sakri 2009: 69)[44]

Efforts to establish more robust infrastructure links with Southeast Asia via a corridor through the northeastern region are burdened by a confluence of factors, including the lack of infrastructure connecting the Northeast with the rest of India; the Indian bureaucracy's notoriously poor implementation record when it comes to connectivity projects;[45] and the rugged terrain and presence of ethnic insurgencies in both the Northeast and Myanmar. All of these challenges are magnified by the relative lip service New Delhi pays to the northeast region.[46] As a result, connectivity projects like the Trilateral Highway and the Kaladan Multi-modal Transit Transportation Project, which aims to use overland and riverine links to connect Kolkata to Sittwe seaport in Myanmar via Mizoram state, have fallen drastically behind schedule. New Delhi has once again pushed back the deadline for completing these projects from 2016 to 2019, a clear indication according to one recent report that 'despite tall claims it just cannot deliver on the ground' (Bagchi 2015).[47]

Security: 'A Difficult Problem for Her'

Similar to the trajectory of its economic interaction with Southeast Asia, India's regional military engagement has also increased greatly. A decade after the Rao government launched the 'Look East' policy with a view toward developing stronger commercial ties with ASEAN, Prime Minister Vajpayee's administration added an explicit security dimension and a broader geographic remit. In September 2003, Foreign Minister Yashwant Singh announced

> India's 'Look East' policy has now entered its Phase–II. Phase–I was focused primarily on the ASEAN countries and on trade and investment linkages. Phase–II is characterized by an expanded definition of 'East' extending from Australia to China and East Asia with ASEAN as its core. Phase–II marks a shift in focus from exclusively economic issues to economic and security issues including joint efforts to protect sea lanes, coordination on counter terrorism etc. (Sinha 2003)

This declaration codified moves that had already been underway for some time. In the early 1990s, New Delhi reportedly attempted to enlist Vietnam, its long-standing diplomatic partner, in a bid to extend India's naval reach into the waters east of the Strait of Malacca by gaining access to the naval and air base at Cam Ranh Bay, a key deepwater port in Southeast Asia. Hanoi turned aside the request but New Delhi renewed it in early 2000, as part of a larger effort to give a stronger security focus to the bilateral relationship. Indian defence minister, George Fernandes, even offered to play an active role in safeguarding regional peace by policing the sea lanes in the South China Sea and seeing to it that 'conflict situations are contained', a reference to Vietnam's festering dispute with China over maritime boundaries. Fernandes declared subsequently that India's maritime area of interest 'extends from the north of the Arabian Sea to the South China Sea'.[48] And in 2002, acting at Washington's request, India provided naval escorts through the Malacca Strait for American cargo ships carrying supplies for the U.S. military campaign in Afghanistan.

The quest for permanent basing rights in Southeast Asia continues to elude New Delhi, though the Indian navy is increasingly a visible feature outside of the Indian Ocean basin. Over the past decade, India has engaged in a steady build-up of naval capabilities in the Andaman Islands and along its eastern seaboard.[49] The Indian navy has established a regular, though far from a standing, presence in the South China Sea through extended, flotilla-sized deployments, and frequently conducts joint exercises in the western Pacific with a number of countries, including the United States, Japan, Australia, Singapore, Vietnam, and the Philippines. It played a high-profile role in the multilateral disaster relief effort in Indonesia, Malaysia, and Thailand following the December 2004 Indian Ocean earthquake and tsunami, and collaborates on maritime patrolling with the littoral states in the Malacca Strait.

In recent years, as the territorial disputes in the South China Sea have grown in prominence, a convergence of maritime security interests has emerged between India and other countries in Southeast and East Asia.[50] In contrast to the 1980s, when some states were suspicious of India's strategic objectives and military modernization, ASEAN countries increasingly look to New Delhi as a positive factor in the regional security order and view the Indian navy as a potential counterweight to China. New Delhi is becoming more vocal in expressing support, in regional fora and in joint statements with other major powers, for the freedom of navigation and overflight in the South China Sea, and is raising the level of its defence cooperation with other countries, especially with the

United States, Japan, and Vietnam. For much of the Look East period, New Delhi maintained fairly low-key military supply and training relationships with Southeast Asian nations, with Singapore and Hanoi being in the forefront, while shying away from transferring advanced military hardware for fear of antagonizing Beijing.[51] But in October 2014, India announced plans to supply naval patrol vessels to Vietnam and has reportedly committed to providing the sophisticated BrahMos anti-ship cruise missile as well (Bagchi 2014).

A large disparity continues to exist between regional expectations and Indian security capabilities, however.[52] Although some Indian commentators advocate taking up the British Raj's expansive regional security functions, it is unclear whether policymakers in New Delhi actually have a desire to embrace a more assertive role.[53] Following on his words at the 2012 Commemorative Summit with ASEAN, Prime Minister Singh proclaimed in May 2013 that India was well placed 'to become a net provider of security in our immediate region and beyond'. Yet less than nine months later, his national security advisor admitted that the Indian government was still mulling over the issue of whether to do so, including in the maritime security sphere (IANS 2014a; Kumar 2013).

Even if Indian officials were inclined to assume a larger regional profile, a series of stubborn constraints stand in their way. New Delhi's national security decision making institutions are widely thought to be antiquated, if not outright dysfunctional, and are notoriously deficient in distilling the country's growing resource base into coherent strategic priorities and force-planning outcomes.[54] India's extraordinary levels of arms imports in recent years captivate global defence contractors but they also put a spotlight on the disquieting reasons it remains so dependent upon foreign sources for advanced weapons technology and lacks an efficient defence production base of its own. Moreover, the defence ministry is staffed with generalist bureaucrats more concerned with prosaic procurement matters and guarding their turf vis-à-vis the military establishment, than with long-term planning, integrating strategic considerations into budgetary decisions, or ramping up international engagement with foreign militaries.

These factors impinge on India's security role in Southeast Asia in a number of ways. They account for the inability to craft high-profile defence supplier relationships that would bring with them enhanced overseas influence, as well as the lack of institutional focus on regional security affairs. As one expert puts it, India has yet to meld 'its bilateral defense relationships with ASEAN states into a coherent regional strategy, which to a significant extent reflects New Delhi's own systemic failures in strategic planning' (Brewster 2013: 158). Another analyst concurs, arguing that the defence ministry 'remains hesitant and is tied down by a lack of institutional depth and political vision to purposefully engage in collective endeavors in the region' (Mohan 2013: 141).

The failure to develop military wherewithal fully commensurate with a rising major power—itself one of the consequences of the economic policy shortcomings detailed in an earlier section—further means that India is bereft of significant expeditionary capabilities that would allow it to project significant force outside of its immediate environs. Funding levels for the Indian navy, the smallest of the armed services and traditionally the most neglected, have grown noticeably in the recent period. But it will take many more years before it is in a position to sustain major operations in the South China Sea or beyond, especially in a hostile environment.[55] Lee Kuan Yew picked up on this deficiency in a May 2010 interview, stating that 'India is too far away' to have a genuine impact on the balance of power in Southeast Asia:

> India's military role will be confined to South Asia and she cannot project her forces into the Pacific. She might be able to project her forces into the Strait of Malacca because it's near the Andaman Islands. But to go beyond Singapore will be a difficult problem for her. (*Straits Times* 2010)

The Importance of 'Act Home'

My experience of six months as Prime Minister says that the whole world is looking at India with expectations. But we are not ready. The world is ready but we are not ready.
—Narendra Modi, address at 'Good Governance Day' celebrations, 25 December 2014 (PTI 2014a)

For the last 60 years, India's involvement with Southeast Asia has been hindered by the lacuna between potential opportunities and actual performance as well as the gap between promises and delivery. Prime Minister Modi's government has vowed to remedy these defects and its 'Act East' initiative portends new vigour for New Delhi's outreach to the region. India is bolstering diplomatic engagement with Bangladesh and Myanmar, the two immediate but problematic neighbours, which will have the most impact on the future course of economic engagement with ASEAN. And it is moving to deepen security cooperation with the United States and Japan, thereby imparting new credibility to India's role in regional security affairs.

Yet most critical to the long-term prospects to the Act East effort is what happens inside India in the coming years. Much will turn on whether New Delhi is able to push the incomplete economic revolution launched in the early 1990s to its next level. The success of 'Act East' is tightly bound up in the ultimate fate of Mr Modi's 'Make in India' campaign to establish India as a global manufacturing hub, and his moves to alter a domestic taxation regime that imposes heavy burdens on Indian companies inside and outside of the country. Likewise key is the building up of modern, world-class infrastructure and resolving the perennial debate over the appropriate role of foreign equity in major economic sectors. Modi has made an impressive entrance upon the Asian leadership stage and his government is right to act on the economic and security opportunities that beckon in Southeast Asia and beyond. But it should be careful not to lose sight of the vital prerequisites at home.

Notes

1. Quotations drawn, respectively, from Guha 2011: 315; Nayar and Paul 2003: 133; and Nehru 1954: 144.

2. Also see Bagchi 2012. In the summer of 2011, the Chinese navy reportedly challenged the passage of an Indian amphibious warfare ship in the South China Sea. See Bland and Shivakumar 2011.

3. Refer also to Samanta 2013; and Saran 2011. For more on the terminological significance, consult Bhatia and Sakhuja 2014; Kaushiva and Singh 2014; Medcalf 2013; and Scott 2012a, 2012b.

4. In a June 2012 address in New Delhi, U.S. Defense Secretary, Leon Panetta, declared that the Obama administration sees India as a 'linchpin' in the rebalancing and 'views India as a net provider of security from the Indian Ocean to Afghanistan and beyond'. See Cloud and Magnier 2012; and Pandit and Parashar 2012. For an example of how Beijing is attempting to use the 'Indo-Pacific' term to its advantage, see Aneja 2014.

5. A similar view, held by a former senior aide to Prime Minister Singh, is expressed in Baru 2009.

6. Also see IANS 2012a.

7. As it turned out, the signing of the parallel trade accord covering services and investments, that was hailed by the Commemorative Summit, was delayed

until late 2014, in part due to inter-ministerial disputes in New Delhi. It is scheduled to enter into force on 1 July 2015.

8. As it is, the highway's anticipated completion date has now been pushed back, first from 2013, then to 2016, and now to 2019. To be sure, the cause of the delay is not entirely on the Indian side. As a recent assessment puts it, 'lack of essential institutional support and government commitments are some of the reasons for the slow progress of the Trilateral Highway. Deeper regional cooperation among the three countries would speed up the development of the highway' (De 2014: 20).

9. The foreign ministry reportedly was 'livid' about the incident (Bagchi 2012).

10. Also see Bayley 2004.

11. For more on this point, see Bharucha 2006 and Mishra 2012. For arguments about the impact of these ideas on modern Indian diplomacy, consult Jaffrelott 2003 and Keenleyside 1982.

12. The quotation is from Nehru's May 1946 letter to Burmese nationalist Aung San, as cited in Stolte 2014: 60. Also see Mani 1998. It's interesting to note that the All-India Muslim League boycotted the New Delhi conference on the grounds that it was 'a thinly-disguised attempt by Hindu Congress to boost itself politically as the prospective leader of Asiatic peoples' (quoted from 'True Character of "Asian Conference"', *Dawn* editorial, 20 March 1947, as cited in Stolte 2014: 58).

13. The Indonesian threat to the islands was a key reason the Indian navy was unable to take offensive action against Pakistan (Brewster 2011: 223).

14. For a good overview of this period, consult Ayoob 1990.

15. The episode is recounted in Muni 2012.

16. Governments in New Delhi have a long tradition of not putting in written form exactly where they stand on important policy issues. The best illustration of this occurred in February 1994 when the Rao government rejected parliamentary efforts to produce a formal whitepaper spelling out India's national security doctrine. The then defence secretary responded that the public pronouncements of government leaders were sufficient for this purpose and that 'the absence of a written document … does not create any confusion or any lack of clarity in this matter' (Babu 2004: 85).

17. See *Hindustan Times*, 6 July 2012. Business journalist Mihir S. Sharma (2015: 76–7) observes that 'every step in the 1991 liberalization was justified only in terms of the crisis that had preceded it, not in terms of the future that might follow'.

18. Former Indian foreign minister Jaswant Singh acknowledges that 'Underlying Indian positions in some international economic negotiations has been a fear of foreign economic looting rooted in our [colonial] history' (Malone 2011: 271).

19. For arguments that the 'original sin' of the 1991 measures is that 'the case for liberal economic reform has never been properly made in India', see Dehejia 2011. Business leader turned public intellectual Gurcharan Das (2014) notes that the country is bereft of 'a liberal party that openly trusts markets and focuses on economic and institutional reform'. For more on the 'reform by stealth' phenomenon, refer to Desai 2009; Jenkins 1999, 2007; and Varshney 1999.

20. For how the rollback on retail liberalization adversely affected the negotiations for the ASEAN services and investment accord, see Basu 2014.

21. For an argument that India perceives international negotiations to be zero-sum in nature, see Narlikar and Narlikar 2014. Also consult Ninan 2015.

22. For more on India's unconstructive role, see Blustein 2008. An Indian expert who earlier served as WTO's deputy director general acknowledges that New Delhi is widely viewed as not contributing positively to global trade talks. See Soni and Sekhani 2015.

23. As part of a U.S.–Indian compromise a few months later, New Delhi signaled its readiness to sign the deal.

24. For more on New Delhi's defensive orientation in trade policy, see Gupta 2014: ch. 7.

25. Despite hopes raised by the January 2015 Obama–Modi summit, a similar theme is playing out with regard to a possible U.S.–India bilateral investment treaty. See Sen 2015. For more on the Indian debate over the appropriate role of foreign capital in the country's economy, see Pandya 2014.

26. For more on the debate in New Delhi, see Basu 2014; Bhattacherjee 2014; and Singhal 2014. According to a media account, the Modi government signed the accord even though an internal government assessment concluded it offered little in the way of benefit. See Srivastava 2014.

27. For more on the fragmentation of the domestic market, consult Choudhury 2014; Kumar and Priya 2014; Mallet 2014; Mehrotra 2014; Nayar 2014, especially ch. 6; Sikarwar 2014.

28. For a worrisome note about India's slow integration into global value-added chains, see *Economic Survey 2014–2015*: 37.

29. Also consult Ninan 2013.

30. According to the World Economic Forum's latest Global Competitiveness Index, port infrastructure in India ranked at 76 out of 144 countries, while Pakistan is pegged at 59 and Sri Lanka at 69 (World Economic Forum 2014).

31. On average, most of India's major ports have turnaround times of about 4.4 days compared with less than a day in Singapore. Were it not for the rapid development of privately managed smaller ports under the jurisdiction of state governments, the situation would be much worse. For more analysis, see Lall and Anand 2014.

32. According to a recent estimate, about 13 per cent of India's container traffic travels via Colombo. If the new terminal there ran at full capacity and dedicated itself to transshipping containers to India, that figure could rise to 28 per cent (*Economist* [Colombo], 8 June 2013). Also consult Simhan 2014.

33. This figure is given in an address by Shyam Saran, 'India's Foreign Policy and the Andaman & Nicobar Islands', in *Security and Development of Andaman & Nicobar Islands Seminar Proceedings*, 15 September 2009. The author wishes to thank Nilanthi Samaranayake for this citation.

34. For an argument that the 'Look East Policy has not been pursued by India in a well-planned and structured manner', see Muni 2011.

35. Haider notes that the label was chosen as a play on Horace Greeley's famous exhortation.

36. In his memoirs, Lee Kuan Yew (2000: 409) recalled warning Rao during this trip that the greatest obstacle to his economic reforms 'was the mindset of Indian civil servants toward foreigners—that they were out to exploit India and should be hindered'.

37. As one analyst notes, 'Such a move by India—to choose Singapore above a former socialist ally, the Czech Republic—would have seemed unthinkable during the Cold War' (Bin Yahya 2008: 69).

38. See Tribune News Service 1998. The dynamics of this episode are complex, involving both ideological rigidity as well as allegations of cronyism and corruption within the Indian civil aviation ministry. For more, consult Das Gupta (9 January; 30 January) 2015. In his memoirs, the civil aviation secretary at the time laments that the 'history of civil aviation in this country would have taken a different trajectory if the Tata Singapore Airlines had been allowed to float an airline' (Kaw 2012).

39. Air India's former executive director attributes the torpedoing of this strategic partnership as a major factor in the decline of the once prestigious national carrier. See Bhargava 2013.

40. For more on the BCIM grouping and the constrained Indian commitment to it, refer to Uberoi 2014.

41. For details about this episode, consult Chandra 2012; Kulkarni 2013; and Huda 2013.

42. For more on the problems of developing connectivity between India and Bangladesh, consult Chaudhury and Basu 2015; Das and Batra 2015.

43. The phrase comes from John Elliott 2015.

44. For more on New Delhi's neglect of the northeastern region, see Bhattacharjee 2014.

45. See, for example, Chandra 2013; Joshi 2015; Kazmin 2014; Limaye 2012; and TNN 1998. For more on how India overpromises and underperforms on its Myanmar policy, including cross-border infrastructure projects, consult Jonah Blank's chapter in this volume and Mallet 2015.

46. For detailed examinations of these challenges, refer to Sanjoy Hazarika's contribution in this volume; Bhaumik 2009, 2014; Downie 2015; G. Das 2012.

47. Just a few months earlier, the Modi government had pledged to finish these projects by 2016 (Roche 2014). On problems relating to the massive *Bharat Mala* highway project, which envisions connecting all of India's Himalayan states with the rest of the country, consult Balachandran 2015.

48. See Brewster 2009, especially 30–3, 35.

49. On the Indian navy's overall expansion, consult A. Singh 2012; Bateman and Ho (eds) 2010; Bipindra 2012; Holmes, Winner, and Yoshihara 2009; Ladwig 2009; Mohan 2012; Pandit 2015a; and Pant 2012. For more on the build-up in the Andaman Islands, consult Pandit 2010, 2015b; P. Das 2011; and *The Economist* 2014.

50. For more on this, see Scott 2013; and Devi and Raja 2012.

51. Good overviews of India's bilateral military collaborations with Southeast Asian states are located in 'Looking East in Defense: Perspectives on India–Southeast Asia Relations' (Basrur and Das 2013). Also refer to Brewster 2014; Jha 2011; and B. Singh 2011.

52. For an argument that there is an incongruity between India's own leadership aspirations in Asia and the perceptions of its own capabilities by other countries in the region, see Brewster 2012. Also refer to Pant 2009a.

53. Consult, for instance, Mohan 2010; and Pant 2009b.

54. For a highly critical assessment, refer to Cohen and Dasgupta 2010.

55. For a view that it 'may take an almost Copernican revolution in strategic thought to help India negotiate the challenges posed' by extraregional operations, see Holmes 2012. For an argument that 'it is doubtful India could do much to counter China so far from its home bases and so near to China's major naval facilities on Hainan Island', see Gordon 2014: 147.

References

Ahluwalia, Montek S. 2002. 'Economic Reforms in India since 1991: Has Gradualism Worked?', *Journal of Economic Perspectives*, 16(3): 67–88.

Aneja, Atul. 2014. 'China Invites India for "Indo-Pacific" Partnership to Counter U.S. Pivot', *Hindu* (Beijing), 6 December; available at http://www.thehindu.com/todays-paper/tp-international/china-invites-india-for-indopacific-partnership-to-counter-us- pivot/article6666919.ece.

Association of Southeast Asian Nations (ASEAN). 2014a. 'External Trade Statistics'; available at http://www.asean.org/resources/2012-02-10-08-47-55/asean-statistics/item/external-trade-statistics-3 (accessed 29 January 2015).

———. 2014b. 'External Trade Statistics', Tables 19 and 24; available at http://www.asean.org/resources/2012-02-10-08-47-55/asean-statistics/item/external-trade-statistics-3.

———. 2012. 'Vision Statement ASEAN–India Commemorative Summit', 21 December; available at http://www.asean.org/news/asean-statement-communiques/item/vision-statement-asean-india-commemorative-summit (accessed 3 January 2015).

Ayoob, Mohammed. 1990. *India and Southeast Asia: Indian Perceptions and Policies.* London: Routledge.

Babu, Shyam. 2004. 'National Security Council: Yet Another Ad Hoc Move?' *Security Beyond Survival: Essays for K. Subrahmanyam*, edited by P.R. Kumaraswamy [SP1]. New Delhi: Sage.

Bagchi, Indrani. 2015. 'India Fails to Walk the "Act East" Talk', *Times of India* (New Delhi), 15 February; available at http://timesofindia.indiatimes.com/india/India-fails-to-walk-the-Act-East-talk/articleshow/46248292.cms.

———. 2014. 'India Ignores China's Frown, Offers Defence Boost to Vietnam', *Times of India* (New Delhi), 29 October; available at http://timesofindia.indiatimes.com/india/India-ignores-Chinas-frown-offers-defence-boost-to-Vietnam/articleshow/44965272.cms.

———. 2012. 'Indo-Pacific Finds Pride of Place in Asean Lexicon', *Times of India* (New Delhi), 20 December; available at http://timesofindia.indiatimes.com/india/Indo-Pacific-finds-pride-of-place-in-Asean-lexicon/articleshow/17697636.cms.

———. 2012. 'Manila Hails Navy Chief's Stand on South China Sea', *Times of India* (New Delhi), 19 December; available at http://timesofindia.indiatimes.com/india/Manila-hails-Navy-chiefs-stand-on-South-China-Sea/articleshow/17671495.cms.

———. 2012. 'ASEAN Nations Lap Up Navy Chief's South China Sea Comment', *Times of India* (New Delhi), 18 December; available at http://timesofindia.indiatimes.com/india/Asean-nations-lap-up-Navy-chiefs-South-China-Sea-comment/articleshow/17668261.cms.

Balachandran, Manu. 2015. 'Is Modi's New $2 Billion Trans-India Highway Project Just Too Ambitious?', *Quartz India*, 29 April; available at http://qz.com/394021/is-modis-new-2-billion-trans-india-highway-project-just-too-ambitious/ (accessed 29 April 2015).

Baru, Sanjaya. 2009. 'It's Time for a "Look Further East Policy"', *Business Standard* (New Delhi) 7 December; available at http://www.business-standard.com/article/opinion/sanjaya-baru-it-s-time-for-a-look-further-east-policy-109120700088_1.html (accessed 16 April 2015).

Basrur, Rajesh and Ajay Kumar Das (Guest eds). 2013. 'Looking East in Defense: Perspectives on India-Southeast Asia Relations', *India Review*, 12(3), Special Issue: 119–224.

Basu, Nayanima. 2014a. 'India–ASEAN Services FTA in Limbo Over Retail FDI', *Business Standard* (New Delhi), 15 April; available at http://www. business-standard.com/article/economy-policy/india-asean-services-fta-in-limbo-over-retail- fdi-114041400972_1.html.

———. 2014b. 'After WTO, India Skips Signing Asean Services Trade Pact', *Business Standard* (Nay Pyi Taw), 27 August; available at http://www. business-standard.com/article/economy-policy/india-puts-off-asean-services-trade-pact- 114082700029_1.html.

Bateman, Sam and Joshua Ho (eds). 2010. *Southeast Asia and the Rise of Chinese and Indian Naval Power: Between Rising Naval Powers*. New York: Routledge.

Bayley, Susan. 2004. 'Imagining "Greater India": French and Indian Visions of Colonialism in the Indic Mode', *Modern Asian Studies*, 38(3): 703–44.

Bellman, Eric and Peter Kenny. 2014. 'India Blocks WTO Agreement to Ease Trade Rules', *Wall Street Journal* (Geneva), 27 July; available at http://www.wsj. com/articles/india-blocks-wto-agreement-to-ease-trade-rules-1406471335.

Bhargava, Jitender. 2013. *The Descent of Air India*. New Delhi: Bloomsbury Publishing India.

Bharucha, Rustom. 2006. *Another Asia: Rabindranath Tagore and Okakura Tenshin*. New Delhi: Oxford University Press.

Bhatia, Rajiv K. and Vijay Sakhuja. 2014. *Indo-Pacific Region: Political and Strategic Perspectives*. New Delhi: Indian Council of World Affairs.

Bhattacherjee, Aparupa. 2014. 'India–ASEAN FTA: Gap Between Expectation and Reality', *Institute of Peace and Conflict Studies*, 5 September; available at http://www.ipcs.org/article/india/india-asean-fta-gap-between-expectation-and-reality-4644.html (accessed 2 February 2015).

Bhattacharjee, Rupak. 2014. 'North East in BCIM–EC: Problems and Prospects', Institute for Defence Studies and Analyses, IDSA Comment Series, 14 October; available at http://www.idsa.in/idsacomments/NorthEast% 20inBCIM-EC_RBhattacharjee_171014 (accessed 11 February 2015).

Bhaumik, Subir. 2014. '"Look East" through Northeast: Challenges and Prospects for India', Observer Research Foundation, Occasional Paper Series, no. 51, June.

———. 2009. *Troubled Periphery: Crisis of India's Northeast*. New Delhi: Sage.

Bland, Ben. 2012. 'Regional Tensions Flare at Asean Summit', *Financial Times* (Phnom Penh), 19 November; available at http://www.ft.com/intl/cms/s/0/e87b2b74-3240-1 1e2- 916a-00144feabdc0.html.

Bland, Ben and Giriji Shivakumar. 2011. 'China Confronts Indian Navy Vessel', *Financial Times* (New Delhi), 31 August; available at http://www.ft.com/intl/cms/s/0/883003ec- d3f6-11e0-b7eb-00144feab49a.html.

Bin Yahya, Faizal. 2008. *New 'Temples' of India: Singapore and India Collaboration in IT Parks*. Leiden: Koninklijke Brill NV.

Bipindra, N.C. 2012. 'Navy Boosting Eastern Flank', *New Indian Express* (New Delhi), 31 December; available at http://www.newindianexpress.com/nation/article1401333.ece.

Blustein, Paul. 2008. 'The Nine-Day Misadventures of the Most Favored Nations: How the WTO's Doha Round Negotiations Went Awry in July 2008', *Brookings Institute*, 5 December; available at http://www.brookings.edu/research/articles/2008/12/05-trade-blustein (accessed 3 February 2015).

Brewster, David. 2014. 'India's Engagement with Southeast Asia: Singapore, Vietnam, and Indonesia', in *The Engagement of India: Strategies and Responses*, edited by Ian Hall, pp. 147–68. Washington DC: Georgetown University Press.

———. 2013. 'India's Defense Strategy and the India–ASEAN Relationship', *India Review*, 12(3): 151–64.

———. 2012. *India as an Asia Pacific Power*. New York: Routledge.

———. 2011. 'The Relationship between India and Indonesia: An Evolving Security Partnership?', *Asian Survey*, 51(2): 221–44.

———. 2009. 'India's Strategic Partnership with Vietnam: The Search for a Diamond in the South China Sea?', *Asian Security*, 5(1): 24–44.

Bruce, Arun. 2014. 'India's Manufacturing Cost Competitiveness: Holding Steady', Boston Consulting Group, 19 August; available at https://www.bcgperspectives.com/content/articles/lean_manufacturing_globalization_india_manufacturing_cost_competitiveness/ (accessed 11 February 2015).

Business Standard (Mumbai). 2015. 'Rao Govt Wanted Tatas to Start Airline but Backed Out: Ratan Tata', 30 January; available at http://www.business-standard.com/article/companies/rao-govt-wanted-tatas-to-start-airline-but-backed-out- ratan-tata-115013000006_1.html.

Chandra, Raghav. 2013. 'Connecting India: It's Still a Long, Bumpy Road Ahead', *Economic Times*, 14 September; available at http://articles.economictimes.indiatimes.com/2013-09-14/news/42062418_1_highway-development-corridor-private-sector.

Chandra, Varigonda Kesava. 2012. 'The Pipeline That Wasn't: Myanmar–Bangladesh–India Natural Gas Pipeline', *Journal of Energy Security*, April; available at http://www.ensec.org/index.php?option=com_content&view=article&id=348:india-bangladesh-and-the-myanmar-bangladesh-india-

natural-gas-pipeline-how-not-to-achieve-energy-s&catid=123:content&-Itemid=389 (accessed 3 February 2015).

Chaudhury, Anasua Basu Ray and Pratnashree Basu. 2015. *India–Bangladesh Connectivity: Possibilities and Challenges*. Kolkata: Observer Research Foundation.

Choudhury, Chandrahas. 2014. 'India's Battle to Become a Single Market', *Bloomberg View*, 18 December; available at http://www.bloombergview.com/articles/2014-12-18/indias-battle-to-become-a-single-market (accessed 28 January 2015).

Clinton, Hillary Rodham. 2011. 'Secretary of State Hillary Rodham Clinton Speaks on India and the United States: A Vision for the 21st Century', U.S. Department of State, 20 July; available at http://www.state.gov/secretary/20092013clinton/rm/2011/07/168840.htm.

Cloud, David S. and Mark Magnier. 2012. 'India Not Sold on Closer Military Ties with U.S.', *Los Angeles Times* (New Delhi), 6 June; available at http://articles.latimes.com/2012/jun/06/world/la-fg-panetta-india-20120607.

Cohen, Stephen P. and Sunil Dasgupta. 2010. *Arming without Aiming: India's Military Modernization*. Washington, DC: Brookings Institution Press.

Colvin, Ross. 2012. 'In China's Shadow, ASEAN Leaders Look to India for Maritime Security', Reuters (New Delhi), 20 December; available at http://www.reuters.com/article/2012/12/20/us-india-southeastasia-idUSBRE8BJ0Q220121220.

Das, Durga. 1969. *India from Curzon to Nehru and After*. New Delhi: Rupa Publications.

Das, Gurcharan. 2014. 'AamAadmi Is Not the Reforming Party India Needs', *Financial Times*, 27 January; available at http://www.ft.com/intl/cms/s/0/0563b53a-81d2-11e3-87d5-00144feab7de.html.

Das, Gurudas. 2012. *Security and Development in India's Northeast*. New Delhi: Oxford University Press.

Das, Pushpita. 2011. 'Securing the Andaman and Nicobar Islands', *Strategic Analysis*, 35(3): 465–78.

Das, Ram Upendra and Nitya Batra. 2015. 'Fresh Perspectives Needed to Boost South Asia Connectivity', East Asia Forum, 21 February; available at http://www.eastasiaforum.org/2015/02/21/fresh-perspectives-needed-to-boost-south-asian-connectivity/ (accessed 23 February 2015).

Das Gupta, Surajeet. 2015. 'Two Decades in the Departure Lounge', *Business Standard* (New Delhi), 9 January; available at http://www.business-standard.com/article/companies/two-decades-in-the-departure-lounge-115010800788_1.html.

Dasgupta, Saibal. 2012. 'Navy Chief Was Fed Words by Media: NSA', *Times of India* (Beijing), 5 December; available at http://timesofindia.

indiatimes.com/india/Navy-chief-was-fed-words-by-media-NSA/article-show/17486187.cms.

Datta-Ray, Sunanda K. 2015. 'The Singapore–India Chronicles', *Business Standard*, 7 August; available at http://www.business-standard.com/article/opinion/sunanda-k-datta-ray-the-singapore-india-chronicles-115080800006_1.html.

De, Prabir. 2014. 'India's Emerging Connectivity with Southeast Asia: Progress and Prospects', Asian Development Bank Institute, *Working Paper Series*, no. 507, December.

Dehejia, Vivek. 2011. 'Don't Blame "Neoliberal" Reforms for Corruption', *Financial Times*, 25 July; available at http://www.ft.com/intl/cms/s/0/e4660ef4-b68c-11e0-ae1f-00144feabdc0.html.

Desai, Meghnad. 2009. 'Economic Reform by Stealth', *Tehelka*, 6(13), 4 April; available at http://www.tehelka.com/2009/04/economic-reform-by-stealth/ (accessed 11 February 2015).

Devi, T. Nirmala and Adlari Subramanyam Raja (eds). 2012. *India and Southeast Asia: Strategic Convergence in the Twenty-First Century*. New Delhi: Manohar.

Downie, Edmund. 2015. 'Manipur and India's "Act East" Policy', *The Diplomat*, 25 February; available at http://thediplomat.com/2015/02/manipur-and-indias-act-east-policy/ (accessed 26 February 2015).

Economic Survey 2014–15. 2015. New Delhi: Ministry of Finance, Department of Economic Affairs, Economic Division.

Economic Times (Hanoi). 2014. 'Sushma Swaraj Tells Indian Envoys to Act East and Not Just Look East', 26 August; available at http://articles.economictimes.indiatimes.com/2014-08-26/news/53243802_1_india-and-asean-countries-east-asia-strategically-important-region.

———. (New Delhi/Geneva). 2013. 'Infrastructure Most Problematic Factor for Doing Business in India: WEF', 4 September; available at http://articles.economictimes.indiatimes.com/2013-09-04/news/41765462_1_global-competitiveness-report-world-economic-forum-report-wef.

Economist (Colombo). 2013. 'China's Foreign Ports: The New Masters and Commanders', 8 June; available at http://www.economist.com/news/international/21579039-chinas-growing-empire-ports-abroad-mainly-about-trade-not-aggression-new-masters.

Elliott, John. 2015. 'India's Remote, Underdeveloped Northeast Quarter', *Asia Sentinel*, 7 January ; available at http://www.asiasentinel.com/society/india-remote-underdeveloped-quarter-assam/ (accessed 10 January 2015).

Express News Service. 2012. 'Navy Chief's Remarks: MEA Asks for Restraint', *Indian Express* (New Delhi), 6 December; available at http://

archive.indianexpress.com/news/navy-chief-s-remarks-mea-asks-for-restraint/1040999/.

Fe Bureau. 2013. 'Indian Industry No Longer an Infant That Needed to Be Mollycoddled, Says Raghuram Rajan', *Indian Express* (Mumbai), 16 November; available at http://archive.indianexpress.com/news/indian-industry-no-longer-an-infant-that-needed-to-be-mollycoddled-says-raghuram-rajan/1195469/.

Forbes, Steve. 2015. 'How Modi Can Make India a Global Superpower', *Forbes India*, 27 May; available at http://forbesindia.com/article/one-year-of-modi-government/steve-forbes-how-modi-can-make-india-a-global-superpower/40287/1.

FICCI and PwC. 2014. *Gateway to the ASEAN: India's North East Frontier*. New Delhi: Federation of Indian Chambers of Commerce & Industry, 27 November; available at https://www.pwc.in/assets/pdfs/publications/2014/gateway-to-the-asean.pdf (accessed 11 February 2015).

Gordon, Sandy. 2014. *India's Rise as an Asian Power: Nation, Neighborhood and Region*. Washington, DC: Georgetown University Press.

Guha, Ramachandra (ed.). 2011. *Makers of Modern India*. Cambridge, MA: Harvard University Press.

Gupta, Ranjit. 2014. *BIMSTEC: Yesterday, Today and Tomorrow: An Interview with Amb Ranjit Gupta*, by Leonora Juergens, 4 June.

Haider, Salman. 2012. 'Look East', *Two Decades of India's Look East Policy*, edited by Amar Nath Ram, 53–62. New Delhi: Manohar.

Hindustan Times (New Delhi). 2012. 'I've Maintained High Standard of Integrity in My Conduct', 6 July; available at http://www.hindustantimes.com/newdelhi/i-ve-maintained-high-standard-of-integrity-in-my-conduct/article1-883969.aspx.

Holmes, James R. 2012. 'Inside, Outside: India's "Exterior Lines" in the South China Sea', *Strategic Analysis*, 36(3) (May–June): 358–63.

Holmes, James R., Andrew C. Winner, and Toshi Yoshihara. 2009. *Indian Naval Strategy in the Twenty-First Century*. New York: Routledge.

Huda, Mirza Sadaqat. 2013. 'Myanmar, Bangladesh and India: Prospects for Energy Cooperation', *National Geographic: Voices* (blog), 13 July; available at http://voices.nationalgeographic.com/2013/07/13/myanmar-bangladesh-and-india/.

Indo-Asian News Service (IANS). 2012a. 'Hillary Clinton Lauds India's Role for Indo-Pacific Region, Urges for Increased Participation', *India Today* (Melbourne), 14 November; available at http://indiatoday.intoday.in/story/hillary-clinton-lauds-indias-role-indo-pacific-region-talks-china-breifly-in-australia/1/229136.html (accessed 29 January 2015).

———. 2012b. 'No Active Deployment of Warships in Pacific: India', *New Indian Express* (New Delhi), 7 August; available at http://www.newindianexpress.com/nation/article584878.ece.

———. 2014a. 'India Needs to Decide on Net Security Provider Role: NSA', *Business Standard* (New Delhi), 12 February; available at http://www.business-standard.com/article/news-ians/india-needs-to-decide-on-net-security-provider- role- nsa-114021201648_1.html.

———. 2014b. 'Northeast India to Be Made Gateway of Southeast Asia: Modi', *Business Standard* (Tripura), 1 December; available at http://www.business-standard.com/article/news-ians/northeast-india-to-be-made-gateway-of-southeast-asia-modi-114120100796_1.html.

Jaffrelott, Christophe. 2003. 'India's Look East Policy: An Asianist Strategy in Perspective', *India Review*, 2: 35–68.

Jenkins, Rob. 2007. 'Political Skills: Introducing Reform by Stealth', *India's Economic Transition: The Politics of Reforms*, edited by Rahul Mukherji, 170–201. New Delhi: Oxford University Press.

———. 2004. 'Introduction', *India Review*, 3(4): 257–68.

———. 1999. *Democratic Politics and Economic Reform in India*. New York: Cambridge University Press.

Jha, Pankaj Kumar. 2011. 'India's Defence Diplomacy in Southeast Asia', *Journal of Defence Studies*, 5: 47–63.

Joshi, Manoj. 2015. 'Building Better Connections', *Mid-Day*, 17 February; available at http://www.mid-day.com/articles/building-better-connections/15994199.

Kak, Radhika. 2014. 'India—Unleashing the ASEAN Opportunity', *Standard Chartered Global Research*, 21 August.

Kaushiva, Pradeep and Abhijit Singh (eds). 2014. *The Geopolitics of the Indo-Pacific*. New Delhi: Knowledge World.

Kaw, M.K. 2012. *An Outsider Everywhere: Revelations from an Insider*. New Delhi: Konark Publishers.

Kazmin, Amy. 'India Struggles to Build Up Infrastructure Dream', *Financial Times* (New Delhi), 29 July; available at http://www.ft.com/intl/cms/s/0/a4152f94-1627-11e4- 89ec- 00144feabdc0.html.

Keenleyside, T.A. 1982. 'Nationalist Indian Attitudes Toward Asia: A Troublesome Legacy for Post-Independence Indian Foreign Policy', *Pacific Affairs*, 55(2): 210–30.

Kripalani, Manjeet. 1997. 'India's Private Airport May Get Grounded', *BusinessWeek* (Bangalore), 11 May; available at http://www.bloomberg.com/bw/stories/1997-05-11/indias-private-airport-may-get-grounded (accessed 30 January 2015).

Kulkarni, Sanket Sudhir. 2013. 'India's Pipeline Diplomacy: Case of Lost Opportunities', *ISSSP Reflections*, 4; available at http://isssp.in/indias-pipeline-diplomacy-case-of-lost-opportunities/ (accessed 3 February 2015).

Kumar, Ritesh Singh and Prachi Priya. 2014. 'Indian States Need a Free Trade Deal', *The Diplomat*, 4 December; available at http://thediplomat.com/2014/12/indian-states- need-a- free-trade-deal/ (accessed 6 December 2015).

Kumar, Vinay. 2013. 'India Well Positioned to Become a Net Provider of Security: Manmohan Singh', *Hindu* (New Delhi), 23 May; available at http://www.thehindu.com/news/national/india-well-positioned-to-become-a-net-provider-of-security-manmohan-singh/article4742337.ece.

Ladwig, Walter C. 2009. 'Delhi's Pacific Ambitions: Naval Power, "Look East," and India's Emerging Influence in the Asia-Pacific', *Asian Security*, 5(2): 87–113.

Lall, Rajiv, and Ritu Anand. 2014. 'Modernizing Transport Infrastructure', *Getting India Back on Track: An Action Agenda for Reform*, edited by Bibek Debroy, Ashley J. Tellis, and Reece Trevor, 138–49. Washington, DC: Carnegie Endowment for International Peace.

Limaye, Sharang. 2012. 'Roadbuilders Stall on Bottlenecks: Corporate India', *BloombergBusiness*, 12 September; available at http://www.bloomberg.com/news/articles/2012-09-12/roadbuilders-stall-on-bottlenecks-corporate-india.

Malik, Preet. 2012. 'India's Look East Policy: Genesis', *Two Decades of India's Look East Policy*, edited by Amar Nath Ram, 23–8. New Delhi: Manohar.

Mallet, Victor. 2015. 'Asian Highway One Mired in Muddy Reality', *Financial Times* (Moreh, India), 23 July; available at http://www.ft.com/intl/cms/s/0/7ee3f1c4- 2f0d-11e5-8873- 775ba7c2ea3d.html#slide0.

———. 2014. 'India is a Nation in Need of a Trade Deal with Itself', *Financial Times* (New Delhi), 3 November; available at http://www.ft.com/intl/cms/s/0/647d1630- 5ec5-11e4-be0b-00144feabdc0.html.

———. 2012. 'Asian Jitters Drive Race for Strategic Ties', *Financial Times* (New Delhi), 26 December; available at http://www.ft.com/intl/cms/s/0/f0ddc1e4-4d36-11e2-a99b-00144feab49a.html.

Malone, David M. 2011. *Does the Elephant Dance? Contemporary Indian Foreign Policy*. New York: Oxford University Press.

Mani, V.S. 1998. 'Nehru's Dreams of an Eastern Federation', *Nehru's Foreign Policy, Fifty Years On*, edited by Surjit Mansingh. New Delhi: Mosaic Books.

Mathur, Akshay. 2014. 'Policy Catalyst: Seven Sisters' Corridor', Mumbai: *Gateway House: Indian Council on Global Relations*, 30 May; available at http://www.gatewayhouse.in/policy-catalyst-seven-sisters-corridor/ (accessed 11 February 2015).

Medcalf, Rory. 2013. 'The Indo-Pacific: What's in a Name?', *The American Interest*, 9(2) : 58–66.

Mehrotra, Kartukay. 2014. 'India to Become Single Market for First Time', *Bloomberg Business*, 6 August; available at http://www.bloomberg.com/news/articles/2014-08-05/india-to-become-single-market-for-first-time-on-modi-tax-u-turn.

Menon, Rajan. 2014. 'The India Myth', *The National Interest*, 134 (November/December): 46–57.

Mishra, Pankaj. 2012. *From the Ruins of Empire: The Intellectuals Who Remade Asia*. New York: Farrar, Straus and Giroux.

Mohan, C. Raja. 2015. 'Modi's Sagar Mala', *Indian Express*, 11 March; available at http://indianexpress.com/article/opinion/columns/modis-sagar-mala/.

———. 2013. 'An Uncertain Trumpet: India's Role in Southeast Asian Security', *India Review*, 12(3): 134–50.

———. 2012. *Samudra Manthan: Sino-Indian Rivalry in the Indo-Pacific*. Washington DC: Carnegie Endowment for International Peace.

———. 2010. 'The Return of the Raj', *The American Interest*, 5(5): 4–11.

Moraes, Frank. 1973. *Witness to an Era: India 1920 to the Present Day*. London: Wiedenfeld & Nicholson.

Muni, S.D. 2012. 'Look East Policy: Beyond Myths', *Two Decades of India's Look East Policy*, edited by Amar Nath Ram, 205–20. New Delhi: Manohar.

———. 2011 . 'India's "Look East" Policy: The Strategic Dimension', Institute of South Asian Studies, Working Paper Series, no. 121, 1 February.

Narlikar, Amrita and Aruna Narlikar. 2014. *Bargaining with a Rising India: Lessons from the Mahabharata*. Oxford, UK: Oxford University Press.

Nayar, Baldev Raj. 2014. *Globalization and India's Economic Integration*. Washington, DC: Georgetown University Press.

Nayar, Baldev Raj and T.V. Paul. 2003. *India in the World Order: Searching for Major-Power Status*. New York: Cambridge University Press.

NDTV. 2004. Interview with P.V. Narasimha Rao, 'Walk the Talk', recorded 11 May 2004; available at http://www.ndtv.com/video/player/walk-the-talk/walk-the-talk-p-v-narasimha-rao/296375 (accessed 4 February 2015).

Nehru, Jawaharlal. 1954. 'Our Policy Is Positive: Address Before the Indian Parliament, 17 March, 1950', *Jawaharlal Nehru's Speeches*, vol. 2. New Delhi: Ministry of Information & Broadcasting.

———. 1941. *Toward Freedom*. New York: The John Day Company.

New York Herald Tribune. 1950. 'India's Position', 5 October.

New York Times. 1950. 'Editorial', 30 August.

Ninan, T.N. 2015. 'The Defensive Crouch', *Business Standard* (New Delhi), 24 July; available at http://www.business-standard.com/article/opinion/t-n-ninan-the-defensive-crouch-115072400766_1.html (accessed 26 July 2015).

———. 2013. 'Why Is India's Garment Industry Stuck in a Stagnant Loom?' *Rediff.com* (New Delhi), 8 July; available at http://www.rediff.com/money/slide-show/slide-show-1-why-is-indias-garment-industry-stuck-in-a-stagnant-loom/20130708.htm.

North Eastern Council. 2008. *North East Region, Vision 2020.* New Delhi: Ministry of Development of North Eastern Region.

Obama, Barack. 2010. 'Remarks by the President to the Joint Session of the Indian Parliament', The White House, Office of the Press Secretary, 8 November; available at https://www.whitehouse.gov/the-press-office/2010/11/08/remarks-president-joint-session-indian-parliament-new-delhi-india (accessed 29 January 2015).

Pandit, Rajat. 2015a. 'Govt Approves Construction of 7 Stealth Frigates, 6 Nuclear-Powered Submarines', *Times of India* (New Delhi), 18 February; available at http://timesofindia.indiatimes.com/india/Govt-approves-con-struction-of-7-stealth-frigates-6-nuclear-powered-submarines/articles-how/46281364.cms.

———. 2015b. 'India to Slowly but Steadily Boost Military Presence in Andaman and Nicobar Islands', *Times of India* (New Delhi), 7 May; available at http://timesofindia.indiatimes.com/india/India-to-slowly-but-steadily-boost-military-presence-in-Andaman-and-Nicobar-Islands/articleshow/47182151.cms.

———. 2012. 'Indian Warships Ready to Sail for Troubled S China Sea if Required', *Times of India* (New Delhi), 3 December; available at http://timesofindia.indiatimes.com/city/delhi/Indian-warships-ready-to-sail-for-troubled-S-China-Sea-if-required/articleshow/17469306.cms.

———. 2010. 'Strategically-important A&N Command to Get a Boost', *Times of India* (Port Blair), 6 February; available at http://timesofindia.indiatimes.com/india/Strategically-important-AN-Command-to-get-a-boost/articleshow/5540325.cms.

Pandit, Rajat and Sachin Parashar. 2012. 'U.S., China Woo India for Control Over Asia-Pacific', *Times of India* (New Delhi), 7 June; available at http://timesofindia.indiatimes.com/india/US-China-woo-India-for-control-over-Asia-Pacific/articleshow/13877405.cms.

Pandya, Sonal S. 2014. 'Why Foreign Investment Still Polarizes India', *The Washington Post: Monkey Cage* (blog), 30 September; available at http://

www.washingtonpost.com/blogs/monkey-cage/wp/2014/09/30/why-foreign- investment-still-polarizes-india/.

Pant, Harsh V. (ed.) 2012. *The Rise of the Indian Navy: Internal Vulnerabilities, External Challenges.* Burlington, VT: Ashgate.

———. 2009a. 'India in the Indian Ocean: Growing Mismatch between Ambitions and Capabilities', *Pacific Affairs*, 82(2): 279–97.

———. 2009b. *Indian Foreign Policy in a Unipolar World.* London: Routledge.

Prakash, Arun. 2011. 'Where Are Our Ships Bound?' *Indian Express*, 1 October; available at http://archive.indianexpress.com/news/where-are-our-ships-bound-/854100/.

Press Trust of India (PTI). 2015. 'Indo-Bangla Rail Project to Suffer for Want of Funds: Tripura Min', *Business Standard* (Agartala), 27 February; available at http://www.business-standard.com/article/pti- stories/indo-bangla-rail-prjct-to-suffer-for-want-of- funds-tripura-min-115022701233_1.html.

———. 2014a. 'World Looking at India with Expectations, but We Aren't Ready: Modi', *Firstpost*, 25 December; available at http://www.firstpost.com/india/world-looking-at-india-with-expectations-but-we-arent-ready-modi-2015655.html.

———. 2014b. 'Centre Suspends New Schemes under NEIIPP with Immediate Effect', *Economic Times* (Guwahati), 3 December; available at http://articles.economictimes.indiatimes.com/2014-12-03/news/56684901_1_neiipp-investment-promotion-policy-new-schemes.

———. 2013. 'Arunachal Pradesh Is "Integral and Important Part" of India: Pranab Mukherjee', *Times of India* (Tanagar), 29 November; available at http://timesofindia.indiatimes.com/india/Arunachal-Pradesh-is-integral-and-important-part-of-India-Pranab-Mukherjee/articleshow/26590025.cms.

———. 2007. 'Vietnam for Greater Economic Engagement with India', *Times of India* (Hanoi), 20 June; available at http://timesofindia.indiatimes.com/world/rest-of-world/Vietnam-for-greater-economic-engagement-with-India/articleshow/2135527.cms.

Ram, Amar Nath. 2012. 'The First Decade of India's Look East Policy: An Insider's Account', *Two Decades of India's Look East Policy: Partnership for Peace, Progress and Prosperity*, edited by Amar Nath Ram, 63–81. New Delhi: Manohar.

Rao, P.V. Narasimha. 2013. *Walk the Talk*, by Shekhar Gupta. NDTV, 31 October; available at http://www.ndtv.com/video/player/walk-the-talk/walk-the-talk-p-v-narasimha-rao/296375 (accessed 29 January 2015).

———. 1994. *India and the Asia–Pacific: Forging a New Relationship.* Singapore: Institute of Southeast Asian Studies.

Ravi, N. 2012. 'India and Southeast Asia', *Two Decades of India's Look East Policy: Partnership for Peace, Progress and Prosperity*, edited by Amar Nath Ram, 169–84. New Delhi: Manohar.

Reuters. 1994. 'Singapore Team's Visit to Spark "India Fever"', *New Straits Times* (Singapore), 24 January; available at https://news.google.com/newspapers ?nid=1309&dat=19940124&id=RztOAAAAIBA J&sjid=zxMEAAAAI BAJ&pg=6764,1407602&hl=en.

———— (New Delhi). 2012. 'Indian Navy Prepared to Deploy to South China Sea', 3 December; available at http://www.reuters.com/article/ 2012/12/03/us-china-sea-india- idUSBRE8B20KY20121203.

Roche, Elizabeth. 2014. 'Highway Linking India to Myanmar, Thailand Likely by 2016: VK Singh', *Livemint.com* (New Delhi), 14 August; available at http:// www.livemint.com/Politics/lXLGGeFzlUmlc3p5hIuKMP/Highway- linking- India-to-Myanmar-Thailand-likely-by-2016-V.html.

Sakri, Rajiv. 2009. *Challenge and Strategy: Rethinking India's Foreign Policy*. New Delhi: Sage Publications.

Samanta, Pranab Dhal. 2013. 'In Signal to China, Manmohan Singh Embraces Japan's Idea', *Indian Express* (Tokyo), 29 May; available at http://archive. indianexpress.com/news/in-signal-to-china-manmohan-singh-embraces- japans-idea/1121761/.

Saran, Shyam. 2011. 'Mapping the Indo-Pacific', *Indian Express*, 29 October; available at http://archive.indianexpress.com/news/mapping-the-indopacific/ 867004/.

————. 2010. 'Time for Just Looking East Over', *Business Standard*, 17 November; available at http://www.business-standard.com/article/opinion/shyam- saran-time-for- just-looking-east-over-110111700028_1.html (accessed 29 January 2015).

————. 2009. 'India's Foreign Policy and the Andaman & Nicobar Islands', *Security and Development of Andaman & Nicobar Islands Seminar Proceedings*, 15 September.

Scott, David. 2013. 'India's Role in the South China Sea: Geopolitics and Geoeconomics in Play', *India Review*, 12(2): 51–69.

————. 2012a. 'India and the Allure of the "Indo-Pacific"', *International Studies*, 49(3–4): 165–88.

————. 2012b. 'The "Indo-Pacific"—New Regional Formulations and New Maritime Frameworks for US–Indian Strategic Convergence', *Asia–Pacific Review*, 19(2): 85–109.

See, Chak Mun Li-Jen Tan, Rahul Advani, and Rinishi Dutt. 2015. *Singapore and India: Towards a Shared Future*. Singapore: Institute of South Asian Studies, National University of Singapore.

Sen, Amiti. 2015. 'India Is in No Hurry to Begin Bilateral Investment Talks with US', *Hindu Business Line* (New Delhi), 13 February; available at http://www.thehindubusinessline.com/economy/india-in-no-hurry-to-begin-bilateral- investment-talks-with-us/article6892638.ece.

Sender, Henny. 2015. 'India: If You Can Make It There …', *Financial Times*, 3 March; available at http://www.ft.com/intl/cms/s/0/dddb842c-c198-11e4-bd24-00144feab7de.html.

Sharma, Mihir S. 2015. *Restart: The Last Chance for the Indian Economy*. Gurgaon: Random House India.

Sikarwar, Deepshikha. 2014. 'Government Plans to Create Unified National Market', *Economic Times* (New Delhi), 12 November; available at http://articles.economictimes.indiatimes.com/2014-11-12/news/56025583_1_market-commission-gst-inter-state.

Simhan, Te Raja. 2014. 'Why Indian Ports Can't Compete with Colombo', *Hindu Business Line* (Chennai), 16 December; available at http://www.thehindubusinessline.com/industry-and-economy/logistics/why-indian-ports-cant-compete-with-colombo/article6698168.ece.

Singh, Abhijit. 2012. 'The Indian Navy's New "Expeditionary" Outlook', Observer Research Foundation, Occasional Paper Series, no. 37 (October).

Singh, Bikash. 2014. 'Union Commerce Ministry Assures to Resume North East Industrial and Investment Promotion Policy', *Economic Times* (Guwahati), 12 December; available at http://articles.economictimes.indiatimes.com/2014-12-12/news/56990502_1_investment-promotion-policy-neiipp-north-east-industrial.

Singh, Bilveer. 2011. 'Southeast Asia–India Defence Relations in the Changing Regional Security Landscape', Institute for Defence Studies and Analyses, Monograph Series, no. 4 (May).

Singh, Manmohan. 2012. 'Opening Statement by Prime Minister at Plenary Session of India–ASEAN Commemorative Summit', Government of India, Ministry of External Affairs, 20 December; available at http://mea.gov.in/Speeches-Statements.htm?dtl/20981/Opening+Statement+by+Prime+Minister+at+Plenary+Session+of+IndiaASEAN+Commemorative+Summit (accessed 29 January 2015).

Singhal, Rajrishi. 2014. 'India–ASEAN's Elusive Services FTA', *Gateway House: Indian Council on Global Relations*, 31 January; available at http://www.gatewayhouse.in/india-aseans-elusive-services-fta/ (accessed 11 February 2015).

Singh, Shri Rajnath. 2014. 'Presidential Speech by Shri Rajnath Singh at BJP National Council Meeting at Ramlila Ground, New Delhi', Bharatiya Janata Party: National Executive, 18 January; available at http://www.bjp.org/

en/documents/national-executive-documents/2014/presidential-speech-by-shri-rajnath-singh-at-bjp-national-council-meeting-at-ramlila-ground-new-delhi (accessed 30 January 2015).

Sinha, Shri Yashwant. 2003. 'Remarks by Shri Yashwant Sinha, External Affairs Minister of India, at the Plenary Session Second India–ASEAN Business Summit', Government of India, Ministry of External Affairs, 4 September; available at http://mea.gov.in/Speeches-Statements.htm?dtl/4843/Remar ks+by+Shri+Yashwant+Sinha+External+Affairs+Minister+of+India+ at+The+Plenary+Session+Second+India++ASEAN+Business+Summit (accessed 2 April 2015).

Soni, Shubh and Richa Sekhani. 2015. 'World Sees India as Not Contributing Much to Trade Negotiations', Observer Research Foundation, Delhi, 2 March; available at http://www.orfonline.org/cms/sites/orfonline/ modules/report/ReportDetail.html?cmaid=79353&mmacmaid=79354 (accessed 3 March 2015).

South China Morning Post. 2012. 'Asean Wants India's Help in China Disputes', 21 December; available at http://www.scmp.com/news/asia/article/1109717/ asean-wants- indias-help-china-disputes.

Srivastava, Shruti. 2014. 'ASEAN FTA Review Shows India "Got Almost Nothing"', *Indian Express* (New Delhi), 3 October; available at http:// indianexpress.com/article/business/business-others/asean-fta-review-shows- india- got-almost-nothing/.

Stolte, Caroline. 2014. '"The Asiatic hour": New Perspectives on the Asian Relations Conference, New Delhi, 1947', *The Non-Aligned Movement and the Cold War: Delhi–Bandung–Belgrade*, edited by Natasa Miskovic, Harald Fischer-Tine, and Nada Boskovska. New York: Routledge.

Straits Times. 2010. 'On power and stabilizing forces', May 17.

Suryanarayana, P.S. 2011. 'China and India Cannot Go to War: Lee Kuan Yew', *Hindu* (Singapore), 24 January; available at http://www.thehindu.com/ news/china-and-india-cannot-go-to-war-lee-kuan-yew/article1119062.ece.

———. 2010. 'Singapore Official's Unflattering Comment', *Hindu* (Singapore), 13 December; available at http://www.thehindu.com/news/national/ singapore-officials- unflattering-comment/article948548.ece.

Szep, Jason and James Pomfret. 2012. 'Tensions Flare Over South China Sea at Asian Summit', Reuters (Phnom Penh), 19 November; available at http://www.reuters.com/article/2012/11/19/us-asia-summit-idUSBRE 8AI0BC20121119.

Talukdar, Sushanta. 2014. 'Northeast Will Be Nurtured, Says Modi', *Hindu* (Guwahati), 2 December; available at http://www.thehindu.com/news/ national/will-nourish-natural-economic-zone-of-northeast-to-benefit-region-modi/article6651698.ece.

The Economist (Port Blair). 2014. 'The Andaman Islands: From Outpost to Springboard', 13 September; available at http://www.economist.com/news/asia/21617000-india-eyes-strategic-opportunity-bay-bengal-outpost-springboard.

Tribune News Service (TNN). 2012. 'Till October NHAI Had Met 6% of Road Contracts Target for Year', *Times of India* (New Delhi), 5 November; available at http://timesofindia.indiatimes.com/india/Till-October-NHAI-had-met-6-of-road- contracts-target-for-year/articleshow/17093101.cms.

―――. 1998. 'Tata Airline Plan Grounded', *Tribune* (New Delhi), 2 September; available at http://www.tribuneindia.com/1998/98sep02/head4.htm.

Tripathi, Suryakanthi. 2012. 'Impress the East, Know the East, Engage the East: India's Relations with ASEAN', *Two Decades of India's Look East Policy: Partnership for Peace, Progress and Prosperity*, edited by Amar Nath Ram, pp. 141–55. New Delhi: Manohar.

Uberoi, Patricia. 2014. 'The BCIM Economic Corridor: A Leap into the Unknown?', Institute of Chinese Studies, Working Paper Series (November).

Varshney, Ashutosh. 1999. 'Mass Politics or Elite Politics?: India's Economic Reforms in Comparative Perspective', *India in the Era of Economic Reforms*, edited by Jeffrey D. Sachs, Ashutosh Varshney, and Nirupam Bajpai, 222–60. New Delhi: Oxford University Press.

World Bank Group. 2014. *India Development Update, October 2014.* Washington, DC: World Bank Group; available at https://openknowledge.worldbank.org/bitstream/handle/10986/20794/AUS103730WP0P100Update0October02014.pdf (accessed 12 February 2015).

World Economic Forum. 2014. *Global Competitiveness Report 2014–2015.* Geneva: World Economic Forum.

Yew, Lee Kuan. 2000. *From Third World to First: The Singapore Story, 1965–2000.* New York: HarperCollins.

2   ASEAN–India Cooperation in Counterterrorism

Evolution and Future

Julio S. Amador III*

ASEAN–India Strategic Relations

The association of southeast asian nations (ASEAN) prides itself as a non-threatening organization that can engage great powers to manage strategic and economic issues in a multilateral forum. Its mechanisms such as the ASEAN Regional Forum (ARF), the ASEAN Plus Three (APT), and the East Asia Summit (EAS) allow great powers to have different platforms for dialogues to build confidence and trust, all of which have achieved a great measure of stability for the region over the last few decades after the Cold War (Ba 2010).

One great power that ASEAN has been engaging is India, which has long been recognized as an important partner to ASEAN. India's attitude towards ASEAN has also evolved over the years and under the new prime minister, Narendra Modi, great strides in the relationship are expected. The historical relationship between ASEAN and India is long;

* I would like to express gratitude to my colleague Jemimah Villaruel for research assistance, Eileene Arquiza for reviewing the initial draft, and the editors for their invaluable comments. The contents of this chapter do not reflect the official position of the Foreign Service Institute, the Department of Foreign Affairs, or the Government of the Philippines. All errors belong to the author alone.

ancient Southeast Asian communities traded with India and Indian ships travelled to the region, bringing food stuff and other trade goods to each other's regions (Paine 2013).

ASEAN and India became full dialogue partners in 1995, which started from a sectoral dialogue partnership in 1992 (ASEAN 2014). Recognizing the growing importance of this relationship, ASEAN and India elevated their ties to that of a strategic partnership on 20 December 2012 during the ASEAN–India Commemorative Summit in New Delhi (ASEAN 2014).

Other chapters in this volume have discussed areas for cooperation between India and ASEAN member states in the field of security. There is agreement that though India is a critical partner to its neighbours in Southeast Asia, that there needs to be deeper engagement between the two sides to make the strategic partnership more effective.

One security issue where both ASEAN and India have found common cause is in fighting terrorism. ASEAN and India have found in each other a partner against the scourge of terrorism; both sides are in the process of finding ways to work more effectively together in this area. This chapter looks into counterterrorism as an important security area where cooperation can be fostered between ASEAN and India. It looks into how ASEAN and India approach terrorism as a security issue and proposes ways forward in promoting cooperation. Some challenges are also identified that can help policymakers improve counterterrorism cooperation.

ASEAN's Counterterrorism Policy

Since the 11 September 2001 (9/11) attacks in the United States, ASEAN member states have been moving towards closer cooperation in countering terrorism within themselves and with external parties. Terrorism, prior to 9/11, was seen as a domestic problem; this was in keeping with ASEAN member states' strong non-interventionist approach to foreign policy, especially with each other (Chow 2005). Responding to terrorism was a matter of national concern and did not take into account regional consensus; thus, counterterrorism cooperation at the regional level had a slow start, even after the Bali Bombing of 2002 (Chow 2005).

ASEAN's post-9/11 response to terrorism is premised on three factors: 1) domestic considerations, 2) attitudes of member states, especially those with Muslim populations, and 3) member states' relationship with the United States of America (Capie 2004; Chow 2005; Gerstl 2010). ASEAN member states have to factor domestic response to any policy concerning terrorism or to the United States, as it is perceived to be driving the counterterror agenda (Capie 2004). Any response to terrorism must also consider its impact on the Muslim population of several Southeast Asian countries. The fear of radicalizing certain sectors, if counterterrorism efforts are perceived to be anti-Islam, is real in member states like Malaysia, Indonesia, and the Philippines.[1] Finally, the member states valued their relationship with the U.S.; even if they were willing to criticize the direction that U.S. counterterrorism was taking with regard to Iraq, they also recognized its continuing military preponderance and strategic guarantor role in the region (Capie 2004; Gerstl 2010).

The challenge to ASEAN post-9/11 was to harmonize disjointed approaches to terrorism (Chow 2005). To address this, ASEAN adopted the Declaration on Joint Action to Counter Terrorism when its leaders met at the 7th ASEAN Summit on 5 November 2001 in Brunei Darussalam (Keng Yong 2005). Further action included training programmes (Keng Yong 2005) and the adoption of the ASEAN Convention on Counter-Terrorism (ACCT), which fully entered into force in 2011 (ASEAN Secretariat 2013). The ACCT sought not only to prevent linking terrorism with 'any religion, nationality, civilization, or ethnic group' but it also strongly expressed the danger that terrorism poses 'toinnocent lives, infrastructure and the environment, regional and international peace and stability as well as to economic development', and that ASEAN saw it as a 'profound threat to international peace and security and a direct challenge to the attainment of peace, progress and prosperity for ASEAN and the realization of ASEAN Vision 2020' (ASEAN 2007).

The ACCT strongly protects the primacy of national governments in responding to terrorism within their territories. Provisions in the convention seek to preserve sovereignty and territorial integrity by preserving jurisdiction within their own territories and emphasizing the importance of domestic laws. However, terrorism is not regarded an existential threat to ASEAN as a whole; while terrorism can have a big impact on ASEAN's long-term goals, it is not enough to challenge the existence of the regional organizations, nor of most of its member states (Gerstl 2010). What ASEAN has done is to securitize terrorism,[2] making it a transnational crime, which in effect removed its political undertones to such a degree that ASEAN member states felt comfortable enough adopting the ACCT as a regional policy framework.

ASEAN's response to terrorism has mostly centred on the ACCT as a framework and promoting cooperation among implementing government agencies of member states. As Gerstl puts it, 'ASEAN's counterterrorism policies reflect… [a]… state- and regime-centric view of security' (Gerstl 2010, p. 67). The provisions of the ACCT seek to preserve the powers of the national governments and protect themselves from external interference. In countering terrorism, ASEAN has a 'pragmatic, realist and voluntarist approach towards regional collaboration' (Gerstl 2010). The ACCT does not diminish the sovereignty of member states; in fact, it reinforces it and puts the primary responsibility on them to implement counterterrorism activities. The ACCT also does not force ASEAN member states to adopt a common, stringent approach to counterterrorism. They are free to define and refine counterterrorism policies and have a free hand in their implementation.

What are the results of ASEAN's counterterrorism policy? In Gerstl's judgement, 'ASEAN's anti-terrorism efforts have not been translated into a robust regional approach: the organization could only agree to securitise terrorism as a transnational crime. Consequently, it has depoliticised and "ASEANised" its anti-terrorism policies, thus enabling its members to co-operate on a legal-technical rather than political basis' (Gerstl 2010). It is difficult to argue with his assessment. Most counterterror activities are still being implemented at the national level.[3] ASEAN is arguably where norm-building on counterterror is done through the various meetings that are meant to strengthen the implementation of the ACCT. The operational aspect is left to the member states who are free to adopt their approaches to counterterrorism. This approach allows ASEAN member states to cooperate with great powers that are willing to work with them on this area. One primary example is the Philippines–USA counterterrorism cooperation.

ASEAN's de-politicization of terrorism has had an arguably positive impact on intra-ASEAN relations as well as relations with extra-regional partners. Without depoliticizing the issue, some ASEAN member states would have found themselves in a quandary as the U.S.-led war against terrorism was fixated against extremist groups of Islamic practitioners. Many ASEAN member states have Muslim populations and had ASEAN committed to using the language of the

U.S.-led coalition, they would have had difficult political issues to deal with at home.

India's Counterterrorism Policy

Terrorist activities in India are products of many different internal conflicts (Kaplan and Bajoria 2008). India's long rivalry with Pakistan has also led some analysts to conclude that the latter is responsible for supporting or abetting terrorism in the former (Jamwal 2003). India's terrorism problems are officially classified into four types: (1) ethno-nationalist terrorism, (2) religious terrorism, (3) ideology oriented terrorism, and (4) state-sponsored terrorism.[4] India's inherent diversity, due to the size of its territory, its history, its multi-ethnic population, and different religious traditions, produces internal and external sources of discontent. In the past 20 years, India has been subjected to multiple terrorist attacks from different sources and from all four types; in 2013, it was among the top 10 countries affected by terrorism (Bora 2014).

State-sponsored terrorism has to be given special attention, however, because of its impact on India's relationship with its neighbours. India views Pakistan as a source of terrorism, a view that has been upheld also by other countries such as the United States.[5] Pakistan's role stems from the dispute over Kashmir and other historical issues; India sees Pakistan's involvement in terrorist activities in Indian soil as a 'deliberate instrument of foreign policy'.[6] From a strategic and policy perspective, Pakistan's involvement in terrorist activities, something which has been admitted (Nelson 2009), creates complications for India since it prevents India from developing strategic trust with its neighbour resulting in the prolonging of their disputes.

From an operational perspective, India views terrorism as a police and intelligence matter; the military is only called in to respond as a last resort, except in certain places. India's counterterrorism policy also focuses on immediate and short-term response, which has been criticized by analysts. Paul Staniland sums up why India has a problem in effectively confronting terrorism: 'The country suffers from a fragmented and inefficient bureaucracy, far fewer resources than developed countries even though it faces a higher threat level, and a political elite focused primarily on electoral politics', leading him to conclude that it 'is likely only a matter of time before another significant terrorist attack occurs' (Staniland

2009). As early as 2003, Jamwal had already identified these hindrances to India's counterterrorism policy. According to Brigadier Gurmeet Kanwal, a retired official and Director of the Centre for Land Warfare Studies, a New Delhi-based think-tank, India's counterterrorism policy is 'mired in systematic weakness', noting that the prevailing perspective is that terrorists have the upper hand in this asymmetric contest (Kanwal 2012).

Under the leadership of Prime Minister Narendra Modi, counterterrorism is seen as a key national security policy arena, with the appointment of Ajit Doval as his national security adviser. Doval, a former director of the Intelligence Bureau, has been dubbed by the scholar Harsh V. Pant as 'an operations man'; however, he is not considered as strategic in outlook as his predecessor (Pant 2014). Modi has stated that the global community must have a 'zero tolerance' policy towards terrorism.[7] At the United Nations, Modi reiterated India's continuing fight against terrorism while also accusing Pakistan of backing terrorist groups (Sengupta 2014).

Terrorism in India, therefore, comes from two primary sources. First, internal conflicts, which are remnants of history, cause dissatisfied sectors to use terrorism as a tool. Second, India views Pakistan as a source and supporter of terrorist attacks. The continuing mistrust in both sides prevents any meaningful attempt at resolving terrorism or engaging in cooperative counterterrorism attempts. In sum, under Modi, India seems to be giving renewed attention to terrorism as a security challenge. It views terrorism as a product of internal conflicts and also a tool of its rival, Pakistan, in destabilizing India. Modi, who is seen as tough on foreign policy issues, is also expected to take on terrorism in a strong manner. While it remains to be seen how effectively his government can combat terrorism, the potential of India as a partner to ASEAN in this area points to a positive direction.

Potential Cooperation

ASEAN and India are not strangers to each other in counterterrorism. The two sides signed the ASEAN–India Joint Declaration for Cooperation to Combat International Terrorism in Bali, Indonesia on 8 October 2003. In the 16th ASEAN Regional Forum in Phuket, Thailand, held on 23 July 2009, ASEAN member states and India both agreed to the ARF Work Plan on Counter Terrorism and Transnational Crime. In October 2010 at the 8th ASEAN–India Summit in Ha Noi, both sides reiterated their commitments to counterterrorism cooperation, among other vital areas for cooperation.

Specifically, the two sides agreed on the following agenda:

Deepen cooperation in combating international terrorism, including under the framework of the 'ASEAN–India Joint Declaration for Cooperation to Combat International Terrorism,' signed in Bali, Indonesia on 8 October 2003, and under the ARF Work Plan on Counterterrorism and Transnational Crime adopted at the 16th ASEAN Regional Forum in Phuket, Thailand on 23 July 2009;

Support the implementation of the ASEAN Convention on Counter Terrorism signed on 13 January 2007 in Cebu, Philippines and the ASEAN Comprehensive Plan of Action on Counter Terrorism endorsed at the 7th ASEAN Ministerial Meeting on Transnational Crime (AMMTC) in Siem Reap, Cambodia, 17 November 2009;

Strengthen capacity-building efforts in the area of combating international terrorism through training and consultations between officials, analysts, field operators, seminars, conferences and operations, as appropriate; Strengthen counterterrorism capacity building cooperation for transport, customs, immigration and quarantine inspections. (ASEAN 2014b)

The agreement focuses on building confidence for cooperation and not on actual operational activities, yet. Official channels must be strengthened so that law-enforcement and counterterrorism government agencies are able to develop the necessary linkages with each other to further deepen their cooperative activities. As a law-enforcement matter for ASEAN member states and India, counterterrorism cooperation gives due attention to customs, immigration, quarantine, and security issues (CIQS).

India is considered a vital partner of ASEAN and the relationship has been upgraded to a strategic partnership level. The two sides have cooperated closely in ASEAN-led mechanisms such as the EAS and the ARF. India has not challenged ASEAN centrality and is supportive of the regional organization's role in the broader Indo-Pacific. India's presence and support of ASEAN in the two aforementioned mechanisms allow ASEAN to push forward its agenda on counterterrorism even as other great powers that participate in the ARF or the EAS attempt to sway other countries to follow their lead. The Plan of Action that ASEAN and India have agreed to implement provides the policy framework for further deepening their cooperation, including in the area of counterterrorism.

ASEAN member states and India may have different experiences and perspectives with regard to terrorism, and future research should look into how bilateral cooperation in counterterrorism has developed over the years between individual ASEAN member states and India. However, as this chapter focuses on the regional aspect of cooperation, that is, between ASEAN as a whole and India, the official declarations and documents are an important start. ASEAN is an inter-governmental organization designed to foster cooperation among its member states primarily, and its external partners secondarily. Regional cooperation, however, is built on strategic trust and confidence in each other; the extent of the strategic trust between India and ASEAN is not studied in depth in this chapter but the lack of implementing activities to the aforementioned regional declarations and agreements all point to the need for ASEAN and India to move forward and take incremental steps to move counterterrorism cooperation forward.

Challenges and Way Forward

Bernard Tai, an analyst, in a book chapter that assesses ASEAN's importance, argues that the process of coming up with ASEAN agreements is quite tedious and while many have been signed, member states still have to overcome their domestic legal and other institutional constraints, thus delaying the implementation process. Another dimension that Tai identifies for further exploration is whether agreements that are being implemented actually achieve their desired results (Tai 2011).

In the case of counterterrorism, problems in implementation are expected. At the strategic or leaders' level, the framework for cooperation is in place. The challenge is in the implementation of programmes and projects that will concretize these commitments. For ASEAN, the implementation of the plan of action is ultimately with the member state. As has been pointed out earlier, ASEAN member states themselves have problems in implementing ASEAN agreements on counterterrorism. It is at the national level where operations are being implemented and it is unclear from publicly available sources if there are true cross-border cooperative ventures. The ACCT's focus on defending sovereignty and promoting non-interference even in the face of terrorism poses a huge challenge to cooperation.

India also has to coordinate with individual ASEAN member states to implement the ASEAN–India Plan of Action, specifically on counterterrorism. India has inked agreements for closer bilateral cooperation with some ASEAN member states. In 2010, India and Malaysia issued a joint statement on their strategic partnership. Both sides condemned terrorism and agreed to 'enhance cooperation in counter-terrorism including through information sharing and the establishment of a bilateral Joint Working Group on Counterterrorism.'[8] India and Indonesia have also agreed to expand their counterterrorism ties and high-level meetings have been held to bolster their cooperation.[9] Myanmar and India have also agreed at the leaders' level to cooperate on counterterrorism.[10] With the Philippines, India has signed a declaration on counterterrorism aside from the ASEAN–India Joint Declaration; the two sides have also established a Joint Working Group on Counter-Terrorism as well as increased cooperation among their agencies that deal with the issue.[11] Thailand and India have signed agreements and have worked together on counterterrorism as well.[12] Singapore and India, according to some reports, have established a Joint Working Group on combating terrorism as early as December 2003 (Singh and Rahman 2010). Vietnam and India have agreed to work closely together on security issues, including counterterrorism (Modi 2014).

India's counterterrorism ties with a majority of ASEAN member states complements the regional level agreement. India needs to have a consistent message on what it wants in its counterterrorism activities with member states. A way forward could be through joint working groups (JWGs) with ASEAN member states that have bilateral counterterrorism ties with India. The JWG should meet regularly and share best practices, views, and other information that each side is comfortable sharing with the other.

Another area ripe for cooperation is capacity building. India, along with several ASEAN member states, could establish a combined training programme that will regularly train law enforcement agents in counterterrorism work. Joint exercises could be held with ASEAN member states which already have agreements with India, while India could host the policy and strategic aspects of the proposed joint training programme.

Intelligence cooperation and sharing is something that India and ASEAN member states should aspire to in the future. This should be one of the goals to establish in the JWGs. India and ASEAN member states could significantly help each other by sharing information on cross-border activities of recognized terrorist groups.

Track 1.5 and Track 2 diplomacy efforts should be essential to ASEAN–India counterterrorism cooperation. That is, both sides should foster academic and policy exchanges at an informal level so as to deepen trust with each other and share analyses on issues related to terrorism. Analyses coming from think-tanks and academic institutions can prove useful to strategists and policymakers.

India has to review its approach to terrorism; it should be strategic and long-term in perspective. As its issues with Pakistan persist, and as it continues to end its internal conflicts, it will face terrorism, and as such a short-term approach will not be sufficient. Modi's government should think strategically when it comes to counterterrorism. Policies, partnerships, and plans must be adopted and implemented to ensure that India can fend off terrorist attacks. Intelligence cooperation with neighbouring countries will be essential along with bilateral or multilateral exercises that promote cooperation and confidence. India needs to break down bureaucratic barriers to cooperation; government agencies must provide better information to each other while finding ways to be more cohesive in counterterror operations.

ASEAN member states have to find better ways to cooperate at an intra-ASEAN level. They need to improve intelligence sharing and must promote multilateral and bilateral exercises between and among their intelligence and counterterrorism agencies. A major challenge to ASEAN is a culture of mistrust that prevents concerned government bodies from cooperating in a manner that reflects the regional community aspirations of its member states. At the domestic level, policymakers have to adopt policies that promote cooperation in counterterrorism. These policies must be reflected at the ASEAN level as well. Without institutionalizing cooperation among its member states, the regional association may find it difficult to engage other countries in multilateral counterterrorism exercises.

What about the Islamic State of Iraq and al-Sham (ISIS)?

An important development is the rise of the Islamic State, a self-styled caliphate that is carving out territories in Iraq and Syria. The ISIS, as it is commonly known, 'follows a distinctive variety of Islam' which focuses on the strict implementation of Shariah and obedience to the Caliph (Wood 2015). It has managed to attract supporters from Southeast Asia and India and should be carefully monitored by leaders of ASEAN and India to prevent future rounds of terrorism. ASEAN has condemned ISIS and like-minded groups noting that these 'not only pose a threat to the people of Iraq and Syria, but also to all countries in Middle East, and if left unchecked, to the rest of the world' (ASEAN, 26 September 2014). There are fears that Southeast Asia may be a potential recruitment ground for ISIS as some radicalized sectors may seek the group out and be enmeshed in its plans, return to their home countries, and sow terror.

India has its own problems with ISIS, with one report noting the wariness of intelligence and security officials with regard to the growing influence of the group in neighbouring countries.[13] There have been reports of Indian nationals joining ISIS but it is still unclear what its goals are in the country. However, it is not in doubt that India is in the radar of the extremist group due to three factors: '1) the relative proximity of the Islamic State's most active South Asia branch (Wilayat Khurasan), 2) its links with home-grown/indigenous Indian Mujahideen members, and 3) the Islamic State's powerful social media channels that proved to be the most enticing medium for aspiring jihadi volunteers' (Roul 2015).

India and ASEAN, through the various frameworks for cooperation that they have signed, can start to work closely together to counter the insidious plans of ISIS that may affect peace and stability of these two neighbouring regions. The early recognition of the dangers that the ISIS brings to India and ASEAN is crucial as it gives the two sides an opportunity to work together against a common antagonist.

***

India and ASEAN have a long way to go in the common goal of countering global terrorism; however, the current state of cooperation is already an achievement as both sides have faced internal constraints that prevent deeper engagement. The existence of a regional agreement, along with bilateral cooperative agreements, suggests that terrorism is an issue that is important to all. There are many avenues for ASEAN–India cooperation and both sides have been using multilateral and bilateral venues to work on counterterrorism.

ASEAN needs to move forward with the implementation of the ACCT and must encourage member states to work together to achieve some level of coherence when it comes to adopting and implementing counterterrorism activities. ASEAN member states must start trusting each other enough to also work on intelligence sharing and operations. This is imperative since ASEAN is nearing its 50th anniversary, yet trust in each other is not a core strength of ASEAN. India must be clear in its own counterterrorism agenda and policy. It should not allow its national policy to be held hostage by political and sub-national interests. India should also provide ASEAN with an array of resources aimed at deepening counterterrorism cooperation.

Further research could look into how intelligence agencies, counterterrorism organizations, and other security-related organizations within ASEAN member states and India cooperate with each other bilaterally or through the ASEAN–India regional level of cooperation. How to move the counterterrorism agenda forward will remain a challenge, especially with the rise of ISIS and the continuing threat by Al Qaeda and other terrorist groups; however, policymakers and scholars should continue to further study this area of ASEAN–India cooperation and see how improvements could be made in this important geo-political relationship.

As the Asian Century progresses, ASEAN and India will probably be drawn in more as both sides are known to respect each other. ASEAN does not have anything to fear from India as opposed to other great powers, and India finds ASEAN to be a useful platform in engaging its rivals and other partners. Commonalities of interest will ensure that both sides will find mutual areas for cooperation, especially on counterterrorism.

Notes

1. Chow 2005 and Capie 2004 examine counterterrorism country case studies in Southeast Asia.

2. While securitization per se means that an issue has become an existential threat, Gerstl argues that terrorism has still been securitized because existential threats can become subjective too. He argues that terrorism was 'ASEANized' or depoliticized so that member states could work together in combating the threat but in a framework that does not threaten the sovereignty and national interests of member states; for further analyses see Gerstl 2010.

3. See, for example, Febrica 2010; Misalucha 2011 further explains that the U.S., in attempting to lead global counter-terror drives, resorted to essentially hegemonic activities, that is, buying influence over individual member states.

4. See Government of India, Second Administrative Reforms Committee 2008.

5. See Government of India, Second Administrative Reforms Committee 2008. For an in-depth analysis of state sponsored terrorism, including Pakistan's role in fomenting terrorism in India, see Byman 2008.

6. See Government of India, Second Administrative Reforms Committee 2008, p. 5.

7. See *Deccan Herald* (Gandhinagar). 2015.

8. See *Hindu* (Putrajaya). 2010.

9. See for example, these news stories: Indo-Asian News Service (IANS) 2012.

10. See *India Digest* 2010.

11. See *First Post* 2013a and 2013b.

12. See Government of India, Ministry of External Affairs 2013.

13. Vasudevan Sridharan 2015.

References

ASEAN. 2007. 'ASEAN Convention on Counter Terrorism.' *International Organization for Migration*. Available at http://www.iom.int/pbmp/ PDF/ASEAN_Convention_Counter_Terrorism_2007.pdf (accessed 23 February 2015).

———. 2014. 'ASEAN Foreign Ministers' Statement on the Rise of Violence and Brutality Committed by Terrorist/Extremist Organisations in Iraq and Syria,' *Association of Southeast Asian Nations*, 26 September; available at http://www. asean.org/images/Statement/2014/Sept/ASEAN_Foreign_Ministers_ Statement_on_the_Rise_of_Violence_and_Brutality_Committed_by_ TerroristExtremist_Organisations_in_Iraq_and_Syria.pdf (accessed on 27 October 2015).

———. 2014a. 'ASEAN Convention on Counter Terrorism,' *Association of Southeast Asian Nations*; available at http://www.asean.org/news/item/ asean-convention-on-counter-terrorism (accessed 23 February 2015).

———. 2014b. 'Plan of Action to Implement the ASEAN–India Partnership for Peace, Progress and Shared Prosperity (2010–2015)', *Association of Southeast Asian Nations*; available at http://www.asean.org/asean/external-relations/ india/item/plan-of-action-to-implement-the-asean-india-partnership-for-peace-progress-and-shared-prosperity-2010-2015 (accessed 23 February 2015).

———. 2014c. 'Overview of ASEAN-India Dialogue Relations', *Association of Southeast Asian Nations*; available at http://www.asean.org/asean/external-relations/india/item/overview-of-asean-india-dialogue-relations (accessed 23 February 2015).

ASEAN Secretariat. 2013. 'ASEAN Convention on Counter-Terrorism Completes Ratification Process', *ASEAN Secretariat News*, 22 January; available at http://www.asean.org/news/asean-secretariat-news/item/asean-convention-on-counter-terrorism-completes-ratification-process (accessed 23 February 2015).

Ba, Alice D. 2010. 'Regional Security in East Asia: ASEAN's Value Added and Limitations', *Journal of Current Southeast Asian Affairs* : 115–30.

Bora, Kukil. 2014. 'Major Terrorist Attacks in India over the Last 20 Years: A Timeline', *International Business Times*, 13 December; available at http://www.ibtimes.com/major-terrorist-attacks-india-over-last-20-years-timeline-1752731 (accessed 26 October 2015).

Byman, Daniel L. 2008. 'The Changing Nature of State Sponsorship of Terrorism', Brookings Institution, Analysis Paper Series, no. 16 (May).

Capie, David. 2004. 'Between a Hegemon and a Hard Place: The "War on Terror" and Southeast Asian–US Relations', *The Pacific Review*, 17(2): 223–48.

Chow, Jonathan T. 2005. 'ASEAN Counterterrorism Cooperation Since 9/11', *Asian Survey*, 45(2): 302–21.

Deccan Herald (Gandhinagar). 2015. 'Modi for Expanding Counter-Terror Web', 12 January; available at http://www.deccanherald.com/content/452930/modi-expanding-counter-terror-web.html.

Embassy of the Philippines. 2014. 'Philippine–India Relations: An Overview', 14 April, New Delhi; available at http://newdelhipe.dfa.gov.ph/index.php/2014-04-14-03-09-43 (accessed 23 February 2015).

Febrica, Senia. 2010. 'Securitizing Terrorism in Southeast Asia: Accounting for the Varying Responses of Singapore and Indonesia', *Asian Survey* 50(3): 569–90.

First Post (Manila). 2013a. 'India, Philippines Set to Upgrade Ties, Reinvigorate Relations', 23 October; available at http://www.firstpost.com/fwire/india-philippines-set-to-upgrade-ties-reinvigorate-relations-1188189.html.

———. 2013b. 'Philippine–India Relations: An Overview', 23 October; available at http://www.firstpost.com/fwire/india-philippines-set-to-upgrade-ties-reinvigorate-relations-1188189.html.

Gerstl, Alfred. 2010. 'The Depoliticisation and "ASEANisation" of Counter-Terrorism Policies in South-East Asia: A Weak Trigger for a Fragmented

Version of Human Security', *Austrian Journal of Southeast Asian Studies*, 3(1): 48–75.

Government of India, Ministry of External Affairs. 2013. 'Joint Statement on Prime Minister's Visit to Thailand', 30 May; available at http://mea.gov.in/bilateral-documents.htm?dtl/21768/Joint+Statement+on+Prime+Minist ers+visit+to+Thailand (accessed 23 February 2015).

Government of India, Second Administrative Reforms Committee. 2008. 'Combatting Terrorism: Protecting by Righteousness', June; available at http://arc.gov.in/8threport.pdf (accessed 26 October 2015).

Hindu (Putrajaya). 2010. 'Joint Statement on the Framework for the India–Malaysia Strategic Partnership', 27 October; available at http://www.thehindu.com/news/national/joint-statement-on-the-framework-for-the-indiamalaysia-strategic-partnership/article852420.ece.

Indo-Asian News Service (IANS). 2012. 'India, Indonesia to Combat Terror, Boost Maritime Security', *India Strategic* (New Delhi), October; available at http://www.indiastrategic.in/topstories1776_India_Indonesia_combat_terror_boost_maritime_security.htm (accessed 23 February 2015).

India Digest. 2010. 'India, Myanmar Boost Counter-Terror, Energy Ties', 1 August; available at https://www.hcilondon.in/indiadigest/Issue316/pdf/4.pdf (accessed 23 February 2015).

Jamwal, N.S. 2003. 'Counter Terrorism Strategy', *Strategic Analysis* 27(1): 1–29.

Kanwal, Gurmeet. 2012. 'India's Counter-Terrorism Policy Mired in Systematic Weakness', *Rediff News*, 24 January; available at http://www.rediff.com/news/slide-show/slide-show-1-indias-counter-terrorism-policy-is-mired-in-systemic-weaknesses/20120124.htm#1.

Kaplan, Eben and Jayshree Bajoria. 2008. 'Counterterrorism in India'. *Council on Foreign Relations*. 27 November; available at http://www.cfr.org/india/counterterrorism-india/p11170#p4 (accessed 23 February 2015).

Keng Yong, Ong. 2005. 'ASEAN's Contribution to Regional Efforts in Counter-Terrorism', Association of Southeast Asian Nations, 21 Februrary; available at http://www.asean.org/resources/2012-02-10-08-47-56/speeches-statements-of-the-former-secretaries-general-of-asean/item/asean-s-contribution-to-regional-efforts-in-counter-terrorism (accessed 23 February 2015).

Misalucha, Charmaine G. 2011. 'Southeast Asia–US Relations: Hegemony or Hierarchy', *Contemporary Southeast Asia*, 33(2): 209–28.

Modi, Narendra. 2014. 'English Rendering of the Prime Minister's Media Statement During the Visit of Prime Minister of Vietnam to India', Press Information Bureau, Government of India, Prime Minister's Office, 28 October; available at http://pib.nic.in/newsite/PrintRelease.aspx?relid=110863 (accessed 23 February 2015).

Nelson, Dean. 2009.'Pakistani President Asif Zardari Admits Creating Terrorist Groups', *Telegraph*, 8 July; available at http://www.telegraph.co.uk/news/worldnews/asia/pakistan/5779916/Pakistani-president-Asif-Zardari-admits-creating-terrorist-groups.html (accessed 26 October 2015).

Paine, Lincoln. 2013. *The Sea & Civilization: A Maritime History of the World*. New York: Alfred A. Knopf.

Pant, Harsh V. 2014.'Narendra Modi Targets Counterterrorism as a Key Policy', *National*, 21 June; available at http://www.thenational.ae/thenational conversation/comment/narendra-modi-targets-counterterrorism-as-a-key-policy.

Press Trust of India (PTI). 2013.'India, Indonesia to Expand Ties, Cooperate on Security Issues', *Economic Times* (Jakarta),11 October; available at http://articles.economictimes.indiatimes.com/2013- 10-11/news/42942431_1_security-cooperation-mutual-legal-assistance-treaty- indonesia-today.

Roul, Animesh. 2015.'India Faces Up to Growing Islamic State Threat', *Terrorism Monitor*, 13(17): 6; available at http://www.jamestown.org/uploads/media/TerrorismMonitorVol13Issue17_02.pdf (accessed on 28 October 2015).

Sengupta, Somini. 2014. 'Narendra Modi, in U.N. Speech, Inserts India into Terrorism Fight', *New York Times*, 27 September; available at http://www.nytimes.com/news/un-general-assembly/2014/09/27/narendra-modi-in-u-n-speech-inserts-india-into-terrorism-fight/.

Singh, Sinderpal and Syeda Sana Rahman. 2010. 'India–Singapore Relations: Constructing a 'New' Bilateral Relationship', *Contemporary Southeast Asia: A Journal of International and Strategic Affairs* 32(1): 70–97.

Sridharan, Vasudevan. 2015. 'Isis: India Concerned Over Growing Tentacles of Terror in Neighbouring Countries', *International Business Times*, 30 September; available at http://www.ibtimes.co.uk/isis-india-concerned-over-growing-tentacles-terror-neighbouring-countries-1521816 (accessed 27 October 2015).

Staniland, Paul. 2009.'Improving India's Counterterrorism Policy after Mumbai', *Combatting Terrorism Center*, 15 April; available at https://www.ctc.usma.edu/posts/improving-india%E2%80%99s-counterterrorism-policy-after-mumbai (accessed 23 February 2015).

Tai, Bernard K.M. 2011. 'Can We Do Anything about the Unimplemented ASEAN Agreements? ' in *ASEAN Matters! Reflecting on the Association of Southeast Asian Nations*, edited by Yoong Yoong Lee, 23–8. Singapore: World Scientific.

Wood, Graeme. 2015.'What ISIS Really Wants', *The Atlantic*, March; available at http://www.theatlantic.com/magazine/archive/2015/03/what-isis-really-wants/384980/ (accessed 27 October 2015).

3   India's Engagement with Myanmar

Regional Security Implications of Acting East Slowly

JONAH BLANK

REGIONAL SECURITY IN ASIA is sometimes portrayed as a two-way struggle, with the U.S. and China each seeking dominance over the Indo-Pacific land, sea, and air. In reality, the security picture is far more complex: neither the U.S. nor China has the resources or the will to become an unfettered hegemon (at least in the near term), and every nation in Asia is primarily concerned with its *own* security calculus rather than that of the region. A key figure in this equation, and one too often under-appreciated, is India. A brief look at India's policy towards the neighbouring state of Myanmar yields some important conclusions— important for the two nations themselves, but also for Southeast Asia, for the security picture of the continent, and for the Indo-Pacific region writ large. One key conclusion: India now has an unprecedented opportunity to add substance to the decades-old rhetoric behind its 'Look East' policy, and doing so would also advance the strategic interests of the United States, Europe, Japan, and most of the emerging democracies of Southeast Asia.[1]

India's engagement with Myanmar is in many ways a microcosm of India's engagement with Southeast Asia. New Delhi measures the present-day relationship against the pre-1990s stasis, and sees a picture of vibrant growth; Southeast Asian nations, however, measure the relationship against their ties to China, Japan, or other states, and see an

India that is lagging far behind. India's narrative is one of steady progress and high hope for the future: grounded in shared history, heritage, and sensibilities (the narrative goes), India's association with Southeast Asia is an organic bond rather than a constructed artifact, and therefore will inevitably continue to grow stronger in the coming years. This narrative, however, is seldom heard in Southeast Asia. From the vantage point of almost all states in the region, long-dormant cultural ties have nowhere near the salience that Indian interlocutors attribute to them; what matters far more (the counter-narrative goes) are economics and security—two areas in which India has yet to prove itself a top-tier partner.

Can the two narratives be harmonized? Perhaps, but it will require time, money, and effort. If India is truly committed to turning 'Look East' into 'Act East', it may wish to start with the Southeast Asian nation on its easternmost border: Myanmar.

Myanmar as a 'Near Neighbour'

Of all the nations in Southeast Asia, only Myanmar shares a land border with India. Moreover, only Myanmar shares a historical legacy of direct consequence to modern politics: both nations were part of the British Raj, and inherited a similar set of colonial-era governing structures at their independence.[2] Myanmar is often seen as the place where South Asia melts into Southeast Asia; Bangladesh is clearly South Asia, Thailand is clearly Southeast Asia, but Myanmar is (both geographically and culturally) somewhere in between. From the standpoint of Indian policy-makers, that makes it a 'near-neighbour'—a category which includes countries India has traditionally considered its own area of proprietary interest.[3]

This near-neighbour status has policy implications, particularly if political or ethnic tension in Myanmar should ever run the risk of spilling over into India's Northeastern states. Under a framework sometimes called the 'Rajiv Doctrine', promulgated by Prime Minister Rajiv Gandhi, India informally asserted the right and duty to maintain stability in its immediate neighbourhood.[4] This doctrine was applied most famously when Rajiv Gandhi sent the Indian Peacekeeping Force to Sri Lanka in 1987, and less publicly through a series of direct and indirect actions in Nepal, Bhutan, and the Maldives in the decades since. Given the range and longevity of insurgencies on both sides of the India–Myanmar border, Delhi can hardly see its eastern neighbour in the same light as (for example) Vietnam. Myanmar, for better or worse, is in a class by itself.

Like the United States' 'Monroe Doctrine', India's Rajiv Doctrine has been applied selectively. In the century after the Monroe Doctrine's issuance, the U.S. chose to overlook colonial incursions into the Western Hemisphere by European powers including Spain, Portugal, France, Britain, and Holland. Likewise, India has uneasily tolerated China's expansion into a region that Delhi considers to be its unique sphere of influence, particularly through the construction of naval facilities in Sri Lanka, Bangladesh, and Myanmar. But just as the U.S. became more assertive in controlling its self-declared exclusionary sphere as its economic and military strength grew, so too may India. Myanmar represents what may be a test-case. With both the rulers and the population actively looking to lessen the degree of China's dominance over the country, will India take advantage of the opening?

To judge by the statements of many officials, India believes it has already done so. In interviews with the author, over a dozen serving and retired officials expressed a nearly unanimous view.[5] In their telling, India made all the right moves in helping guide Myanmar out of its long isolation, and was well-placed to reap the policy rewards for its foresight; specifically, India took a principled stance in supporting the democracy movement led by Aung San Suu Kyi in 1988, then deftly engaged with the Burmese military since the turn of the current century in order to lay the foundation for political reform. As many of those interviewed noted, Aung San Suu Kyi lived in New Delhi in her youth (her mother, Khin Kyi, was Burma's ambassador to India from 1960 to 1967), and was friends with the young Rajiv Gandhi.

In Myanmar, however, the story is almost precisely inverted. In interviews in Yangon, both Burmese citizens and long-time foreign observers told the author a tale of India being consistently wrong-footed, and winding up with nothing whatsoever to show for its efforts:[6] Whatever popular goodwill India may have gained from its support for the democracy movement was destroyed by Delhi's subsequent courting of the junta, and the feebleness of India's outreach to the Burmese military prevented it from challenging China for influence. If Aung San Suu Kyi had any warm feelings left over from childhood, they were wiped away by India's perceived failure to support the reformists during the Saffron Revolution of 2007. Since the 2011 decision by Myanmar's reformist president Thein Sein to engage with Suu Kyi and the West, India has (interviewees said) been virtually a non-presence. 'I never hear India even mentioned by the Burmese, at least not at the government level', said one Yangon-based diplomat. 'But China—people talk about China all the time.'

The chasm separating India's view of its own policy from the view of so many in Myanmar presents an opportunity: if India can bring its actions in line with its rhetoric, it will receive a warm welcome. In geopolitical terms, Myanmar's post-2011 engagement with the world has created two rival camps. The reformist camp includes most of the Burmese population (including Aung San Suu Kyi, the democracy movement, and many of the minority ethnic communities that have struggled against the Burmese state for decades), most ASEAN members (Thailand, Singapore, Vietnam, and Malaysia with greater enthusiasm, Laos and Cambodia with less), and open democracies ranging from Japan and South Korea to the European Union and the U.S. The *status quo ante* camp, again roughly, includes much of the leadership of the Tatmadaw (the Burmese military), and the People's Republic of China.[7]

India's interests lie squarely with the reformist camp. Despite India's attempts during the late 1990s and early 2000s to woo the military junta, the Tatmadaw never had much to offer Delhi beyond border security (which it could not reliably enforce) and neighbourly stability (which, from 2007 onward, it seemed increasingly unlikely to deliver). A Myanmar committed to political and economic reform, weaned away from its over-reliance on the patronage of China, and willing to abide by international norms, would be a much better fit for India's goals. The reform camp's goals are by no means identical: India, for example, sees cross-border drug trafficking as a major threat, while some of the minority communities in Myanmar's highlands see it as a valuable source of income. The overall goals of Burma's internal reformists, however, are a better fit with the goals of both India and nearly every other state except China. Policymakers in the U.S., Europe, and the nations of South and East Asia can advance their own interests by helping India engage more deeply with Myanmar.

How Did the Paths of India and Myanmar Diverge?

At their birth as independent nations (less than six months apart), India and Burma seemed less like neighbours than siblings. Their experience during World War II had been similarly conflicted, with Indian and Burmese troops fighting valiantly for—and, in a smaller number of cases, against—their colonial rulers. Throughout the subsequent decade they were united by a post-colonial world-view, and when Jawaharlal Nehru led the movement to create a community of non-aligned states proudly rejecting affiliation with either the U.S. or Soviet blocs, Burma's first prime minister, U Nu, was keen to sign up. Relations began to cool as the Burmese military assumed more control over the government. The increasingly powerful army saw Communist plots behind every corner (often accurately, since Maoist China was indeed actively sponsoring both Communist parties and underground cells in Burma at the time). The military viewed ethnic minorities with suspicion, some because of their links to China, others simply because these groups rejected the control of a government dominated by the Bamar majority. In 1962 General Ne Win ordered the expulsion of much of the country's ethnic Indian population, which had formed a majority of the capital city's population shortly before independence.[8] For nearly three decades after this, a period during which Ne Win governed as autocrat, India had little to do with its neighbour.

India's stock with the Burmese people, however, may have reached its peak when its interaction with the Burmese government was at its nadir. The '8888 Revolt', named because it broke out on the eighth day of the eighth month of 1988, brought Aung San Suu Kyi to international prominence. The daughter of Burma's founding father, Aung San, Suu Kyi soon became the leader of a pro-democracy movement. In 1990, the military junta (officially, the State Law and Order Restoration Council, or SLORC) misjudged its popular support and permitted a relatively free election—which Suu Kyi's party won handily. In the aftermath of the military's rejection of the poll and crackdown on Suu Kyi's followers, India provided sanctuary to many Burmese activists. In 1992, India sponsored a U.N. resolution condemning Myanmar's human rights violations.

For the rest of the 1990s, India and Myanmar had little engagement. When Prime Minister P.V. Narasimha Rao unveiled India's 'Look East' policy in 1992, his aim was to link his nation to such 'Asian Tigers' as Thailand, South Korea, and Singapore; Myanmar was no economic tiger, and any eastward glance skipped over a nation which appeared to have little to offer India.[9] Myanmar's ominously acronymed SLORC, for its part, had no real interest in international outreach: a junta which had been created decades earlier in part to combat subversion by Chinese

Communists was now almost entirely dependent on the patronage of Communist China.

After the Bharatiya Janata Party (BJP) formed its first government in 1998, however, India's foreign policy began to change across a wide range of issues.[10] The BJP, with no vested interest in upholding the orthodoxies of a foreign policy establishment dominated by its rival Congress party, was quite willing to break from established positions. Almost as soon as it took office, the new government broke a 24-year moratorium on nuclear tests, and launched a deep re-evaluation of India's relationship with the U.S.; in September 2000, prime minister Atal Bihari Vajpayee became the first Indian leader in 15 years to receive a State Dinner at the White House. India's policy towards Myanmar following the 1988 military crackdown had been shaped by Congress prime minister Rajiv Gandhi, and in 1993 it was Congress prime minister Narasimha Rao who presented the Jawaharlal Nehru Award (named, of course, after the first Congress prime minister) to Aung San Suu Kyi; this pro-reformist stance was upheld by three other prime ministers who began their careers in the Congress party,[11] and after the BJP victory it faced a re-examination along with other traditional Congress positions.

Vajpayee downplayed support for Aung San Suu Kyi and the reformists, avoiding any actions which could be seen as interference in Myanmar's domestic affairs. The shift was likely due to the politics of India rather than those of Myanmar—the BJP had traditionally bristled at international criticism of India's own internal policies in areas such as Kashmir—but it occurred just when Myanmar's own political balance was beginning to move away from continued rule by the Tatmadaw. In 2000, Delhi made its first arms sale to the Burmese junta, a deal worth $5 million (SIPRI 2015).

The shift towards the junta and away from the reformists was maintained, and even deepened, when Congress came back into power in 2004. India made another arms deal with the junta in 2006, worth nearly twice as much as the Vajpayee-era sale.[12] During the junta's 2007 crackdown on reformist protesters in the 'Saffron Revolution', Prime Minister Manmohan Singh refrained from criticizing the Burmese military. Over a month after the junta's heavy-handed arrests of protesters began, and days after the U.S. president condemned the actions in an address to the United Nations and announced unilateral sanctions, an Indian government spokesman merely declared that Delhi was 'concerned at and is closely monitoring the situation in Myanmar', and hoped 'all sides will resolve their issues peacefully through dialogue' (PTI 2007).

The Saffron Revolution was a tipping point for the Tatmadaw: by beating, incarcerating, and killing not merely students but Buddhist monks, the military regime lost much of the support it might have still have enjoyed. After the additional self-inflicted blow of an incompetent response to Cyclone Nargis the following year, high-ranking generals began to recognize the inevitability of reform. India, however, did not appear to have made any such recognition. In 2010, Prime Minister Singh hosted junta leader Than Shwe for a rare five-day state visit, promising tens of millions of dollars' worth of aid to the general who had led the suppression of the Saffron Revolution (Mukherjee 2010).

India's narrative of constant support for reform, therefore, strikes many Burmese as far removed from reality. Close observers of Myanmar's politics report that Suu Kyi and her supporters have not forgiven India for what they regard as a deep betrayal during the Saffron Revolution. The question for Indian policymakers is not whether such a view of the relationship is accurate, but—given that it exists, and has widespread currency in Myanmar—what to do about it. To judge by the actions New Delhi has taken, and failed to take, since the reform movement reached critical mass in 2011, the answer appears to be: not very much. Just as India has refrained from decisive action in the political arena, it has held back from meaningful engagement in the economic and security spheres as well.

India–Myanmar Economic Connections: Trade and Infrastructure

India's trade with Myanmar has been growing steadily over the past 15 years (see Figure 3.1), but this growth is impressive only when viewed in isolation. Between 2000 and 2011, for example, India's trade with Myanmar grew from about $227 million to $1.7 billion. An eye-popping metric of economic success—except when set beside the figures for China: during the same period, China's trade with Myanmar started out just under $400 million greater than India's, and increased that gap more than tenfold, to $4.8 billion. Moreover, China's trade more than doubled during precisely the period when its political influence was beginning to wane: in 2009, after both the Saffron Revolution and Cyclone Nargis, China's trade with Myanmar totalled $2.9 billion; in 2011, the year when

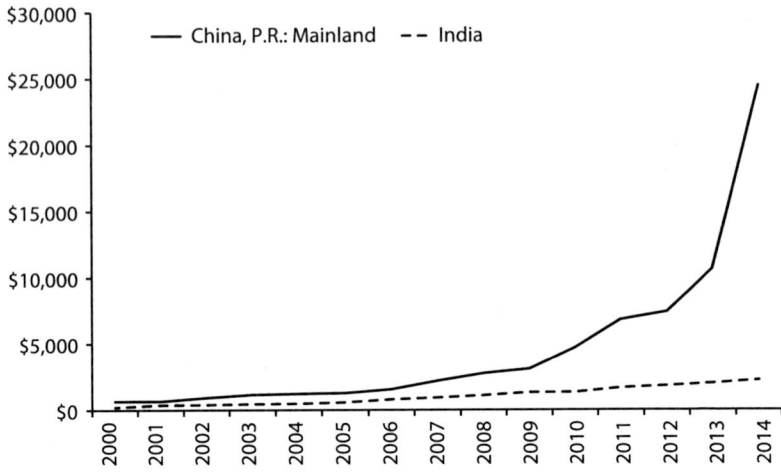

Figure 3.1 Myanmar's Bilateral Trade with India and China (U.S.$ millions)

Source: International Monetary Fund 2015. For details on methodology, see Blank et al. 2015, p. 84.

President Thein Sein began reform in earnest, trade totalled $6.5 billion. During the same period—that is, the period during which Delhi had an opportunity to cash in its supposed chits earned during years supporting the democracy movement—India's trade increased by about $300 million: less than 10 per cent of the dollar-amount China's trade grew (International Monetary Fund 2013).[13]

India exports pharmaceuticals and steel to Myanmar, and buys agricultural products in return—but India is not even one of Myanmar's top half-dozen suppliers of trade goods. China, Thailand, Singapore, South Korea, Japan, and Indonesia all export more to Myanmar than India does (United Nations 2015). Moreover, these figures account for only the licit sectors of the economy: if illicit trade were factored in, particularly the lucrative commerce in drugs, small arms, trafficked persons, illegally harvested timber, and illegally mined gemstones, the imbalance towards China (as well as Thailand) would likely be far larger.

During a visit by Burmese president Thein Sein to New Delhi in 2011, Prime Minister Singh promised a line of credit worth $500 million to support infrastructure projects (PTI 2012). Whenever Indian policy-makers discuss economic goals in Southeast Asia, the word 'connectivity' is quick to come up. In this context, connectivity typically is shorthand for the physical infrastructure needed for the transportation of trade goods: that is, roads, ports, and railways. It is no exaggeration to say that India's goals for economic outreach to Southeast Asia run, quite literally, straight through Myanmar. And are stuck at the border.

The two infrastructure plans most commonly discussed for building connectivity by land are a highway and a railway linking India's road and rail networks to those of mainland Southeast Asia. When either project is completed, advocates promise, it will be possible to travel by land from Kolkata to Yangon, Bangkok, or Hanoi in less than a day. The Tri-Nation Highway is projected to run from the town Moreh in India's Manipur state to the Burmese city of Mandalay, and then onward to Yangon and into Thailand via Mae Sot. The railway project would follow a similar path, laying new track from the railhead at Dimapur, in India's Nagaland state, to the Burmese rail-line at Mandalay.

So far, neither project has made an inch of headway into Myanmar. While India has modestly upgraded its own highway system in some of the Northeastern states, in mountainous terrain the largest of these highways become extremely basic two-lane roads unsuitable for significantly increased trade, let alone containerized traffic; as Sanjoy Hazarika notes in Chapter 5, New Delhi's concrete commitment to the economic development of its seven Northeastern states has generally lagged well behind political rhetoric. Beyond Moreh, no work has been done to upgrade the Burmese portion of the road, which is in even worse condition than that on India's side of the border. Despite the lack of any substantive progress, India and Myanmar agreed in August 2013 to set a 2016 deadline to complete the highway linking 'Guwahati in Assam to Burma's border with Thailand via Mandalay and the former capital Rangoon' (Nelson 2013).

As daunting as road construction in the Burmese highlands may be, the construction of a modern rail system is considerably more challenging. During the colonial period, British engineers linked all major parts of what are now the nations of India, Pakistan, and Bangladesh together in a single rail network; due partly to the great logistical difficulties involved, this system was never linked to the colonial-era railway system in British-administered Burma. There is at least one additional obstacle: most of India's rail lines are broad gauge, many of those in its mountainous Northeast are narrow gauge—and neither would easily be able to share rolling stock with Myanmar's metre gauge trains.[14] Even in the best of circumstances, railway construction in highland Myanmar is an arduous prospect. Perhaps the most noteworthy example is the last venture on a scale envisioned by India: imperial Japan's 1942–3 attempt to build new railway lines in occupied Burma. The effort is portrayed (in a fictional form, but one which does not overstate the hardships of those forced to labour on the project) in the book and movie *The Bridge on the River Kwai*.

It does not take more than a quick glance at a map to see that India's ambitions for land connectivity to Southeast Asia must run through Myanmar. Less obvious, but still closely tied to geographical realities, is the fact that India's plans for expanded maritime connectivity run through Myanmar as well. As C. Raja Mohan (2012) and others have noted, the maintenance of free navigation through the Indian Ocean and the southern Pacific is one of India's most pressing security concerns; this strategic necessity helps explain the fact that the Indian Navy has been more forward-leaning on its engagement with the U.S. and other nations than have the Indian Army or Indian Air Force. India's primary point of maritime entry to Southeast Asia, for civil and military shipping alike, will remain the Strait of Malacca for the foreseeable future; but open passage through the strait is an interest shared by the U.S., China, Japan, and every state in the region—India's interests are unlikely to be threatened without the interests of far more powerful military and economic forces being threatened as well. In short, India has little need to spend its scarce resources ensuring free navigation through the strait, or upgrading nearby port facilities (such as those in Singapore) which are already more capable than Indian ports.

India's signature maritime connectivity project, therefore, is located not in peninsular Malaysia, but on the western coast of Myanmar. The Kaladan Multi-Modal Transit Transport Project is envisioned as a network reaching from port to canal to river to road. Its hub would be Sittwe port, a dilapidated naval facility in Myanmar's Rakhine State. When completed, the Kaladan project would enable goods to be shipped from Kolkata, Chennai, or any other Indian port not only to mainland Southeast Asia, but even to the landlocked states of India's Northeast.

The project at Sittwe involves not only modernizing and upgrading existing structures, but dredging the harbour so that it can accommodate deepwater ships. The new facilities would have two commercial routes flowing north into Mizoram: one via the Kaladan River (suitable for low-draft vessels), the other via an upgraded 158-kilometre road to Paletwa, another 129 kilometres to the border post of Myeikwa, and an additional road to meet a new extension of India's National Highway 54.

Like the land connectivity projects, the Kaladan infrastructure plans remain largely speculative. Little work has been done even at Sittwe port, and even less on the more ambitious plans to link the port to commercially viable modes of transporting goods to Mizoram. Two international observers interviewed by the author in Yangon (both involved in infrastructure development on a daily basis) were unaware of any Indian work at Sittwe; a Western diplomatic source was able to confirm that some work was indeed going on, but at a very slow pace.[15] By contrast, Chinese construction of a port facility at Kyaukphu (just south of Sittwe), and a pipeline stretching nearly 800 kilometres from Kyaukphu to the Chinese province of Yunnan, took about three years; in 2013, China began importing natural gas from offshore fields and transporting it straight across Myanmar (Hook 2013).

India–Myanmar Security Connections

India and Myanmar both have a strong interest in border security, since the mountainous region where the two nations meet provides ample sanctuary to insurgent groups and transnational criminal networks. As described in detail by Bertil Lintner in Chapter 4, rebels in Northeastern Indian states such as Manipur and Nagaland often enjoyed safe haven, with or without Tatmadaw complicity, in Burmese territory. The Khaplang faction of the Nationalist Socialist Council of Nagaland (NSCN) has maintained quasi-permanent camps in Myanmar, as has the People's Revolutionary Party of Kangleipak.[16]

Myanmar has faced even more serious insurgencies throughout its independent existence. Most of these armed rebellions have been launched by highland minority communities, sometimes by groups with cultural or commercial linkages across the Indian border. Throughout the 1980s and 1990s Myanmar was a major source of poppy cultivation, and from the mid-1990s onward has been a source of methamphetamine production; India is a transit country for narcotics and a source for precursor chemicals for processing methamphetamine. Alliances among traffickers in drugs and persons have supplied ample funding for violent rebels and violent criminals on both sides of the border. The Burmese military has promised to take action against Indian insurgent groups in Myanmar, while India has permitted Myanmar to conduct 'hot pursuit' operations against its own insurgents on India's side of the line (Jha 2011: 54–5).

One of the largest elements of India's 2006 arms sale to Myanmar was the transfer of four British-origin BN-2 Defender Islander maritime patrol aircraft. When London objected to the sale, New Delhi promised to strip the aircraft of all armaments, and make them suitable for use 'exclusively on relief and humanitarian missions' (India Defence 2007). India has also sold light artillery and armoured personnel carriers, and a month before the Saffron Revolution broke out in August 2007, there were press reports that India was planning to sell Myanmar its indigenously designed Advanced Light Helicopter (*The Financial Express* 2007).[17] In 2006 India offered to provide special warfare training to Tatmadaw troops, and repeated the offer when Myanmar's armed forces commander, General Min Aung Hlaing, visited New Delhi in August 2012 (Sakhuja 2012).

These military sales and offers of training, however, are utterly dwarfed by the security relationship Myanmar continues to maintain with China (see Figure 3.2). Given the poor timing of New Delhi's initiatives, perhaps the light footprint was fortunate: military hardware from the

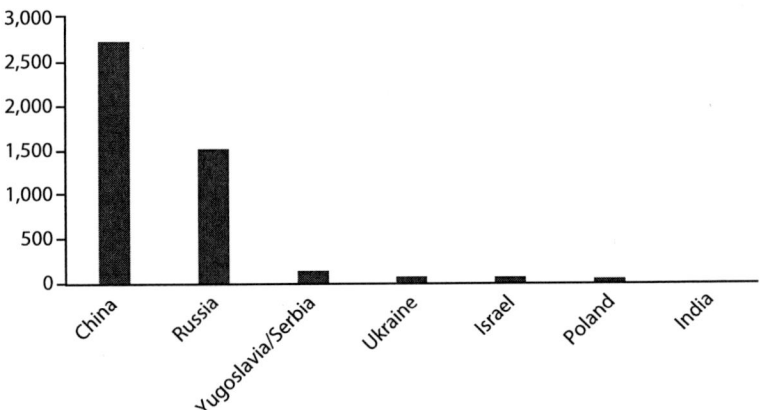

Figure 3.2 Myanmar Arms Purchases from Top 7 Suppliers, 1990–2014 (U.S.$ millions)

Source: Stockholm International Peace Research Institute (SIPRI). 2015. SIPRI Arms Transfer Database, available at http://armstrade.sipri.org/armstrade/html/export_values.php (accessed 8 May 2015).

2006 arms sale, representing the high point of India's commercial security relationship with Myanmar, may have still been in the delivery pipeline even as Burmese troops were attacking Buddhist monks during the protests of September 2007.

In one type of security engagement, however, India has succeeded in securing some measure of goodwill from both the population of Myanmar and from its military rulers. That type is military humanitarian assistance and disaster relief (HA/DR), provided during the period when Cyclone Nargis took over 100,000 Burmese lives. In Operation Sahayata, two Indian Air Force aircraft brought tents and medical supplies to Yangon on 8 May 2008, at a time when the junta was denying access to the U.S. and almost all other would-be donors. Two Indian naval vessels, the INS *Rana* and the INS *Kirpan*, were permitted to unload additional relief supplies near Yangon (*The Hindu* 2008). India was one of only two nations (the other was Thailand) whose nationals were allowed to conduct relief efforts in-country: during the two weeks before this permission was revoked, Indian military doctors treated about 15,000 victims of the cyclone (Samaranayake, Lea, and Gorenburg 2014: 26).

Can Closer Ties with India Help Wean Myanmar Away from Reliance on China?

Throughout the first two decades of Burma's post-colonial history, China covertly provided material support to an array of Communist groups seeking to overthrow the national government. By the late 1980s, about a dozen years after the death of Mao Zedong, China had become the foremost external patron of Myanmar's military regime. The shift was both an expression of realism (all of the Communist insurgencies had fizzled out in the 1950s and 1960s), and of opportunism: with the suppression of the 8888 Revolt, Myanmar was internationally isolated— and in desperate need of at least one powerful patron. China served as that patron throughout the next two decades of Myanmar's seclusion, supplying huge amounts of arms and providing much-needed diplomatic support. But this alliance has never been a truly harmonious one, and many Burmese have long resented China's dominant role in their nation's economy and exploitation of its natural resources. An essential component of the post-2011 reform package has been outreach to the international community, not merely in order to remove Western economic sanctions, but also to diversify Myanmar's cohort of friends.

Why might Myanmar welcome closer ties with India? A warmer relationship with its neighbour could bring security to some of its volatile highland areas. Perhaps the greatest existential threat to Myanmar comes from an internal rather than an external source: unless it can make peace with its panoply of ethnic minorities, Myanmar's rulers (whether they be military or civilian) could find themselves ruling over a rump Bamar state surrounded by *de facto* minority statelets. India can help prevent such a scenario—or, if relations were to deteriorate severely, could help accelerate it. While India has done little to back up its promise to build connectivity infrastructure, Myanmar would very much like to see such plans come to fruition. Perhaps most importantly from the view of Myanmar's leadership class: unlike China or (in the imagination of at least some Tatmadaw generals) the U.S., India poses little threat of economic, political, or military domination.

From New Delhi's perspective, Naypyidaw provides mirroring benefits: cooperation in combating insurgencies in its unruly Northeast, the possibility of direct land and multi-modal connectivity to Southeast Asia, and a partner in the effort to offset China without provoking an open conflict. Given this harmony of interests, why has India not been more proactive in its policy towards Myanmar? Several explanations present themselves, none of which is a legitimate basis for continued inaction:

- Until 2011, India would have been unable to engage much more significantly without jeopardizing its self-image as a nation firmly committed to democracy, protection of minority rights, and representative government. New Delhi's forays into collaboration with the junta, during periods of both BJP and Congress rule between 2000 and 2010, demonstrated the difficulty of such a policy: China can form its alliances without fear of domestic opposition and with little care for international criticism, but Indian leaders have no such luxury. The first point is demonstrated by 2007 protests in Delhi and Kolkata in support of the Saffron Revolution, the second by European rebukes to India's arms sales to the junta in the face of global sanctions.
- India's policy towards Southeast Asia has traditionally been characterized by inattention and inertia. The first articulation of an international policy was Jawaharlal Nehru's dream of Non-Alignment;

it formed at least the rhetorical basis for strategy until the death of his daughter, Indira Gandhi, but its relevance for Southeast Asia did not last much after the Bandung Conference of 1955. The 'Rajiv Doctrine', which was promulgated by Nehru's grandson and asserted India's leadership role throughout the sphere of near-neighbours, has yet to recover from the wounds suffered during India's bloody 'peacekeeping' mission in Sri Lanka. The 'Look East' policy of Narasimha Rao has been upheld in principle by his successors, but has seldom moved beyond the realm of aspiration. Several of India's leaders have earnestly wished to engage more meaningfully with Southeast Asia—but none has been able to summon the sustained focus to devote sufficient resources and attention to such a programme.

• Perhaps as a result of these two impediments, Indian leaders have created a third: self-delusion. In the view of many policy-shapers, India does not need to deepen its engagement with Myanmar—it already *has* a profound strategic partnership with its neighbour. Given that such a *bhai-bhai* (brotherly) bond is seldom recognized in Myanmar itself, this attitude prevents India from realizing the relationship's true potential.

* * *

Despite optimistic rhetoric and the benefits of geography, shared history, and overlapping demographics, India and Myanmar remain remarkably unconnected. India seems to be a less significant player in Myanmar than China, the U.S., Thailand, Japan, South Korea, or Singapore. Even Vietnam is a more visible economic presence in Yangon than India is. A sense of the physical disconnect can be seen in flight data: at the start of 2013, India's national carrier ranked only 20th in weekly capacity to Yangon airport, with a single weekly flight from Kolkata carrying up to 836 passengers; by contrast, two Thai airlines had a weekly capacity of more than 27,500.[18]

Despite India's claim of having softened the Burmese military up for political change, India was only Myanmar's seventh-largest supplier of arms from 1989 to 2013, a period during which China's arms transfers totalled nearly $2.8 billion and Russia's totalled over $1.5 billion (see Figure 3.3).[19] Unlike Western and ASEAN states, however, India's lack

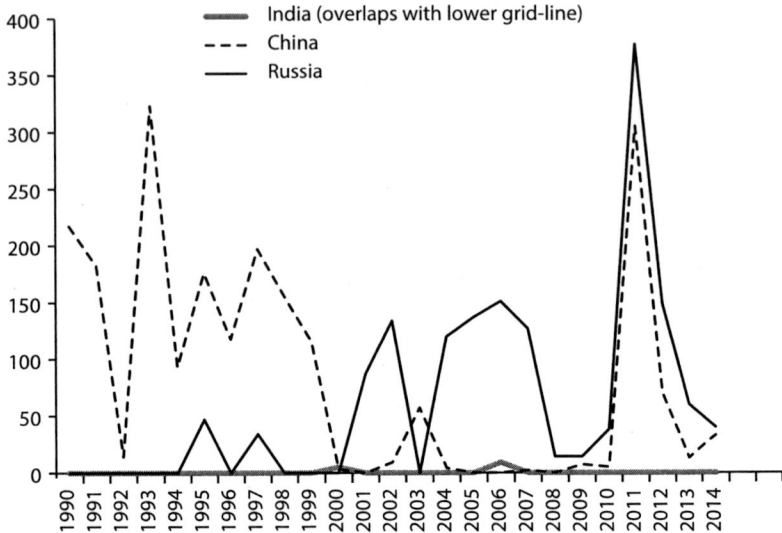

Figure 3.3 Arms Sales to Myanmar by Year (U.S.$ millions)

Source: Stockholm International Peace Research Institute (SIPRI). 2015. SIPRI Arms Transfer Database, available at http://armstrade.sipri.org/armstrade/html/export_values.php (accessed 8 May 2015).

of security engagement has not been offset since the post-2011 reforms by corresponding trade or investment.

The future, however, need not be a replay of the past. India's slow pace in implementing its 'Look East' policy has had more to do with domestic political realities than with international strategic choices. Every prime minister from P.V. Narasimha Rao to Manmohan Singh presided over a coalition government, and therefore were forced to devote a great deal of political and budgetary capital to internal priorities. Prime Minister Narendra Modi, the first Indian leader in a quarter-century to enjoy an absolute Lok Sabha majority, has greater political freedom to 'Act East' (as he has vowed) than his seven immediate predecessors. If he uses this political space to significantly increase India's engagement with Myanmar, such a course will serve the interests of his nation, of democratic nations in Asia, Europe, and the Americas, and of the mass of the citizens of Myanmar themselves.

Notes

1. Throughout this chapter, I have drawn on research conducted for a larger publication on relations between India and Southeast Asia (Blank *et al.* 2015). I am indebted to my co-authors—Jennifer D.P. Moroney, Angel Rabasa, and Bonny Lin—for their contributions to every aspect of that project. In this chapter, all observations and analysis (as well as any errors or shortcomings) are strictly my own.

2. India, attaining independence in 1947, has kept the framework of Westminster-style parliamentary democracy in place for all but two years of its history (the 1975–7 'Emergency'). Myanmar, called the Union of Burma at its 1948 independence, abandoned meaningful parliamentary democracy following a 1962 military *coup d'etat*, and is in the process of re-creating it. Two other Southeast Asian nations, Malaysia and Singapore, grew out of the British colonial Straits Settlement rather than British Indian Raj; the political, legal, and administrative history of the Straits Settlement shares many features with that of the Raj, but also many differences. For discussion of India's more ancient cultural ties to Myanmar and other parts of Southeast Asia, see Blank 2000: 105–9.

3. For perspective of an Indian policymaker on Myanmar's place in the 'near neighbour' category see former foreign secretary Nirupama Rao 2013.

4. Scholarly sources using the term 'Rajiv Doctrine' in this manner include Jaffrelot 2011: 685–6 and Hagerty 1991: 352; Sidhu and Smith 2000: 34 refer to the 'Indira and Rajiv Doctrine'.

5. These officials included retired flag-rank military officers and Cabinet-level civilians. Quotations from these interviews can be found in Blank *et al.* 2015.

6. These interviewees included Burmese private citizens, diplomats from Southeast Asian and Western countries stationed in Myanmar, and representatives of international organizations based in Yangon. Details and excerpts can be found in Blank *et al.* 2015.

7. This dichotomy is, of necessity, rather rough. It remains unclear whether the Rohingyas and certain other minority groups will do better or worse under democratic Myanmar. Powerful warlords and traffickers in illicit items, some of them also serving as legitimate leaders of ethnic-minority armies, have much to lose from reform. The degree of President Thein Sein's own commitment to reform remains to be seen. Perhaps the only nation other than China which stands to lose from political reform in Myanmar would be North Korea, whose relationship with the Tatmadaw has been close and covert.

8. Until it was officially renamed Yangon in 1989, the largest city in Burma was known as Rangoon. It was the capital of independent Burma (officially Myanmar from 1989) until 2006, when the seat of government was moved to the newly

constructed city of Naypyidaw. In 1941, 56 per cent of Rangoon's population was Indian, and slightly less than one-third was Bamar (Than 1993: 586).

9. There was at least one noteworthy instance of security cooperation during the tenure of Narasimha Rao: Operation Golden Bird, a joint India–Myanmar operation conducted in April–May of 1995 against insurgent groups based in three northeastern Indian states (Assam, Nagaland, and Manipur). This episode, however, did not lead to a sustained engagement in the security, diplomatic, or economic spheres.

10. The BJP first attempted to form a government in May 1996, but party leader Atal Bihari Vajpayee could not forge a majority coalition and resigned as prime minister after thirteen days.

11. The 8888 Revolt occurred during the tenure of Rajiv Gandhi (1984–9), and India's 'Look East' policy towards Southeast Asia was formulated by Narasimha Rao (1991–6). Prime Ministers V.P. Singh (1989–90), H.D. Dewe Gowda (1996–7), and I.K. Gujral (1997–8) led Janata Dal governments, but began their political careers in the Congress party. The only leader during this period without a Congress background was Chandra Shekhar, who held power for less than eight months (1990–1), and had little impact on foreign policy.

12. The 2006 arms sale was worth $9 million (SIPRI 2015).

13. The figures cited here are based on RAND analysis of data contained in the subscription-only portion of the database, current as of 13 June 2013. See Blank et al. 2015.

14. It is possible for a train to run on different gauges of track switching out the bogies (undercarriages). Mass-conversion of existing stock, however, is a formidable task.

15. These interviews took place in April 2013. At the time of writing, neither the Sittwe port upgrading nor any other part of the Kaladan project had moved noticeably closer to completion.

16. The continued importance of this issue is highlighted by the attack on 3 May 2015 by Khaplang Faction rebels on an Indian army post in the Mon district of Nagaland, which left eight soldiers dead (Kashyap 2015).

17. The Indian government denied the report, and the sale appears not to have gone forward. The helicopter components were of European Union (EU) origin, and at the time such a sale would have violated EU sanctions on Myanmar.

18. Five Chinese carriers had a weekly capacity over ten times that of India; Malaysia and Singapore each carried about eight times as many as India; even countries as far away as Australia, Vietnam, and Qatar carried twice or three times as many passengers as India did (Centre for Aviation 2013).

19. Between 2001 and 2008, China, Russia, Serbia, and Ukraine, countries not known for their steadfast devotion to democracy, supplied $1.1 billion in arms to Myanmar: 81 times as much as India did; to the extent that security

engagement with the pre-Saffron Revolution junta can be seen as having influenced the junta's decisions, any reformist message from India would clearly have been overshadowed by the *realpolitik* message of these other states. All figures from SIPRI arms transfer database.

References

Blank, Jonah. 2000. *Arrow of the Blue-Skinned God: Retracing the Ramayana through India*. New York: Grove.

Blank, Jonah, Jennifer D.P. Moroney, Angel Rabasa, and Bonny Lin. 2015. *Look East, Cross Black Waters: India's Interest in Southeast Asia*. Santa Monica: RAND Corporation.

Centre for Aviation. 2013. 'Myanmar Poised for More Rapid Growth in 2013 as Foreign Carriers Expand and Local LCC Launches', *CAPA Centre for Aviation*, 10 January; available at http://centreforaviation.com/analysis/myanmar-poised-for-more-rapid-growth-in-2013-as-foreign-carriers-expand-and-local-lcc-launches-93666 (accessed 8 May 2015).

Hagerty, Devin T. 1991. 'India's Regional Security Doctrine', *Asian Survey*, 31(4) (April): 351–63.

Hook, Leslie. 2013. 'China Starts Importing Natural Gas from Myanmar', *The Financial Times*, 29 July; available at http://www.ft.com/cms/s/0/870f632c-f83e-11e2-92f0-00144feabdc0.html#axzz3ZZUUWFYv (accessed 8 May 2015).

India Defence. 2007. 'Indian Navy to Transfer BN2 Maritime Surveillance Aircraft to Myanmar', 12 May; available at http://bharatdefence.blogspot.com/2007/05/indian-navy-to-transfer-bn2-maritime.html (accessed 10 December 2015).

International Monetary Fund (IMF). 2013. *Direction of Trade Statistics Database 2013*. Washington, D.C.: International Monetary Fund.

———. 2015. *Direction of Trade Statistics 2015*. Washington, D.C.: International Monetary Fund. Available at http://elibrary-data.imf.org/finddatareports.aspx?d=33061&e=170921.

Jaffrelot, Christophe. 2011. *Religion, Caste, and Politics in India*. London: Hurst & Co.

Jha, Pankaj Kumar. 2011. 'India's Defence Diplomacy in Southeast Asia', *Journal of Defence Studies*, 5(1): 47–62.

Kashyap, Samudra Gupta. 2015. 'Nagaland Ambush: A Day Before, NSCN(K) Had Warned of Attack', *The Indian Express*, 5 May; available at http://indianexpress.com/article/india/india-others/nagaland-ambush-a-day-before-nscnk-had-warned-of-attack/ (accessed 7 May 2015).

Mohan, C. Raja. 2012. *Samudra Manthan: Sino-Indian Rivalry in the Indo-Pacific.* Washington, D.C.: Carnegie Endowment for International Peace.

Mukherjee, Krittivas. 2010. 'India Courts Myanmar Junta with Stronger Ties', *Reuters*, 27 July; available at http://in.reuters.com/article/2010/07/27/idINIndia-50428220100727 (accessed 7 May 2015).

Nelson, Dean. 2013. 'India to Open Super Highway to Burma and Thailand', *The Telegraph*, 8 August; available at http://www.telegraph.co.uk/news/worldnews/asia/india/9297354/India-to-open-super-highway-to-Burma-and-Thailand.html (accessed 8 May 2015).

Press Trust of India (PTI). 2012. 'India Extends $500 Million Line of Credit to Myanmar', *Economic Times*, 28 March; available at http://articles.economictimes.indiatimes.com/2012-05-28/news/31877180_1_thein-sein-myanmar-president-myanmar-foreign-trade-bank (accessed 8 May 2015).

———. 2007. 'Political Reform in Myanmar Should Be Broad-Based, Says India', *Times of India*, 26 September; available at http://timesofindia.indiatimes.com/india/Political-reform-in-Myanmar-should-be-broad-based-says-India/articleshow/2406090.cms? (accessed 8 May 2015).

Rao, Nirupama. 2013. 'America's "Asian Pivot": The View from India', paper presented at the Spring 2013 Brown–India Initiative Seminar Series, Brown University, Providence, Rhode Island, 4 February 2013; available at http://www.brown.edu/initiatives/india/sites/brown.edu.initiatives.india/files/uploads/NirupamaRao-America'sAsianPivotTheViewfromIndia-Brown-IndiaInitiativeSeminar2.4.2013.pdf (accessed 10 December 2015).

Sakhuja, Vijay. 2012. 'India and Myanmar: Choices for Military Cooperation', *Indian Council of World Affairs Issue Brief*, 11 September; available at http://www.icwa.in/pdfs/IBindiamyanmar.pdf (accessed 8 May 2015).

Samaranayake, Nilanthi, Catherine Lea, and Dmitry Gorenburg. 2014. *Improving U.S.–India HA/DR Coordination in the Indian Ocean.* Arlington, VA: Center for Naval Analyses.

Sidhu, Waheguru Pal Singh and Chris Smith. 2000. *Indian Defence and Security: Industry, Forces and Future Trends.* London: Jane's Information Group.

Stockholm International Peace Research Institute (SIPRI). 2015. 'SIPRI Arms Transfer Database', SIPRI; available at http://www.sipri.org/databases/armstransfers (accessed 8 May 2015).

Than, Tin Maung Maung. 1993. 'Some Aspects of Indians in Rangoon', in *Indian Communities in Southeast Asia*, edited by K.S. Sandhu and A. Mani, 585–623. Singapore: Institute of Southeast Asian Studies.

The Financial Express. 2007. 'India Rejects Amnesty Report on Copter Sale to Myanmar', 17 July; available athttp://archive.financialexpress.com/

news/india-rejects-amnesty-report-on-copter-sale-to-myanmar/205257 (accessed 8 May 2015).

The Hindu. 2008. "'Operation Sahayata' to Help Myanmar', 8 March; available at http://www.thehindu.com/todays-paper/tp-national/operation-sahayata-to-help-myanmar/article1254354.ece (accessed 8 May 2015).

United Nations. 2015. *United Nations Commodity Trade Statistics Database;* available at http://comtrade.un.org/db/ (accessed 8 May 2015).

4   The Indo-Myanmar Border and India's Security Problems in the East

BERTIL LINTNER

INDIA'S 1,643-KILOMETRE-LONG BORDER with Myanmar is not receiving nearly as much attention from security planners as its other international frontiers. But it is in, along, and across this largely neglected, porous frontier in the east that India is facing some of its most important foreign-policy challenges. In brief, India's interests in Myanmar should be motivated by four major concerns. The first is New Delhi's 'Look East' policy. Myanmar is the obvious link between India and lucrative markets in Southeast Asia—and the highway on which one day it will be possible to travel from India to Singapore will go through Myanmar. New Delhi's security planners also want to ensure that ethnic Assamese, Manipuri, and Naga rebels are deprived of cross-border sanctuaries in the remote hills of northwestern Myanmar, from where they can launch raids into India and smuggle guns into India's volatile northeastern region. Thirdly, India's rapidly expanding economy also needs energy, and New Delhi has shown interest in importing more oil, gas, and perhaps even hydroelectric power from Myanmar. Lastly, India wants to keep China's influence in Myanmar at acceptable levels.

A New Myanmar?

There is no doubt that many important events have taken place in Myanmar since a quasi-civilian government led by Thein Sein, a former army general, assumed office in March 2011. Political prisoners have been released, the media is freer than at any time since the military seized power in 1962, and political parties can now operate more or less openly. Those changes have resulted in vastly improved relations with the West, which had slapped sanctions on Myanmar's ruling military elite because of its gross violations of human rights. But it would be naïve to believe that recent policy changes in Myanmar—and the West's warm response to the overtures—are driven by a sudden democratic awakening among the country's ruling military elite. Nor are Western powers, despite their rhetoric and posturing, placing progress on democracy and human rights at the top of their policy priorities. There is hypocrisy on both sides—and the main issue of concern, which neither side would acknowledge publicly, is without doubt China's economic and strategic push south through Myanmar to the Indian Ocean and the rest of Southeast Asia (Lintner 2015b).

After years of pursuing a policy of isolation and condemnation, the West realized that those moves had only pushed Myanmar into the hands of China, which had become the country's main trading partner, investor, and supplier of military hardware. When it was discovered in the early 2000s that Myanmar and North Korea had established a strategic partnership, the U.S. decided that an entirely new approach was needed. North Korea was providing Myanmar with tunnelling expertise, heavy weapons, radar and air defense systems, and—it is alleged by Western as well as Asian intelligence agencies—even missile-related technology.

At the same time, the Myanmar military was also worried about becoming too dependent on China. As early as August 2004, a classified, 346-page document entitled 'A Study of Myanmar–US Relations' was compiled at Myanmar's prestigious Defense Services Academy in Pyin Oo Lwin. It stated that Myanmar's reliance on China as a diplomatic ally and economic patron had created a 'national emergency' that threatened the country's independence. Therefore, the report concluded, Myanmar must normalize relations with the West after electing a government, so that the regime can deal with the outside world on more acceptable terms.[1]

A general election was indeed held in Myanmar in November 2010, which led to Thein Sein's rise to power. It may have been blatantly rigged and fraudulent, but it was just the opportunity that Washington needed. Myanmar suddenly had a new face and a country run by a constitution, not a junta. It was also the perfect time for Myanmar's generals to launch their charm offensive in the West, and for the U.S. and other Western countries to begin the process of détente—and of pulling Myanmar from its uncomfortable Chinese embrace and close relationship with North Korea.

While emphasizing democracy and human rights publicly, the West has welcomed the 'new Myanmar' with open arms. But that the 'China factor' was also important, and even more so than Myanmar's 'reform process', became clear after Thein Sein announced on 20 September 2011 that his government had suspended a U.S.$3.6 billion joint venture hydroelectric dam project with China that threatened environmental damage in the country's northern Kachin State (Fuller 2015; Nomi 2011). The dam, located at Myitsone where the Mali Hka and Nmai Hka Rivers converge to form the Ayeyarwady (formerly the Irrawaddy), would have flooded more than 766 square kilometres of forest land, an area bigger than Singapore, and 90 per cent of the electricity was scheduled for export to China (Harvey 2011). Once online, the dam and its huge reservoir would have done grave harm to the Ayeyarwady, the nation's economic and cultural artery. Western policies and sanctions did not cause Myanmar's economic, and strategic, push into 'the hands of the Chinese', as many foreign observers have argued, though Western policies certainly made it easier for China to implement its designs for Myanmar. In 2011, all that began to change. After the suspension of Myitsone, once-isolated Myanmar turned from being a pariah state to the darling of the West.

Myanmar Turning to the ASEAN and India

To strengthen its position vis-à-vis China, Myanmar turned to its partners in the Association of Southeast Asian Nations (ASEAN) for trade, especially Thailand, Malaysia, and Singapore. Even more significantly, when Gen. Min Aung Hlaing, who was appointed commander-in-chief of Myanmar's military in March 2011, went on his first foreign trip in mid-November, he did not go to China as his predecessors had done, but to China's traditional enemy, Vietnam. Myanmar and Vietnam share the same fear of their common, powerful northern neighbour, so it is reasonable to assume that Min Aung Hlaing had a lot to discuss with his Vietnamese hosts.

Myanmar is also seeking to improve its relations with India. Immediately after the 1988 pro-democracy uprising in Myanmar, India expressed support for the opposition, led by the iconic Aung San Suu

Kyi, the daughter of Myanmar's independence hero Aung San. New Delhi gave shelter to Myanmar refugees and allowed dissidents to operate freely from Indian territory. That, of course, was not for entirely altruistic reasons: the policy was viewed widely as India's way of countering China's influence in Myanmar. But it soon became obvious to policymakers that the pro-democracy opposition would not assume power anytime soon, so India began to re-evaluate that strategy around 1993, out of concern that its policies had achieved little except to push Myanmar closer to Beijing. The result was a dramatic shift in policy aimed at patching up relations with Myanmar's ruling generals. In turn, Myanmar signalled to India to take greater interest in improving bilateral relations to lessen its heavy dependence on China.

As stated above, India's interests in Myanmar are motivated by four major concerns. The first is New Delhi's 'Look East' policy. Myanmar is the obvious link between India and trading partners and lucrative markets in Southeast Asia—and the highway from India to Singapore will go through Myanmar. New Delhi's security planners also want to ensure that ethnic Assamese, Manipuri, and Naga rebels in the Northeast are deprived of sanctuaries inside northwestern Myanmar, where they are able to launch raids into India. Thirdly, India's rapidly expanding economy needs energy, and New Delhi has shown strong interest in importing more oil, gas, and perhaps even hydroelectric power from Myanmar. And then, of course, India wants to keep Chinese influence in Myanmar at acceptable levels.

The construction of gas and oil pipelines from the coast of Myanmar to Yunnan in China was especially worrisome for New Delhi because that would also need an extensive signals intelligence network in the Indian Ocean sea lanes along which the fuel is transported. China has no naval bases in Myanmar, which some Indian newspapers have reported, but it has helped Myanmar upgrade its own naval facilities in exchange for access to intelligence gathered from newly installed radar stations in the region (Sudarshan 2000).[2] India has not taken lightly the prospect of another major player in a strategically important maritime area that it considers its own lake. This concern provides a new aspect to the age-old strategic rivalry between India and China.

Not surprisingly, the U.S.'s Barack Obama administration has expressed its support for New Delhi's 'Look East' policy. On 23 November 2011, the then U.S. deputy National Security Advisor for Strategic

Communication Ben Rhodes said: 'The President very much welcomes India's Look East approach. We believe that just as the United States, as a Pacific Ocean power, is going to be deeply engaged in the future of East Asia, so should India as an Indian Ocean power and as an Asian nation' (PTI 2011). Then came, of course, the September 2014 visit to the U.S. by India's new prime minister, Narendra Modi, and Obama's return visit to India in January 2015.

The more recent anti-Chinese stance taken by Myanmar's new government was music to the ears of India's security planners. India rolled out the red carpet for Thein Sein when he first visited New Delhi in October 2011 in an effort to reduce Myanmar's heavy dependence on China and make more room for India. That visit has been followed by several other high-ranking exchanges between India and Myanmar.

Obama's 'Asian pivot' has also seen Washington reaffirming its alliances with Japan, South Korea, the Philippines, Indonesia, and Thailand—all of them traditional strategic partners in the region. The U.S. has even strengthened ties with its old foe Vietnam, but given that the U.S. and Vietnam, a sworn enemy of China, are on the same side in this new Cold War in Asia, this is not surprising. Myanmar, however, is the only example of how the U.S. has managed to expand its influence at the expense of China's. 'It's a rollback situation', says a military analyst in Southeast Asia.[3] It is easy to see that Myanmar's reform process was never what it seemed—nor was the West's response to it. The main issue for the U.S. that no one wants to talk about too openly is, of course, the rising power and influence of China—and here, there has been a meeting of minds between America's politicians and Myanmar's generals.

China's Push South through Myanmar

In this context, it is also important to remember that Myanmar remains of vital economic and strategic importance for China, which cannot just 'hand over' Myanmar to the U.S. and possibly also India. As a result, China is playing a complex diplomatic game in Myanmar. In 2012 Chinese arms dealers supplied the United Wa State Army (UWSA), a militia operating along the Sino-Myanmar border, with not only assault rifles, machine guns, rocket launchers, and the HN-5 series man-portable air defence systems or MANPADS, but also PTL-02 6x6 wheeled 'tank destroyers' and another armoured combat vehicle identified as Chinese 4x4 ZFB-05.

Jane's Defence Weekly reported in its 29 April 2013 issue that China had supplied the UWSA with several Mi-17 medium-transport helicopters armed with TY-90 air-to-air missiles (Davis 2013).

All of this comes in the wake of a remarkable thaw in relations between the United States and Myanmar, and while supporting the UWSA, including through the provision of arms, China has become involved in the peace process with the rebel Kachin Independence Army (KIA), a powerful ethnic rebel army in the far north of the country. While waving a carrot in front of the Myanmar government—a promise to solve the bloody conflict in Kachin State and, in January 2013, pledges of generous loans in the order of U.S.$527 million for infrastructure development and other projects—China's big stick is its support for the UWSA. Few observers, however, believe that China would want the UWSA to actually go to war against the government, but the MANPADs, armoured vehicles, and now helicopters supplied to the UWSA serve as a deterrent and will make the Myanmar military hesitate to launch an offensive against the Wa. They are also a reminder of the fact that China, unlike the U.S., is Myanmar's immediate neighbour and has the means to interfere in its internal conflicts—and that it can, and is willing to, step up the pressure if Myanmar moves too close to the U.S.

It remains to be seen what China's next step will be and if the U.S. is prepared to counter it with increased support, including possible military-to-military engagement, for the Myanmar government. But whatever those moves may be, Myanmar has been dragged into a superpower rivalry that it may not be able to handle as the competition for influence intensifies. It is already the country where Obama's pivot comes into greatest contact with China's own strategic designs for the region, and where China's and India's strategic and economic interests clash.

Cross-Border Insurgencies and the Role of China

In the early 1960s, Naga separatist rebels who had been driven out of India established cross-border sanctuaries in the remote mountains of northwestern Myanmar. From there, they trekked through Myanmar's Kachin State to China's Yunnan province, where from 1968 to 1976 they received military training and returned to the Indo-Myanmar border with Chinese-supplied arms and ammunition. Ethnic Mizo rebels also went to Yunnan for training in the 1970s, and a small group of Manipuri rebels underwent training in Tibet in the late 1970s.[4]

China's support for the ethnic rebels in northeastern India was a direct outcome of the 1962 border war between Asia's two giants, and, I could argue, also the way in which the Chinese wanted to 'teach India a lesson' for allowing the Dalai Lama to set up a Tibetan government in exile in India. Direct aid, however, ceased after Mao Zedong's death in 1976 and the rise to power of Deng Xiaoping, who was more interested in trade and economic expansion than exporting revolution to China's neighbours. That has not prevented India's rebels from being able to buy weapons in China.

The biggest seizure of arms destined for India's Northeast occurred in Chittagong, Bangladesh, in April 2004. Ten truckloads of mostly Chinese-made assault rifles, sub-machine guns, rocket propelled grenades launchers, hand grenades, and assorted ammunition were seized. The munitions had been shipped from Hong Kong, then on to Singapore where more weapons, not Chinese-made, were added. The ship then continued to Sittwe on Myanmar's Rakhine coast of the Bay of Bengal, where the load was transferred to two smaller fishing trawlers, which ferried the weaponry to Chittagong (Karlekar 2014). The shipment was destined for at least two major rebel groups in India's Northeast, the United Liberation Front of Asom (ULFA) and the Nationalist Socialist Council of Nagalim-Isaac and Muivah (NSCN-IM), and was worth an estimated U.S.$4.5–7 million. ULFA's military commander, Paresh Barua, was at Chittagong at the time, but managed to escape, and left Bangladesh a few years later. On 30 January 2014, a special court in Chittagong sentenced Barua and 13 others to death for having masterminded the shipment of arms from China (Sikkimfirst.in 2014).

The shipment to Chittagong came only four months after the Bhutanese army, assisted by the Indian military, had launched 'Operation All Clear' and pushed ULFA and some smaller separatist groups from their sanctuaries in the hills and jungles of southeastern Bhutan. ULFA then lost vast amounts of weapons, and the stocks had to be replenished. The next setback for ULFA was in November 2009 when Bangladesh's new government led by the Awami League—which, unlike its predecessor from the Bangladesh Nationalist Party had little or no interest in supporting Indian rebels—had ULFA chairman, Arabinda Rajkhowa, and its deputy commander-in-chief, Raju Barua, arrested along with eight other Assamese militants. They were later handed over to India (BBC News 2009; Kashyap 2009). In September 2010, Rajkumar Meghen, better known as Sana Yaima, the leader of Manipur's United National Liberation Front (UNLF), was arrested in Dhaka and bundled off to India (Bhaumik 2010). At about the same time, the main arms procurer of the Naga rebels and a frequent visitor to China, Anthony Shimray, was arrested at Kathmandu airport in Nepal and ended up in Indian custody (Chaudhury 2013).

The loss of Bhutan and Bangladesh as sanctuaries leaves northwestern Myanmar as the only remaining haven for India's Northeastern rebels. ULFA and its Naga and Manipuri allies maintain several camps in the mountains north and northwest of Singkaling Hkamti in Myanmar's Sagaing region. The main camp is at Taka on a western tributary of the Chindwin River, and that is where Paresh Barua is also based when he is not in China. Some weapons from China are still reaching those bases, usually smuggled from Yunnan down to Mandalay and Monywa in central Myanmar, and from there to the Indian border. It is uncertain whether China's security services are involved in this traffic, or if the weapons have been obtained on the Chinese black market—which, in any case, has always been more grey than black.

According to Rajeev Bhattacharyya (2014), an Indian journalist who trekked across the border into Myanmar's northwestern Sagaing region in late 2011, Assamese, Manipuri, and Naga rebels are ensconced in a string of camps west of the Chindwin, where they are treated with benign neglect by the Myanmar Army. From those sanctuaries in northwestern Myanmar—well beyond reach of the Indian Army—Assamese, Manipuri, and Naga rebels have been able to carry out cross-border raids into northeastern India. India's attempts to persuade Myanmar's military authorities to engage in joint operations against those ethnic insurgents have fallen on deaf ears. Combating insurgents from northeastern India is evidently not a priority of the Myanmar Army, which is engaged in battles against its own ethnic insurgents elsewhere in the country.

The Civil War in Myanmar and the Present 'Peace Process'

Shortly after Thein Sein assumed presidency in 2011, he reached out to the country's ethnic rebels, offering them talks about what was termed a 'Nationwide Ceasefire Agreement' (NCA). So far, however, little or no attention has been paid to the Myanmar military's strategic thinking in regards to the so-called 'peace process'. Discussions have centred on 'a nationwide ceasefire', after which a 'political dialogue' may be held. The government's own outfit, the Myanmar Peace Center, has received massive funding from the European Union and other international donors, while a cabal of foreign 'peacemakers' and 'reconciliation experts' are flocking to the country to get their share of the pie. A foreign human rights activist familiar with the situation in the frontier areas even described Myanmar's foreign-dominated peace industry as 'a cabal of carpetbaggers and conmen whose real contribution to the peace process is shrouded in self-laudatory assessments that have no basis in reality.'[5]

The problem is that few if any of those 'foreign experts' have a very deep understanding of the complexities of Myanmar's ethnic problems. And, as critics are also eager to point out, these 'experts' are paid more in one month than an ordinary Myanmar worker can earn in five years or more. 'Peacemaking' has become a very lucrative industry in Myanmar— at least for the foreign experts and their organizations. And so far, no one has discovered that it is, in fact, a very shrewd strategy designed to outmaneuver and neutralize the non-Bamar ethnic groups without giving in to any of their demands.

While some leaders of the ethnic armies are being bribed with car-import licenses and other economic incentives, many of their followers are unhappy with those arrangements. The result is discord and even splits within those groups and between the various ethnic armies, making this an effective divide-and-conquer game to defeat the ethnic resistance. On 15 October 2015, the Myanmar government signed what it termed 'a Nationwide Ceasefire Agreement' with 'eight armed ethnic groups' in what some observers and foreign dignitaries, including UN Secretary General Ban Ki-moon, described as a historic accomplishment (UN News Center 2015).

However, the event was more of a face-gesture as only eight groups signed the accord—and of those only two (the Karen National Union and the Shan State Restoration Council) could be described as armed resistance forces. Another Karen faction, the Karen Peace Council, is a Thailand-based NGO and the other five groups are small and insignificant. None of Myanmar's main ethnic armies, among them the 8,000–10,000 strong Kachin Independence Army KIA and the 20,000–30,000-strong UWSA, signed the deal.[6]

The reason for the failure to attract the major groups to sign the deal is that in most other peace processes, talks are held first and agreements are signed when a consensus has been reached. No signatures are required for the preceding ceasefire that could be agreed upon verbally. But in Myanmar, the government and the foreign peacemakers put the cart before the horse, asked for an agreement to be signed first and then vague promises of talks later.

The model for that kind of strategy would be a somewhat similar peace process in the Indian state of Nagaland. In 1997, the insurgent NSCN-IM signed a ceasefire agreement with the Indian government. Today, 18 years later, no less than 80 rounds of talks have been held in what clearly amounts to delaying tactics on the part of the Indian government. Meanwhile, the NSCN's fighters are getting used to a comfortable life in so-called 'peace camps'—and the Naga public is turning against them. They continue to demand 'taxes' from the public while the leaders are becoming corrupt, spending the money they have collected on new houses and cars.[7]

An accord between the Government of India and the NSCN-IM was eventually signed in August 2015, but it remains to be seen if it is going to solve decades of civil strife and conflict in Nagaland. The NSCN-IM is claiming huge tracts of land in the neighboring states of Manipur, Assam, and Arunachal Pradesh to be included in a 'Greater Nagaland', a demand that is unlikely to be accepted by those states or the government in New Delhi. If that demand is pushed any further, it could lead to more civil unrest in areas which the Nagas claim but where local populations would be opposed to such a move (Husein 2015). Meanwhile, NSCN-IM leaders are enjoying the benefits of their deal with the central government.

A similar development with rebel leaders who became corrupt and lost sense of what they were fighting for could be seen in Kachin State between the KIA's signing of a ceasefire agreement in 1994 and when the government decided to break it in 2011. During those 17 years, the KIA lost much of the popular support it had preciously enjoyed—while the government's attacks over the past two and a half years have galvanized the Kachin nation and made the rebels heroes in the eyes of most Kachins.

The KIA is not likely to repeat the mistake it made in 1994—nor would the 'Naga model' work in Myanmar. The NSCN is only one group and it wants to separate Nagaland from India. Myanmar has more than a dozen ethnic armies, and they want federalism, a far more reasonable and realistic demand.

So, will killing Myanmar's ethnic groups with endless talks about the technicalities of a ceasefire agreement, and no substantive political discussion, work? The events of 15 October 2015 will not change that approach to the problem—and the Myanmar government is still hoping that other, more powerful rebel armies will sign the agreement later. First of all, one has to consider why Myanmar's ethnic rebels took up arms in the first place. A nationwide ceasefire agreement will only freeze the problem, not solve it. The non-Bamar ethnic groups want a political dialogue to begin before they sign any NCA. Even more importantly, they see the peace process as the first step towards re-establishing the federal structure Myanmar had before the military seized power in 1962 and abolished the 1947 Constitution.

However, the Myanmar military, which stands behind the government, sees federalism as a first step toward disintegration of the country, and therefore, unacceptable. Certain political issues can be discussed in Parliament, but 'non-disintegration' of the country is one of six basic principles enshrined in the new, 2008 Constitution.

On the other hand, the ethnic resistance groups have not articulated their demand for federalism either. What kind of federal union would they want Myanmar to be? How should power be divided between the states and the central government? And what exactly is the 'federal army' some of the groups have begun talking about? Unless those issues have been made clear, there is little or no hope of the military changing its mind about federalism.

Many models have been mentioned: the U.S., Canada, Germany, and even multi-ethnic Malaysia. The U.S. has a federal system, but it is not based on ethnicity, which is what Myanmar's ethnic groups are demanding. There is no Anglo-Saxon, Irish, Polish, Mexican, Chinese, or Italian state in the U.S. The states there are purely geographical entities where a multitude of different peoples live.

Canada has a province with a French-speaking majority, Quebec, and the country has two official languages, English and French. In 1999, the predominantly Inuit-speaking parts of the Northwest Territories became a new territory, Nunavut, and there are other autonomous areas in Canada. But, by and large, Canada, like the U.S., is a country made up of various groups of immigrants and it is not a federal state based on ethnicity.

Malaysia is multi-ethnic, but there is no Malay, Chinese, or Indian state in that federation. Malaysia's federalism is based on the traditional Malay sultanates and some former British colonies and protectorates. But there are different ethnic groups living in all 13 Malaysian states. This is similar to the Federal Republic of Germany, which is made up of old kingdoms and principalities that were united in the late nineteenth century, except that the resulting nation-state was, and still is, overwhelmingly German in its ethnic composition.

There are, in fact, very few federations that are—or rather were—based along ethnic or linguistic lines. One was the former Soviet Union, which was dissolved in 1991. Another was Yugoslavia, which fell apart in the 1990s following bitter wars between the country's different ethnic groups. A third would be Belgium, which has only two major ethnic groups—the Dutch-speaking Flemish people and the French-speaking people of Wallonia—and a smaller German-speaking community in the east. But even with so few ethnic groups, Belgium has had immense problems maintaining its unity, let alone forming functioning central governments.

So, are there any successful models Myanmar could follow? There seems to be only one: India. India has twenty-eight states and seven union territories, and although the Indian constitution does not mention 'federation' or 'federalism', the basic structure of the country is federal. India's constitution has three lists that empower the union and the states to legislate on various matters. For instance, each state has an elected legislative assembly, its own official language, and its own police force. But defence is the responsibility of the central government. India has ethnic units in its armed forces, but it is not a 'federal army'; it is all under central command. Any other model would be unworkable. The third list contains issues where both the union and the various states can legislate. It is a fine balance, but despite all India's internal ethnic conflicts, it is working. Unlike the Soviet Union and Yugoslavia, India has not fallen apart, nor is it as dysfunctional as Belgium.

But if Myanmar is going to follow the Indian model, it should be prepared for all the problems that would entail. There is not a single state or region in Myanmar that has only one ethnic group. There are frictions between Shans and Kachins in Kachin as well as Shan States; the Pa-O rebellion in Myanmar broke out in the 1950s, not against the central government but the dominance of the Shan *sawbwas*, or local princes. The

United Wa State Army, which is active in northeastern and eastern Shan State, wants a separate state for its people. And while there is a Mon State, the Mon people are perhaps the most assimilated of Myanmar's many ethnic groups.

Myanmar's 1947 Constitution, its first, could serve as a basis for discussion, but little more. Its most controversial clause is in Chapter X: The Right of Secession, which said that 'every State shall have the right to secede from the Union' after 10 years of independence from British colonial rule. But other clauses stipulate that this right does not apply to Kayin or Kachin States, so it was only Shan State and Kayah State that could, at least in theory, secede from the Union.[8] In any case, the clause was not meant to be exercised, but was put there to make the then proposed Union of Myanmar more palatable for the non-Bamar peoples to join. The Mon, Chin, and Rakhine States were not established until 1974, and therefore not covered by the 1947 Constitution.

Nor did the new constitution that was adopted in 1974 have any provisions for federalism or regional autonomy—all that had disappeared after the 1962 military takeover in Myanmar. The 2008 Constitution is not federal in nature either. There is no difference between the states and the regions, and regional and state assemblies do not have nearly as much power as, for instance, India's state legislatures or those of non-ethnic federations such as the U.S. or Canada.

So what could a federal Myanmar look like? When the government embarked on its peace plan in 2009, the ethnic resistance armies were invited to become 'border guard forces'—but that was a very ill-conceived idea. Border security in nearly all countries is the responsibility of the central government. In India's northeastern states, adjacent to Myanmar, border security is in the hands of the paramilitary Assam Rifles, which is under the control of the Ministry of Home Affairs in New Delhi.[9] There are also other centrally controlled border guard forces, and sometimes local police may assist but not be responsible for border security.

On the other hand, Nagaland, Manipur, Mizoram, and other Indian states have their own armed police forces that are under the command of their respective state governments. If that system was adopted, the KIA or the Shan State Army could be absorbed into a Kachin State or Shan State Armed Police Force, but not into locally commanded 'border guard forces', which could easily degenerate into bands of border bandits and smugglers.

The Myanmar government and the country's armed resistance groups need to find a model that works, and the most viable solution would be to study the Indian model. It is also important to remember that when the Shans, the Kachins, and the Chins signed the Panglong Agreement with Aung San on 12 February 1947, it was clearly stated that 'full autonomy in internal administration is accepted in principle' (Panglong Agreement 1947). That was the principle upon which an independent Myanmar was founded, and it is still the only solution that would satisfy the aspirations of the country's non-Bamar ethnic groups.

The Future?

It is evident that Myanmar's decades-long civil war between government forces and ethnic rebels, and the inability of successive Myanmar governments to find a sustainable solution to its ethnic problems, is not 'an internal Myanmar affair'. Indian rebels have cross-border sanctuaries in Myanmar, weapons—and also drugs—are flowing through Myanmar to northeastern India, and the instability of the border areas is a major reason why India's Look East policy has been only partially successful.

In June 2015, India's security authorities finally lost their patience with the Myanmar government's turning a blind eye to the presence of Indian rebels on its soil, and launched two raids across the border, targetting camps where Assamese, Manipuri, and Naga rebels had been ensconced for years. The Nagas there belong to the NSCN-Khaplang (named after its leader, a Myanmar Naga called Shangwang Shanyung Khaplang), a group that has a separate ceasefire agreement with the Myanmar government and was not included in the deal struck on 15 October 2015. It was the first time Indian troops carried out such a raid across the border, and it served as a stern warning to Myanmar authorities that India would no longer tolerate the presence of Indian rebel camps inside their country. The Myanmar government did not protest, and a statement from the presidential office in the capital Naypyitaw, issued the day after the attacks took place, asserted that fighting had only broken out on the Indian side, still denying that any 'outside forces' were using Myanmar as a staging ground for attacks into India (Lintner 2015c). Those problems are likely to continue to cause problems in the relations between India and Myanmar, and therefore, also for the efforts to implement India's 'Look East' policy.

China's role is another major factor that has to be taken into consideration. Myanmar's policy shift from being more or less a Chinese client state to enjoying cordial relations with the West, India, and Japan has prompted China to re-evaluate its Myanmar policies. Recent events indicate that the 'stick' is becoming sharper. The UWSA, which, in effect, is controlled by China's security services, is not involved in any direct military confrontation with the Myanmar army, and, until recently, it did not to any significant extent share its vast stocks of arms and ammunition with other ethnic armies. But that is changing. In early 2015, Kachin, Palaung, Shan, and Kokang Chinese (Kokang district in northeastern-most Shan State is populated mainly by ethnic Chinese) rebels formed an alliance—with the UWSA supplying them with arms and ammunition.

This is an alliance of convenience, and partly grown out of a feeling that the West has let the ethnic rebels down. The Kachins, for instance, would not deal with the Chinese and the UWSA if they had a choice.[10] General Gun Maw, the then deputy commander of the KIA, did visit the U.S. in April 2014, but received little support for the federal aspirations of his movement. Instead, according to multiple Kachin sources, the Americans are putting pressure on the KIA to sign the NCA. Myanmar's ethnic rebels—and political and religious organizations representing the ethnic minorities as well—are not asking for any military or other material support, but they want the international community to get involved in helping them initiate a genuine peace process aimed at solving decades of ethnic strife and civil war. And that would mean political talks now, not later.

A second general election was held in November 2015 resulting in a landslide victory for Aung San Suu Kyi's National League for Democracy (NLD). However, she could not assume the presidency because her two sons are not Myanmar citizens, but she has become the *de facto* leader of the country as state councillor, a position created for her after the NLD's election victory. The new official president is her close associate Htin Kyaw, the first civilian to be Myanmar's head of state since the military first seized power in 1962. The policies of the new government when it comes to ethnic issues are still unclear, although Aung San Suu Kyi has mentioned the possibility of a 'second Panglong'. But despite the formation of an NLD-led government, the military remains the country's most powerful institution. The three most important ministers—defence, home affairs, and border affairs—are appointed by the military. It also takes orders from the commander-in-chief, not the president. Thus, national security issues, including the so-called peace process, will also remain in the hands of the military.

India's Look East policy, and any prospect of successful connectivity between the Indian subcontinent and Southeast Asia, depends on peace in Myanmar—and how China's designs for the region can be contained. A more sophisticated approach than just rallying behind the Myanmar government's deeply flawed 'peace process' is therefore needed to solve the problem. Ethnic sensitivities must also be considered by all parties. India could also play a constructive role in finding a sustainable solution to Myanmar's ethnic problems, which, if achieved, would also serve to stabilize its volatile eastern border and, therefore, also be beneficial to India's other interests in the east. India could promote its federal principles, which are working, and, in a modified form, would be more suitable for Myanmar's needs than any other model. The alternative is another few decades of turmoil, which will be detrimental to the interests of India as well as the West.

Notes

1. A copy of the 346-page dossier is in the author's possession. It is a classified document that was circulated only among Myanmar's top military leadership.

2. For an exaggerated version of China's involvement, see Vasan 2014. R.S. Vasan claims that Myanmar's 'Coco Island...has been leased by Myanmar to China'. There is no evidence to support that claim. Chinese experts helped the Myanmar Navy install electronic equipment on Coco Island, but the island has not been leased to China.

3. Interview with a Bangkok-based military analyst who wished to remain anonymous, Bangkok, 4 January 2013. See also German-Foreign-Policy.com 2013.

4. For a complete list of Indian rebel missions to China, see Lintner 2015a: 262–7.

5. Interview with the foreign human rights worker who requested anonymity, Chiang Mai, 26 February 2015.

6. For an overview of the ceasefire deal, see Moe and Fuller 2015.

7. Interviews with local residents in Kohima and Dimapur, December 2013 and October 2014.

8. See *The Constitution of the Union of Burma*, Rangoon: Government Printing and Stationery, 1947, 58–9 (for Kachin State not enjoying the right to secede from the Union, p. 178, and for Karen State not enjoying that right, p. 53.).

9. For the status of the Assam Rifles, see Assam Rifles, n.d., available at http://www.assamrifles.gov.in/ (accessed 11 April 2015).

10. These views were expressed in interviews with KIA leaders at their Laiza headquarters, December 2012.

References

Assam Rifles. n.d. Available at http://www.assamrifles.gov.in/ (accessed 11 April 2015).

BBC News. 2009. 'Assam Rebel Leader Handed Over to India', 4 December; available at http://news.bbc.co.uk/2/hi/south_asia/8394508.stm (accessed 11 April 2015).

Bhattacharyya, Rajeev. 2014. *Rendezvous with Rebels*. New Delhi: HarperCollins Publishers.

Bhaumik, Subir. 2010. 'Indian Separatist Leader Arrested in Bangladesh', *BBC News*, 13 October; available at http://www.bbc.com/news/world-south-asia-11532737 (accessed 11 April 2015).

Chaudhury, Mithu. 2013. 'NIA Report Reveals NSCN(IM)–China Link', *North East NewsPortal*, 14 January; available at http://northeastnewsportal.blogspot.com/2013/01/nia-report-reveals-nscnim-china-link.html (accessed 11 April 2015).

Davis, Anthony. 2013. 'China Sends Helicopters to Myanmar Separatists', *Jane's Defence Weekly*, 25 April.

Fuller, Thomas. 2011. 'Myanmar Backs Down, Suspending Dam Project', *New York Times*, 30 September; available at http://www.nytimes.com/2011/10/01/world/asia/myanmar-suspends-construction-of-controversial-dam.html?_r=0 (accessed on 11 April 2015).

German-Foreign-Policy.com. 2013. 'Roll Back China's Influence', 3 May; available at http://www.german-foreign-policy.com/en/fulltext/58530 (accessed 11 April 2015).

Harvey, Rachel. 2011. 'Burma Dam: Why Myitsone Plan Is Being Halted', *BBC News*, 30 September, available at http://www.bbc.com/news/world-asia-pacific-15123833 (accessed 11 April 2015).

Husein, Wasbir. 2015. 'Naga Peace Accord Remains Hazy and Full of Pitfalls', *The Wire*, 18 August; available at http://thewire.in/2015/08/18/naga-peace-accord-remains-hazy-and-full-of-pitfalls-8712/ (accessed 16 October 2015).

Karlekar, Hiranmay. 2014. 'The Great Chittagong Arms Haul and India', *The Daily Pioneer*, 8 February; available at http://www.dailypioneer.com/columnists/edi/the-great-chittagong-arms-haul-and-india.html (accessed 11 April 2015).

Kashyap, Samudra Gupta. 2009. 'ULFA Chairman Arabinda Rajkhowa Arrested in Bangladesh', *The Indian Express*, 2 December; available at http://archive.

indianexpress.com/news/ulfa-chairman-arabinda-rajkhowa-arrested-in-bangladesh/548924/ (accessed 11 April 2015).

Lintner, Bertil. 2015a. *Great Game East: India, China and the Struggle for Asia's Most Volatile Frontier*. New Haven and London: Yale University Press.

———. 2015b. 'Myanmar Morphs into US–China Battlefield', *Asia Times Online*, 2 May; available at http://www.atimes.com/atimes/Southeast_Asia/SEA-01- 020513.html (accessed 11 April 2015).

———. 2015c. 'Mysterious Motives: India's Raids on the Burma Border', *The Irrawaddy*, 30 June; available at http://www.irrawaddy.org/contributor/mysterious-motives-indias-raids-on-the-burma-border.html (accessed 16 October 2015).

Moe, Wai and Thomas Fuller. 2015. 'Myanmar and 8 Ethnic Groups Sign Cease-Fire, but Doubts Remain', *New York Times*, 15 October; available at http://www.nytimes.com/2015/10/16/world/asia/myanmar-ceasefire-armed-ethnic-groups.html?_r=0 (accessed 16 October 2015).

Nomi, Alek. 2011. 'Burma Suspends Controversial Myitsone Dam', *Earth Rights International*, 30 September; available at http://www.earthrights.org/blog/burma-suspends-controversial-myitsone-dam (accessed 11 April 2015).

Panglong Agreement. 1947. Panglong, 12 February; available at http://peacemaker.un.org/sites/peacemaker.un.org/files/MM_470212_Panglong%20Agreement.pdf (accessed 11 April 2015).

Press Trust of India (PTI). 2011. 'US Wants India to Play Key Role in the Pacific', *IBN Live*, 23 November; available at http://ibnlive.in.com/news/us-wants-india-to- play-key-role-in-asia-pacific/204859-7.html (accessed 11 April 2015).

Sikkimfirst.in. 2014. 'Bangladesh Awards Death Sentence to Paresh Barua, 13 Others in Chittagong Arms Haul Case', 30 January; available at http://sikkimfirst.in/2014/01/30/bangladesh-awards-death-sentence-to-paresh-barua-13- others-in-chittagong-arms-haul-case/ (accessed 11 April 2015).

Sudarshan, V. 2000. 'The Doublespeak Spin', *Outlook*, 4 December; available at http://www.outlookindia.com/printarticle.aspx?210508 (accessed 11 April 2015).

The Constitution of the Union of Burma. 1947. Rangoon: Government Printing and Stationery, 58–9.

UN News Center. 2015. 'Myanmar: UN Chief Welcomes "Milestone" Signing of Ceasefire Agreement', 15 October; available at http://www.un.org/apps/news/story.asp?NewsID=52278#.ViENa7cnZnQ (accessed 16 October 2015).

Vasan, R.S. 2014. 'India: The Importance of Setting Up of a Radar Station at Narcondam', *South Asia Analysis Group*, 25 June; available at http://www.southasiaanalysis.org/node/1553 (accessed 11 April 2015).

5   Making People's Voices Count

Northeast India and Its Neighbourhood

SANJOY HAZARIKA

THE INDIAN NORTHEASTERN REGION of eight states stands on the cusp of South and Southeast Asia, cupped by the Eastern Himalaya and the Patkai ranges, watered by the powerful Brahmaputra and 53 other rivers. Indeed, not less than 96 per cent of the region's borders are with other countries; only 4 per cent is connected to the rest of India—what is often described in this area as the 'mainland' or the 'mainstream'. Lightly researched and poorly governed, its ethnic diversity and the contending political aspirations of its many groups have nourished demands for separate homelands independent of India, or simply seeking separate states within the country. It has seen no less than three wars involving the national armies, air force, and other security forces of Pakistan and China—the India–Pakistan war of 1965, the 1962 border war with China, and the 1971 Bangladesh Liberation War. The border with China remains unresolved despite one conflict and many rounds of negotiations over many years; both sides claim the largest state of the region, Arunachal Pradesh, which borders Tibet. In Chinese maps, it is defined as Southern Tibet. India has had physical possession of this region since the colonial era and the dispute dates to 1914 when Britain and Tibet signed a demarcation of the border which China refused to join.

Uniquely Disadvantaged by Partition

The Northeast remains uniquely disadvantaged by Partition and the legacy of colonial rule but with new policies of economic opportunity and regional cooperation opening up; this could change in the next decades.

The region suffered the impact of not one but three Partitions. The first was the separation of Burma (annexed by the British in 1885) in 1946, which split the Nagas and Mizos between two sovereignties, devastating kinship relations, disrupting traditions of self-governance and trade connectivity. Then followed the Partition designed by Sir Cyril Radcliffe which divided the Khasis, Garos, Hajongs, and Rabhas of Assam from their kin in East Pakistan and also the Chakmas and Reangs of Tripura, apart from the exchange of populations on religious lines which was starkest and bloodiest on the western part of the subcontinent. Finally, the breakup of Pakistan in 1971, as Bangladesh emerged from East Pakistan's demise. Thus, the Mizos find themselves in three countries: India, Bangladesh, and Myanmar.

This is India's frontier land, where migrations from other parts of India and Southeast Asia have taken place over millennia. In its extremely complex ethnic population mosaic there are groups with links to Myanmar and China (for example, the Lisu of Arunachal Pradesh, Naga, Chin, Tai-Ahom, and Khamti to name just five) while some are believed to have their origins in Kampuchea (the Khasis of Meghalaya state).

In fact, the region has been one of the most globalized parts of the subcontinent for well over a century. It was where the prosperous tea gardens and companies in the Assam and Barak valleys were set up, connecting to international markets especially in London. Steamers and ferries took goods and people from as far as Dhaka and Kolkata to Dibrugarh in Upper Assam and back. Some 54 rivers pour and surge across the hills and valleys, transformed by rain and flood into over 500 during the heavy monsoons (Bandhyopadhyay 2014).

Large reserves of oil and gas were discovered here in the nineteenth century, which still supply a substantial part of India's energy needs. Partition and the India–Pakistan wars shut down the river route and it is only in recent years that Bangladesh and India have negotiated legal instruments of reopening trade, commerce, and navigation on these rivers which are the lifelines for tens of millions of people.

Innumerable local ethnic 'mutinies' have exploded into major internal conflicts with anti-India antagonists within the Northeast fighting against New Delhi in not less than seven of the eight states which make up the NER (North Eastern Region): Nagaland, Mizoram, Manipur, Assam,

Tripura and, to a lesser degree, Meghalaya and Arunachal Pradesh. Large contingents of the Indian Army and other security forces have been tied down by successive insurgencies. However, one state, Sikkim, located north of West Bengal, and physically distant from the other states, has escaped the heat of insurgent conflict. Once an independent Himalayan kingdom, Sikkim was militarily and politically subsumed by India in 1974.

Many of the conflicts are rooted in the ethnic and political complexity of this tiny region. Taking advantage of traditional links to Southeast Asia by culture, language, diet, history, and conquest, the Government of India has pressed ahead with a major initiative to change the geo-strategic architecture of the NER and its borderlands. This was earlier known as the Look East Policy[1] and now has been tweaked through Prime Minister Narendra Modi's word-smithery, to become the 'Act East Policy'.

Today, as internal conflicts in the NER abate and as conditions in the neighbourhood, especially Bangladesh and Myanmar, appear to improve, India's ambitions as well as those of China, seem, consequentially and sequentially, to rise in the Asian arena.

Yet, for long, 'Geography has conspired with economics, faulty planning and poor implementation to give the region a weak hand', says Professor Mohendro Singh (2011) of Manipur.

Between the 1960s and 1970s, external issues, linkages, and concerns such as Chinese and Pakistani assistance to rebels in the NER drove India's internal politics and policies toward this marginalized area. The anti-India armed movements began first in the Naga Hills district of Assam, on the Burma borderland, in the 1950s and moved in a southerly wave, embracing one ethnically different area after another, before curving west to the Brahmaputra Valley of Assam. Thus, by 1966, the Mizo Hills district of Assam had erupted demanding independence followed by Manipur in the 1970s; Tripura's tribals embarked on their separatist campaign after 1980 and by the end of that decade, United Liberation Front of Asom (ULFA) was picking up intense energy and visibility in Assam. Meghalaya was disrupted by occasional organized outbreaks of violence while the Nagas spread their activities to the eastern most districts of Arunachal Pradesh. To complete the circle of unrest, members of the Bodo tribe began a bloody campaign for separation.

There were extensive fears of 'Balkanization' and concerns that conditions of long-term instability in the NER could spill over into other parts of Eastern India, such was the sharpness and scale of the internal conflicts and the depth of Chinese and Pakistani support to the insurgents. Between 1966 and 1976, China hosted and trained groups from Nagaland and Mizoram in Yunnan Province, which went back and fought the Indian army and other security units in bitter and protracted battles and ambushes; the Chinese hosted at least one unit from Manipur and imparted political and armed training. However, after India and China resumed full diplomatic relations in 1976, the Chinese stopped all direct assistance to the rebels.

Pakistan, meanwhile, had provided funds, training facilities, and arms from an earlier period when it still comprised of West and East Pakistan and the latter had not broken away to become Bangladesh. The journalist and South East Asian security expert Bertil Lintner speaks of 'north-east India's battlefields' at the time, emphasizing the severity of the fighting as well as the depth of the crisis that India faced not just to its periphery but to its survival (2012: XII). Over nearly a half century, extensive fighting pinned down over 20,000 government troops and led to widespread violence against civilian populations and human rights abuse by both government troops and militants. Although conditions have eased extensively, linkages between insurgent groups and intelligence networks in Bangladesh, Myanmar, and Pakistan have continued even after the creation of Bangladesh in 1971. Lintner talks of extensive travel by Naga rebels based in Thailand to Yunnan in the 1990s to purchase weapons from Chinese arms dealers (Lintner 2012: 339).

Closing of the Chinese Door

With the closing of the Chinese door, the focus of the Northeastern rebels turned to armed groups in Myanmar where they paid for food and board as well as for training and weapons, and also to organize safe houses, bank accounts, and travel routes in Bangladesh.[2] The first cracks in the insurgent armour appeared in 1986, when the Mizo National Front signed an accord under whose terms it accepted the Constitution of India, disbanded the rebel army, ended its war against India, converted itself into a democratic party involved in the election process, and extracted statehood and special funding by the Central Government as its political price.

Yet, despite this, from the 1990s, at least four armed organizations,[3] with support from Bangladeshi intelligence officials and local Myanmar authorities, established camps and safe houses in both countries. But from 1997 onward, the armed movements in the Northeast suffered a series of major setbacks. In the first, the major faction of the National Socialist Council of Nagalim (NSCN), the region's oldest and most powerful insurgency, agreed to talks and a ceasefire with the Government of India. The leaders came in from locations in Bangkok and now live in India, shuttling between a large camp in Nagaland, where their cadres and colleagues also stay, and a government bungalow in New Delhi. All travel and facilities are funded by the Central Government; the ceasefire continues with this group although a smaller faction recently abrogated its peace by attacking security units in Nagaland. Yet, the desire for peace remains strong. The scholar Udayon Misra has remarked that 'The process of alienation of certain segments within the movement which started in the late 1950s has reached such a point today that the need for reconciliation and unity within the movement seems to override all other factors' (Misra 2011: 79).

The push for peace with the Nagas signalled similar efforts with ULFA and the National Democratic Front of Bodoland (NDFB), and although the United National Liberation Front (UNLF) of Manipur has held out against negotiations, the violence levels in that state also have gone down.

While breakaway factions of the Bodo (NDFB-S) and Garo tribes (Garo National Liberation Army or GNLA) continue to strike at vulnerable civilian populations, public support for them has waned and the main groups from these ethnic communities are in talks with New Delhi.

Three armed groups[4] established over thirty camps in Bhutan's foothills in the late 1990s but they were driven out in 2003 in fierce fighting by the Bhutanese Army,[5] led by King Jigme Singye Wangchuk[6] and his son, the Crown Prince, with the full backing of the Indian army. The latter did not, however, directly intervene but provided logistic support and took control of the detainees and others who surrendered. In December 2009, the Bangladesh government handed over to Indian authorities a set of India's most wanted fugitives and leaders of armed movements in the Northeast, who had been living in and around Dhaka, effectively breaking the back of a set of movements which had destabilized the region for nearly half a century.

When Bangladeshi intelligence detained Northeastern militant leaders and handed them over to Indian security, they were effectively and officially closing their land as a sanctuary for Indian rebels after nearly 50 years of tacit and open support, first under the Pakistanis and then under Bangladesh's own Directorate General of Field Intelligence (DGFI), which retained strong links to the ubiquitous Inter Services Intelligence (ISI) of Pakistan. The remnants of the Northeastern fighters were left with little option to fall back upon but the thick forests of Northern Myanmar and the camps of a Burmese Naga leader, SS Khaplang.

Khaplang had fought the Burmese since 1964 in campaigns for freedom in addition to leading a faction that also fought the Indian forces in Nagaland. However, after the military junta in Myanmar relaxed its relentless crackdown against ethnic groups and began a process of democratic reform in 2011, he too decided to bury the hatchet. In another development, coincidentally also after 50 years of conflict and confrontation (the same time frame as the peace overtures in the Indian Northeast were taking place), Khaplang signed a ceasefire with the Burmese (Mishra 2012). His nominees are also able to participate in local elections and hold political power. A Naga semi-autonomous territory was officially demarcated for the first time in Burma's history (Mishra 2012). This meant that for the first time in decades his area would be free from army pressure and reports from the region indicate that several Northeastern armed groups are taking shelter under his wing and have recently formed a new anti-India alliance. The Burmese government has not taken tough action against Khaplang despite nudging from New Delhi, including the 3 June attack on an army convoy that took the lives of over 20 Indian soldiers, the worst such incident in peacetime in nearly two decades (Roy 2015). The Centre struck back within a week, authorizing a counter-attack on an insurgent camp, which Indian intelligence sources said was located in Burma's western region, inside Burmese territory. The number of those killed in the riposte has never been clearly stated, with estimates published in the media wildly fluctuating from seven to twenty-two and even over 50. Jingoistic narratives appeared both in the print and broadcast media (PTI 2015) while a junior government minister stirred a furious controversy by saying that similar 'hot pursuit' on India's western border (with Pakistan) could not be ruled out (Razdan 2015).

The Burmese Government affirmed, however, that no incident took place inside its territory. It maintained that there was an event along the border but no intrusion across it; media coverage of the attacks was minimal in Burma and relied upon reports out of India. Burmese scholars and officials[7] have indicated that the official reluctance to respond to Indian concerns is drawn from an assessment that the NSCN, with about 1,000 armed cadres, is no longer a major threat to its internal security.

In less than half a century, through the dual process of attrition and negotiation— what the analyst Subir Bhaumik calls its *tan-dhan-man-bhed* approach based on discussions, bribery, mental stress, and force— the Indian State had managed to reduce a major threat to its territorial and political integrity to an internal problem.

These examples show how the security–diplomatic core of India's public policy towards its neighbours has been affected by the changing dynamics in its own domestic political, social, and economic conditions. Growing political confidence, aligned to robust economic growth and internal stability in India and its NER now appear to be driving those policies as India reaches out to its neighbours and seeks to carve a greater space for itself in Asia through its Northeast.

However, if this grand design is to actually take shape and substance, a wide range of political, economic, and social issues need to be addressed and resolved, partially, if not completely. These are considered in the following section of the chapter and its conclusions.

Indeed, some ground conditions in the region appear to contradict and confuse the preceding narrative. This is part of the complexity of the challenges facing policy makers.

Consider the following: Assam state has India's worst Maternal Mortality Ratio. The region is one of the slowest growing areas of the country. Governance is poor. Over 80 per cent of the population in the eight states is rural. Conflicts at different levels exist in seven of the eight states.

Yet, organized violence by non-State actors has dramatically and drastically diminished in the past twenty years with the growth of ceasefires between the Central Government and these groups. Until earlier this year, not a single Indian soldier had fallen in combat in nearly a decade (Sahni 2012) to the bullets or bombs of non-State actors in Nagaland, the state where insurgency began in India. Across the region, the number of casualties suffered by security forces appeared to drop (Sahni 2012) while those among armed groups rose. Yet, the number of civilian casualties has shown an equally steep rise with ordinary people facing unacceptably high levels of violence. This is partly the result of a proliferation of armed factions in not less than five states of the region.

The sprouting of these armed groups is also an outcome of both the peace processes and the prolonged conflicts; the latter spawn divisions in strategy and approaches among different leaders, leading to breakaway factions. The peace processes on the other hand give rise to a new form of rivalry among the armed combatants: in numerous cases, those which settle or negotiate with the Government are denounced as traitors by others who claim to represent the real interests of the people. The effort is to push the Central Government to open negotiations with this new group. There are more fundamental concerns for the armed groups—each wants a greater share of an extensive extortion racket where government officials, politicians, business persons, professionals, and even teachers are taxed for the 'national cause'.[8] This process has been active for decades in Nagaland state and is also currently extensive in Manipur, although limited to business and professional and some government circles in Assam. They pay 10 to 25 per cent[9] of their incomes as tax to the groups, which use them to run their parallel governments, pay, feed and train their cadres, and fund travel and even weapons.

A significant but slow change is the growing resistance in the public to acquiescence. Earlier, this attitude was based on a fear of retribution from the armed groups.[10] Public rallies of opposition to tax notices from the groups, despite threats from the latter, have taken place in Nagaland. An official committee demanding not just government probity but accountability from the armed factions[11] has been set up. According to the *Morung Express* (25 March 2015), Justice K.H. Sema, formerly of India's Supreme Court and Chairman of the High Powered Committee, issued the summons to seven 'Naga Political Groups (NPGs)' and went on to identify them by their abbreviations as rival factions fighting for Naga rights.

The Centre's inability to handle this sensitive issue, which affects a large number of government employees and private citizens, shows clearly the difficulties of handling problems that go beyond ceasefires and paper agreements. Despite over sixteen years of a ceasefire and a set of ground rules which urged the armed groups to look into issues of extortion, neither the Government of India (which is the principal negotiating entity at the peace talks) nor the State Government of Nagaland have tackled the Naga factions head-on. Ultimately, years after the negotiations began, it was left to the state government to set up the review committee; it took another year for the committee to begin its work.

'No one wants to upset the apple cart or their places at the table', said a Naga rights activist.[12] 'Everyone wants business as usual, unaccounted money to come and go, it gives them power and creates not just a parallel economy but a parallel government'.

This is one of the most critical issues before the Indian Government, and one which it has failed to resolve in nearly two decades of discussions. In turn, this has seriously dented its credibility in Nagaland and elsewhere in the Northeast: it is seen as acquiescent with the continuous and open efforts by armed organizations to raise funds from the public and reluctant, if not unable, to do anything about it. 'The concern is that it could disrupt the peace process', said one senior official[13] who has handled discussions with the Nagas, underscoring one of the principal worries of New Delhi. It was unwilling to take the issue to a head and risk the fragile peace that was holding.

The question here is whether such a stand strengthens or otherwise affects India's medium and long-term security interests. These obviously lie in a stable region and neighbourhood. Interviews[14] with a cross section of residents of Nagaland and Manipur, held in June and October 2014 and April 2015, indicate widespread cynicism about government initiatives to promote regional growth and spur investment there as well as connectivity to Myanmar and Southeast Asia.

Several interviewees, who declined to be named, said that they expected large parts of Indian funding for hill and plains infrastructure through four-lane highways, bridges, and railways, to be diverted to benefit senior politicians and officials in the region as well as contractors with links to the armed groups. One interviewee said that many of the senior UGs—or underground—as the armed groups are commonly known, were known to support specific contractors in return for a commission on the value of the overall project.

The mesh and clout of such networks is vast, stretching from the Northeast to New Delhi. Both State and successive Central governments have failed repeatedly to crack the whip of financial discipline and accountability of major projects. This is an issue that is hampering India's accessibility within and outside the region. Last year, the road between Dimapur and Kohima, the Nagaland capital, less than 100 km, was so horrendous with potholes and broken stretches that travellers could complete it in four to five hours.

This year, the Dimapur–Kohima stretch was surprisingly smooth. Yet, visitors were puzzled by the sight of hundreds of trees being felled on the hillocks above the road and digging and excavation along the highway. These are apparently preparations for a four-lane highway that is being built at the Central Government's initiative, converting what is a perfectly good two-lane road for the Look/Act East Policy. The plan is to connect products 'made in the North-east' or other parts of India to Manipur, Myanmar, and to the markets of Southeast Asia.

But without good internal road connectivity which benefits local communities, such grand plans may remain distant dreams caught up in the mesh of delays, corruption, and demands of multiple stakeholders, which include the armed groups.

Ambassador Richard Varma remarked at a conference in Kolkata[15] that financial inclusivity and good governance go together. He emphasized repeatedly that 'ordinary people must benefit' from ambitious government schemes. That is why it is important to assess, given the current pace of implementation and the capacity of both the Centre and the state governments, whether government plans are on track and if not, what should be done to tweak and change them.

Connectivity

The idea of connecting to our neighbourhood should be supported; but the Northeast is itself poorly connected within the region. To travel between Kohima and Imphal on a national highway, a distance of barely 100 km, may take four hours on a back-breaking road through historic and truly beautiful hillsides and lush valleys. In the Second World War, this was the sector where critical battles pushed the Japanese and the Indian National Army of Subhash Bose out of India. Yet, this is also the key link road to the proposed connectivity corridor to Myanmar and other ASEAN (Association of Southeast Asian Nations) countries. If we are to look at Pan Asian Connectivity, we need first to be connected competently within even a small region like the Northeast.

My experience on this highway in the Assam plains underlined that while the road was smooth, life in the villages alongside could not have been easy. The number of modern, finished houses of brick and mortar dwellings could be virtually counted. Most of these were either school buildings, forest offices, or police posts. Village after village were mostly built of thatch and mud and/or bamboo with some electricity lines. Off the smooth highway, the lanes were of dirt and dust but probably muddy and slippery during the rainy season.

The Government of India needs to ask hard questions of states like Assam and Nagaland and demand answers on where the money supposedly pumped into projects has gone. Conversely, civil society groups, researchers, and state governments in turn need to ask the Central Government why it proposes to spend vast amounts[16] on four-lane highways in Nagaland while its hill ranges are notoriously soft and fickle, which even an amateur geologist could say. Civil society groups need to assert their right to information and demand details of these projects to gain an assessment of the principal beneficiaries. After all, no four-lane highway has been built on any part of the Himalayas between Jammu and Kashmir and Arunachal Pradesh; there must be sound scientific reasons for this. One of them could be the soft nature of the soil; the other is the vulnerability of the region to high seismicity, as the recent earthquakes in Nepal have shown.

The proposed infrastructure growth needs also to be seen in Japan's plans for the Northeast, clearly in collaboration with India, and possibly as a posit to China's ambitious plans of dams, roads, and rail projects in Tibet, Myanmar, and Southeast Asia. Japanese Foreign Minister Fumio Kishida[17] told a New Delhi audience that '...for the enhancement of connectivity between SAARC and ASEAN, Japan will strengthen its assistance by supporting development initiatives in North East India, which will serve as a connective node between the two regions'.

A 'connectivity node' means essentially a hub, which would also involve transit and trade and some manufacturing. That is a vision of where the Look East Policy (LEP) and the Act East Policy could take the Northeast. This underlines another point about which there has been so much misunderstanding: the LEP is a Government of India policy for all of India, not for one part of it. The Northeast has come into the picture only in recent years. While the region has geographical and locational advantage, the volume of goods that can be moved over land and by river transport can be extensive. It is important to energize plans for multi-nodal transport that could take advantage of the region's great water resources: inland water transport remains the cheapest form of transport in most parts of the world, especially when commodities are moved in bulk over river routes (six of Asia's great rivers are in Northeast India and Southeast Asia: the Brahmaputra, Meghna/Barak, Chindwin, Irrawaddy, Salween, and Mekong). Although most international trade is conducted over sea routes, the use of river routes could help the Northeast to offset, to a degree, the advantage that states like West Bengal, Andhra Pradesh, Orissa, and Tamil Nadu, with large functional seaports, enjoy.

There is another issue which the scholar M. Myilvaganan pointed out in a 2013 essay for the International Policy Digest (Mayilvaganan 2013), that there is an LEP 3.0, a new policy that addresses issues of geo-strategic importance and not the softer issues of trade and culture which the original Look East Policy prioritized. '… increasing trade ties between India and Southeast Asia has contributed to the expansion of relations in the areas of defence and security. As a result, relations between India and the region have acquired strategic characteristics in recent years', he said.

> India's Look East Policy 3.0 refers to India's strategy of strengthening its relations with states in Asia–Pacific that are beyond the South East Asia region, extending to East Asia. It is safe to assume that the new version of India's Look East Policy has been shaped partly by China's rise and the manner in which Beijing is strengthening its position in the South and Southeast Asian regions both in terms of strategic ties with countries in the region and technological advancements like anti-ship ballistic missiles (ASBM).

'Disturbed Region'

The Government of India has been promoting efforts to garner domestic and international investments for the Northeast. However, the results have been poor. One of the reasons is that the region remains 'disturbed' in security terms in the eyes of the Indian Government, with the overwhelming presence of army and paramilitary troops in the region to tackle insurgencies and ethnic conflicts. Their presence has caused extensive public discord. In addition, the Armed Forces (Special Powers) Act (AFSPA), which was legislated by the Parliament in 1958 to tackle the rise of the Naga insurgency, now applies to the entire region barring the state of Sikkim. This sweeping legislation empowers central security forces to open fire on suspicion and even kill suspects (whose relatives do not have the right of recourse to judicial appeal). Its powers are focused in the hands of the Centre and can be enforced without consulting local governments. This law has been challenged in courts and in 2006, a major Government review committee called for its repeal, describing it as having become a symbol of hatred and oppression, and its replacement by a more humane law sensitive to human rights concerns as well as security concerns of the State. The review of the Act in 2004 was prompted by public outrage in Manipur and across the country about the alleged rape and killing of a young woman, a militant suspect in Manipur, by paramilitary troops. One of the country's human rights icons, Irom Sharmila, has been on a hunger strike for ten years in Manipur to protest the law and is kept alive by a nasal drip. A Supreme Court authorized investigation to check on allegations of unlawful killings by security forces in Manipur found the charges, based on random sampling, to be accurate. The Report was never tabled in the Parliament nor discussed by the Centre, barring at a few public events, and in February 2015, there were reports that it was being rejected by the Narendra Modi Government (Tripathi 2015).

Rejection of the Reddy Committee Report is an assertion of faith in the force of arms to tackle sensitive political challenges. It also rejects the very processes which the Government itself has advocated for so long—patient negotiations and ceasefires leading to a peace dividend. The Central Government has to assert its confidence in the peace process in the region and the improvement in the security conditions. It should consider the withdrawal of AFSPA from most areas by dropping the enabling legislation, the Disturbed Areas Act (an area such as a district or a state has to be declared 'Disturbed' before the Centre can deploy troops under AFSPA). However, it could maintain a minimal, visible, highly mobile, and well trained deterrent Central security force. Few investors, domestic or international, and travellers (barring the occasional, brave one) are likely to go to places where the Government itself has proclaimed a state of unrest and, in effect, is asking to stay away from.

Another area where the Central Government would need to move robustly is in tackling extortion by different armed groups. Any group in a ceasefire agreement with India cannot be allowed to intimidate and extort the public or levy tolls on passengers and freight; those who break the law should be prosecuted under relevant rules and not allowed to shelter behind threats that such actions could jeopardize the ceasefire. Other extortion groups which are not part of any peace pact require to face the full force of the law. Police and security agencies need to be instructed by the Government to act robustly and assured that they, in turn, will be supported.

'Export' Peace Building

The Government of India could share its extensive experiences in peace building and dialogue with armed groups with neighbouring countries like Myanmar and Bangladesh through a process of collaborative seminars, workshops, and conferences which would bring in representatives of all sides, including civil society groups. It could be one of the 'smart' exports that India could develop, along with sending its soft power of musical talent (rock groups/heavy metal bands/traditional performers) and sports persons (national level footballers/international boxers like Mary Kom) and others to perform at regular festivals and cultural exchanges as well as media visits to Myanmar, Thailand, and Bangladesh: these are three key countries where Indian insurgents have long had bases and extensive networks.

Finally, India, Bangladesh, and Myanmar need to work out verifiable collaborative programmes which bring armed groups, which are working against the interests of any of the three countries, under the scanner. Thus, although the Khaplang group of the NSCN has a peace accord with the Myanmar government, it would need to be restrained by Yangon from any activity in the Indian state of Nagaland which would adversely affect India. Similarly, if there are armed groups from the NER which are taking shelter in the Naga Semi-Autonomous Area, Myanmar would need to urge the Khaplang group to end its support of these groups and send them out of Myanmar territory. Yangon is unlikely to take unilateral action on such issues because it is deeply conscious of the impact of such decisions on the overall peace process in Myanmar, especially with the powerful ethnic nationalities. It is in areas such as this, as also with 'exporting' peace process and building dialogue, where the United States could play a key role as convenor of such dialogues and facilitator of discussions. The creation of a secure and robust region between the Northeast, Myanmar, Bangladesh, and Thailand would be in the long-term U.S. strategic interests here, given its diverse ethnicities and faiths as well as its enormous natural resources, mineral wealth, and access to the Bay of Bengal.

Thailand's former Foreign Minsiter Surin Pitsuwan has suggested (*Assam Tribune* 2013) that India needed to bring top leaders of Southeast Asia to the region and encourage dialogue and discussions through 'a meeting of the ASEAN+India ... on the banks of the Brahmaputra', if the Northeast if to benefit from the LEP.

India's own role in its eastern neighbourhood would be influenced also not just by the control of its recalcitrant ethnic minorities but by building peace processes through inclusive local initiatives which would emphasize an investment in peace building. For a start, it needs to get its act together on delivering high quality infrastructure which would benefit its own people before expanding and exporting that work to the neighbourhood. It would need to stress cultural affinity, a shared history, and a common commitment to security among the many diverse communities and ethnic groups which comprise this exasperatingly difficult but enchanting area.

Notes

1. According to M. Myilvaganan in the *International Policy Digest*, 'India's Look East Policy was initiated in 1992 following the end of the Cold War and the start of the liberalization policy to reintegrate India within South East Asia (SEA), economically and culturally. This policy is commonly mentioned as LEP 2.0 as the initial LEP refers to Indian influence in SEA from the 6th to the 15th century B.C. According to Prime Minister Manmohan Singh "it was also a strategic shift in India's vision of the world and India's place in the evolving global economy"'.

2. Author's interviews with Indian security officials, in 2000, 2003, and 2010, at New Delhi, Guwahati, and Shillong, and with Bangladeshi diplomats and media professionals in Dhaka, in September 2012, October 2014.

3. United Liberation Front of Asom (ULFA), National Democratic Front of Bodoland (NDFB), All Tripura Tigers Force (ATTF) and National Liberation Front of Tripura (NLFT).

4. ULFA, NDFB and the Kamatapur Liberation Organization (KLO).

5. The then Queen Ashi Dorji Wangmi Wangchuck reflects on this in her book, *Portrait of Bhutan*.

6. Author's interview with Prime Minister Jigme Yosier Thinley of Bhutan, 19 May 2010, Thimpu.

7. Author's interviews with Burmese scholars and government officials during a visit to Burma, 20–4 October 2015.

8. Interview with senior media professional in Dimapur, Nagaland, on 12 April 2015, who did not want to be further identified.

9. Author's interview with former Nagaland Government official, Kohima, 1 June 2014; he was not to be further identified.

10. Author's interview with Kekhiye Sema, a retired government official and leader of the Action Committee against Unabated Taxation, which has publicly taken on the armed groups.

11. The High Powered Committee was set up by the Nagaland Government in March 2014.

12. Author's interview with with former Nagaland Government official in New Delhi, 4 September 2014.

13. Author's interview with Government official, New Delhi, 20 September 2010.

14. Author's interviews in Dimapur, Kohima, Mao Gate, Senapati, and Imphal.

15. Remarks during Ambassador Varma's address to the Conference on Building Pan Asian Connectivity, Kolkata, 11 March 2015.

16. In May 2015, National Transport Minister Nitin Gadkari announced a Rs 10,000 crore package for road infrastructure in Arunachal Pradesh, Meghalaya, and Nagaland.

17. Special Partnership for the Era of the Indo-Pacific, address at Sapru House, Indian Council for World Affairs, New Delhi, 17 January 2015.

References

Assam Tribune (Guwahati). 2013. 'Involve Northeast in Look East Policy: ASEAN Leader', 9 March; available at http://www.assamtribune.com/scripts/mdetails.asp?id=mar0913/at045 (accessed 14 December 2015).

Bandhyopadhyay, Jayanta. 2014. Presentation to the Indo-Bangladesh Water Dialogue, Kolkata, 27 October, Maulana Abul Kalam Azad Institute for Asia Studies.

Lintner, Bertil. 2012. *Great Game East, India, China and the Struggle for Asia's Most Volatile Frontier*. New Delhi: HarperCollins Publishers India.

Mayilvaganan, M. 2013. 'Examining India's Look East Policy 3.0', *International Policy Digest*; available at http://www.internationalpolicydigest.org/2013/11/21/examining-indias-look-east-policy-3-0/ (accessed 14 December 2015).

Mishra, Rahul. 2012. 'Why India is wary of a NSCN-K-Myanmar Agreement', 24 May available at *www.rediff.com* (accessed 9 March 2015).

Misra, Udayon. 2011. 'The Issues of Nagaland and the Nagas'. *Conflicts in the North East: Internal and External Effects*, edited by Sanjoy Hazarika and V.R. Raghavan. New Delhi: Vij Books India Pvt Ltd.

Morung Express (Dimapur). 2015. 'HPC Summons Naga Political Groups', 25 March; available at http://morungexpress.com/hpc-summons-naga-political-groups/ (accessed 14 December 2015).

Press Trust of India (PTI). 2015. 'Myanmar Ops: Intellectuals Attack Jingoist Sentiments', *Times of India*, 16 June; available at http://timesofindia.

indiatimes.com/india/Myanmar-ops-Intellectuals-attack-jingoist-sentiments/articleshow/47692466.cms (accessed 14 December 2015).

Razdan, Nidhi. 2015. 'PM Modi Ordered Hot Pursuit after Manipur Ambush', *NDTV*, 10 June; available at http://www.ndtv.com/india-news/after-manipur-ambush-pm-narendra-modi-ordered-hot-pursuit-union-minister-rajyavardhan-rathore-to-ndt- 770230 (accessed 14 December 2015).

Roy, Esha. 2015. 'Manipur Ambush: 18 Army Men Killed, 11 Injured', *Indian Express*, 5 June; available at http://indianexpress.com/article/india/india-others/at-least-10-army-men-killed-in-ambush-by-manipuri-insurgents/ (accessed 14 December 2015).

Sahni, Ajay. 2012. 'The North East: Troubling Externalities', *South Asia Intelligence Review* (SAIR) 10(38), Weekly Assessments and Briefings, 26 March; available at www.satop.com (accessed 9 March 2015).

Singh, Mahendro. 2011. 'Impacts of Conflict in the North-East: Manipur'. *Conflicts in the North East: Internal and External Effects*, edited by Sanjoy Hazarika and V.R. Raghavan. New Delhi: Vij Books India Pvt Ltd.

Tripathi, Rahul. 2015. 'Rajnath Singh Rejects Jeevan Committee's Report to Remove AFSPA from North East: Report', *India Today*, 27 February; available at http://indiatoday.intoday.in/story/rajnath-singh-armed-forces-act-north-east-jeevan-committee-afspa/1/421454.html (accessed 14 December 2015).

II

Trade

6   India and the Potential of Trade East

Rani D. Mullen

India's new government, under the leadership of Prime Minister Narendra Modi, has prioritized India's relationship with its East Asian neighbours, with Minister of External Affairs of India Sushma Swaraj stating that the time has come for India to change its 'Look East' Policy to one of 'Act East' Policy (Philip 2014). Crucial to the success of the Act East Policy will be the opening up and facilitation of trade between India and its eastern neighbours, with large benefits to the overall economy and per capita incomes in India as well as its eastern neighbours. A strong India Trade East policy has the potential to transform the South and Southeast Asian region into an engine of growth for Asia. In 2013–14 Singapore became the largest source of foreign direct investment (FDI) for India, accounting for about 27.5 per cent of total FDI (Reserve Bank of India 2014), and between 2008–9 and 2013–14 India's trade with all the fifteen East Asian countries in the Association of Southeast Asian Nations (ASEAN) and the Bay of Bengal Initiative for Multi-Sectoral Technical and Economic Cooperation (BIMSTEC) plus China, or Trade East countries for short, tripled in volume.[1]

While the potential for increased trade between India and its eastern neighbours and its benefits are large, there remain significant barriers to structurally transforming India's eastward trade. Intra-Asian trade among the South Asian Association for Regional Cooperation (SAARC) and Indian trade with its eastern neighbours as a percentage of India's overall trade in 2013–14 was at an abysmal 5 and 21 per cent respectively, and India's trade with its eastern neighbours was only 12 per cent of India's overall trade if one excludes China. Significantly, India's formal trade with its border countries of Bangladesh and Myanmar, both of which are crucial to any overland trade with the East, were only 0.87 per cent and 0.29 per cent respectively of India's total trade in 2013–14 (Government of India 2014).

This article will examine the steps needed to get to an engaged India Trade East policy. It will do so by exploring the political changes undergirding India's Act East Policy and the current patterns of trade flow with India's eastern neighbours, the opportunities the Act East policy represents for deeper engagement with regional associations in South and Southeast Asia, and the bilateral trade relationship with the crucial nodal eastern border countries of Bangladesh, Bhutan, and Myanmar. It also will highlight the key issues that need to be addressed in order to improve India Trade East before concluding and presenting recommendations.

A quarter century of India's 'Look East Policy' and recent foreign policy focus on an 'Act East Policy' hold great potential for increasing trade in the world's least integrated region of South Asia. However, a precondition for increasing trade with India's eastern neighbours will be addressing the massive infrastructure deficit and bureaucratic barriers to trade that exist on the Indian side of the borders. The ASEAN countries already trade significantly among themselves and in 2010 when the ASEAN–China Free Trade Area (ACFTA) came into effect China overtook the United States to become ASEAN's third largest trading partner (Moore 2009). By contrast India's ASEAN–India Free Trade Area, which also has been in effect since 2010, is less than a third of China's. In order to Act East, India will have to invest in its eastern areas and enable conditions for a Trade East policy.

The Changing Political Engagement and Patterns of Trade Flow with India's Eastern Neighbours

India and many of its East Asian neighbours have experienced high economic growth rates over the past decade and their overall trade volumes have also increased during this time period. Yet despite the significant economic growth and external trade volumes and despite India's Look East foreign policy focus since 1991, India's trade with the dynamic economies to its east has remained virtually stagnant aside from China and Singapore. This stagnation in India's relationship with its eastern countries is due for the most part to a foreign policy approach that into the first decade of the twenty-first century remained rhetorical, rather than one focused on creating the conditions for enhanced foreign and trade engagement.

Since India's independence, its political and economic orientation has been westward. In the aftermath of the Cold War and spurred by the 1991 economic balance of payments crisis in India, the government of Prime Minister P.V. Narasimha Rao sought to reorient its foreign policy focus closer to home by launching the 'Look East Policy'. This policy aimed to access and become part of the economic growth and growth opportunities that East and Southeast Asia were experiencing. Steps made towards this eastward reorientation were primarily focused on fostering strategic and economic relations with India's dynamic eastern neighbours, with the aim of countering China's rising regional and global status as well as boosting India's own status. It was essentially a *realpolitik* change in India's foreign economic policy.

The barriers to implementing the economic and trade aspect of the Look East Policy were significant in three main areas. First, India's economic policies up to the early 1990s were protectionist and inward-focused compared to the export-oriented East Asian economies and changing this orientation would take time. Second, land connectivity to the eastern countries through Bangladesh and Myanmar, with whose territories India had enjoyed a flourishing trade prior to independence, were blocked politically as well as due to the neglected east-west infrastructure. And third, India had neglected economic investments in its eastern states of West Bengal and especially the Northeastern states. This led to a widening of economic development indicators between these crucial border-states and the Indian average, and thwarted the economic development of the Northeastern states, thereby also denying them their own resources to invest in trade-facilitating infrastructure. The low levels of economic development indicators in the border-states included infrastructure and connectivity—crucial to cross border trade. All three barriers to greater trade with India's eastern neighbours still plague India's trade east relationship today.

On a macro-level, and given the increasingly globalized world of the 21st century, India's continued levels of trade with its eastern neighbours has increased in diversity as well as volume, yet given the historical trade links and geographic proximity, still remain well below its potential.

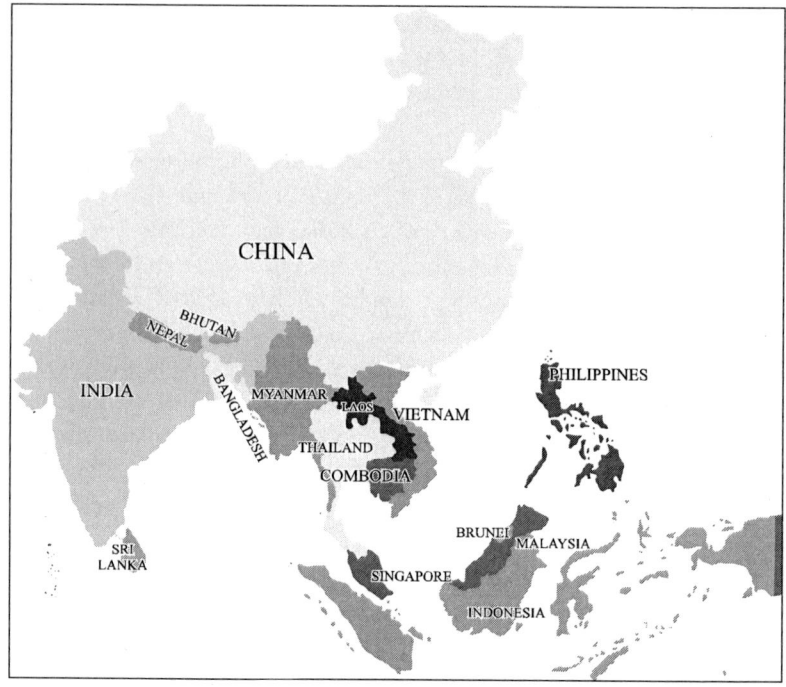

Figure 6.1 Map of India and the 15 Trade East Countries

Source: Map created by Indian Development Cooperation Research, Centre for Policy Research, New Delhi.

Note: Map not to scale and does not represent authentic international boundaries.

Overall, India's foreign trade levels continued to rise into the twenty-first century in volume and value from the low levels of the early 1990s. In 1997–8, India's total trade was over U.S.$76 billion. By 2014–15, its total trade volume had increased nine-fold to over U.S.$692 billion. In 2013–14, China replaced the USA as India's largest trading partner. Indonesia, Korea, Singapore, and Malaysia were not among India's top twelve trading partners seventeen years earlier, yet by 2014–15 they were India's seventh, ninth, tenth, and twelfth largest trading partners respectively. Furthermore, the more high-income western countries of the United Kingdom, Belgium, and Italy as well as the high-income eastern countries of Japan and Australia were no longer among India's top twelve trading partners. As seen in figure 6.2, by 2014–15 half of

Figure 6.2 India's Top 12 Trading Partners, 1997–8 versus 2014–15 (April–February), in U.S.$ million

	India's Top 12 Trading Partners in 1997–8	Total Trade Volume in 1997–8	India's Top 12 Trading Partners in 2014–15	Total Trade Volume in 2014–15
Rank	Country	Total Trade		
1	USA	10,449.58	CHINA PR	66,675.81
2	UK	4,535.68	USA	58,277.35
3	GERMANY	4,449.40	UAE	54,104.09
4	JAPAN	4,036.97	SAUDI ARABIA	36,624.04
5	BELGIUM	3,883.39	SWITZERLAND	19,852.87
6	Petroleum Products	3,697.83	GERMANY	18,620.55
7	UAE	3,104.61	INDONESIA	17,288.63
8	SWITZERLAND	3,007.35	HONG KONG	16,550.40
9	SAUDI ARABIA	2,410.06	KOREA RP	12,600.64
10	HONG KONG	2,245.02	SINGAPORE	15,758.65
11	ITALY	2,008.09	NIGERIA	15,650.51
12	AUSTRALIA	1,923.81	MALAYSIA	15,505.32
	Total of Top 12 countries	45,751.79		352,098.84
	India's Total	76,141.43		691,783.72

Source: Data from the Export Import Data Bank, Ministry of Commerce, Government of India, available at http://www.commerce.nic.in/eidb/Default.asp (accessed 15 May 2015).

India's twelve main trading partners were in East Asia compared to three in 1997–8.

Yet despite this rise in volume and the increased dependence of the economy on foreign trade, global trade grew at similar rates, leading India's share of world merchandise exports, for example, to only reach 2 percent (Chandrasekhar and Ghosh 2012), similar to rates it had reached in 1950–1 (Jain *et al.* 2009: 285). Moreover, the share of trade with India's Trade East neighbours (see Figure 6.1) among the top twelve trading partners, excluding China, increased only from 10 per cent in 1997–8 to 22 per cent in 2014–15—an increase nowhere near its potential.[2] However, if one includes China, the percentage of trade volume with India's eastern

Figure 6.3 India's Trade East (with ASEAN–BIMSTEC–China) in U.S.$ million between 1997–8 and 2014–15

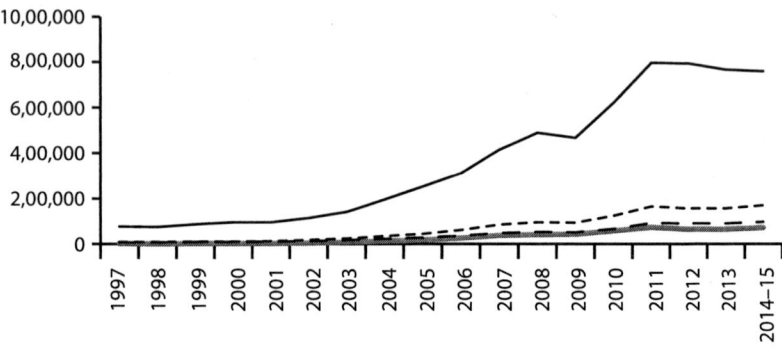

▬▬▬ Trade between India and China
— — India's total trade with Eastern neighbours between 1997–8 and 2014–15 (excluding China)
- - - - India's total trade with Eastern neighbours between 1997–8 and 2014–15 (including China)
——— India's total trade

Source: Data from the Export Import Data Bank, Ministry of Commerce, Government of India, available at http://www.commerce.nic.in/eidb/Default.asp (accessed 15 January 2016).

neighbours among the top twelve trading partners increases to 41 per cent. The increase in trade with India's eastern neighbours is largely a story of the increased trade with China. India's quarter-century old 'Look East' Policy focused on the political front and by 2015 had not yet yielded a significantly increased trade relationship with its close eastern neighbours, particularly as a percentage of India's overall trade, except with China.

India's Engagement with Regional Free Trade Associations in the East

Since India's political engagements under its Look East Policy did not lead to significant increases in volume of trade between India and its eastern neighbours (see Figure 6.3), India's endeavours to increase its eastward trade have largely focused on multilateral as well as bilateral free trade agreements. By the end of 2015, India was engaged in or had established a dozen bilateral or regional trade agreements with countries and organizations in the East Asian and Pacific region. Among the regional trade agreements, the agreements with ASEAN, BIMSTEC, Bangladesh, China, India, and Myanmar (BCIM), and South Asian Growth Quadrangle (SAGQ) were the main agreements, while the bilateral agreements with its eastern neighbours of Sri Lanka and Singapore have been among the key ones to fostering India's eastward trade.

ASEAN

By far the largest regional economic organization with which India has sought to foster closer ties is the ASEAN. If ASEAN were a single economy it would be the world's seventh largest (ASEAN 2015) as well as the world's fourth largest exporter, making it a clear focus from the beginning of India's Look East Policy in 1992 when India became a dialogue partner of ASEAN. In 2014, India and ASEAN signed free trade agreements on trade in services and investments, an area where India sees itself as having a comparative advantage, after having signed one on free goods, where ASEAN countries have a relative comparative advantage, a few years earlier. While the FTA in goods has been operational for several years, the agreement on services and investments was supposed to come into effect by the end of 2015, after ratification by all ASEAN member countries. However, by the spring of 2016 several of the ten ASEAN countries had still not ratified these agreements, leaving India with a sense of not being able to capitalize on its comparative advantage in the enhanced trade relationship with ASEAN countries.

India's trade relationship with ASEAN holds great potential for boosting India's eastward external trade and is an economic relationship. ASEAN countries have an advantage in the export of goods while India has an advantage in the export of services. India's trade value with ASEAN in U.S.$ has increased fifteen-fold since 1997, though trade with the ASEAN region as a percentage of India's total trade has remained in the range of between 7 and 10 per cent since 1997. Moreover, despite India being ranked just behind ASEAN in terms of the size of their respective economies (IMF 2014), ASEAN is more important to India than India is to ASEAN with India's share of ASEAN's overall trade having hovered around 2.7 per cent over the past five years. If the free trade agreement in investment and services does become fully operational, India would be able to leverage its competitive expertise in information technology, medical tourism, telecommunications, finance, and higher education services and could hope to balance its trade deficit in goods with ASEAN (Mehra 2014).

Studies of the India–ASEAN free trade agreement have shown the great potential of and complementarities in this trade relationship for both. A study based on the Global Trade Analysis Project (GTAP) database found that once the free trade agreement is fully implemented, India's trade with ASEAN would rise substantially, while the market share of the rest of the world in India and the ASEAN area would decrease, including a loss of market share in China and Bangladesh (Sikdar and Nag 2011). Other studies have found complementarities in trading in energy, consumer durables, and food items and particular gains to India if it can become part of East Asia's production network (Banik 2014).

However, the signing of free trade agreements by itself will not be enough to increase the share of trade with ASEAN countries in India's total trade. In order for India to be able to take advantage of the increased trade possibilities with ASEAN, several studies point to the need for India to address poor physical infrastructure, high tariff and non-tariff barriers, differences in standards, and the poor institutions and governance (De 2011; Osius and Mohan 2013; Banik 2014).

BIMSTEC, BCIM, and SAGQ

In addition to ASEAN, India's Look East Policy and its interest in fostering increased trade with its eastern neighbours also led to a variety of other regional economic associations. Key to understanding India's focus on regional organizations to its east, particularly since the election of Prime Minister Modi, is a realization in India's policy circles that unlike the thirty-year-old SAARC in India's immediate neighbourhood, regional economic associations to India's east are not hostage to the perennial politics of India–Pakistan and therefore present greater opportunities for trade growth and integration.

Three of the major regional associations on India's eastern borders are the BIMSTEC, the BCIM regional grouping, and the SAGQ. BIMSTEC, which was founded in 1997 to foster technical and economic cooperation among Bangladesh, India, Myanmar, Sri Lanka, Thailand, Nepal, and Bhutan, specifically identified increased cooperation in trade and investment as one of its priority areas of focus. BIMSTEC has great potential to act as a land bridge, connecting trade between South and Southeast Asia. BIMSTEC countries have identified fourteen priority areas of cooperation, ranging from trade and transport to energy and communication, and each member country has taken the lead responsibility in at least one priority area. India is the lead country on cooperation in the areas of communication and transport, environment and natural disaster management, as well as counterterrorism and transnational crime.

Yet despite that greater potential for trade and even though member nations have signed a BIMSTEC Free Trade Area agreement (FTA) for the trade of goods, this agreement has not yet come into force due to negotiations in the individual member countries. The framework agreement also envisages free trade in services and investments as well as an agreement for energy and grid interconnection, all of which had yet to be addressed by May 2015. However, Dhaka was expected to host the BIMSTEC commerce ministers during the summer of 2015 where several agreements related to the BIMSTEC FTA were expected to be signed.

Moreover, despite the lower political barriers to trade among BIMSTEC countries and even if signing and implementation of BIMSTEC agreements should progress in the near future, the physical barriers to eastward trade are significant and the main bottleneck to eastward trade. Trade among India and BIMSTEC countries has historically been low, averaging approximately 3 per cent between 1997–8 and 2013–14, while inter-regional trade among member countries hovered around 5 per cent. This is despite all countries being in the same region and bordering each other. The state of the physical infrastructure at the BIMSTEC countries' borders and the logistics of being able to carry through trade across the borders is particularly important to enabling the free trade of goods and are the main impediments to enhancing trade amongst the member countries. For example, infrastructure quality and non-tariff barriers inhibit land transport. Many of the roads used for passenger and freight movements across borders are inadequate for modern transport, there is little coordination between countries on the development of roads and visas issues, and other barriers often inhibit formal trade across borders, including railroad gauges differing between India, Bangladesh, Thailand, and Myanmar (Kellogg Brown and Root Pty Ltd. 2008). Moreover, the Indian states that are crucial to building India's eastward overland trade, West Bengal and the Northeastern states, are poorer states relative to the Indian average, with the Northeastern states in particular having few financial and human resources of their own to undertake the political negotiations and enormous infrastructure investments that are needed to facilitate overland trade.

BCIM is another eastward focused sub-regional forum for integrating trade and investment among the four countries of Bangladesh, China, India, and Myanmar. The concept of BCIM has been under discussion since the late 1990s and representatives of the four countries had met at twelve BCIM forums by the end of 2015 with the aim of linking the four neighbouring countries and the Bay of Bengal with India's landlocked northeastern region and China's landlocked southwestern regions, which are both underdeveloped despite being crucial to any transport between these four countries. In 2009, the member countries proposed an economic multi-modal corridor linking India and China and passing through Myanmar and Bangladesh, a plan that India approved at the end of 2013 (Dasgupta 2013). This BCIM economic corridor would start in China's Yunnan province, pass via Yangon and Mandalay in Myanmar, Chittagong, Dhaka, and Sylhet in Bangladesh, India's northeastern states, and end in Kolkata, India (Bhattacharjee 2014). Yet by mid-2016 the idea of a BCIM economic corridor was still confined to the realm of strategy papers, with little concrete measures to show for it.

Trade between these four member countries has increased significantly since 1997, growing twenty times in U.S.$ value between 1997–8 and 2014–15. Moreover, the percentage of intra-BCIM trade as a percentage of India's trade overall has grown from 3 to 10 per cent during this sixteen year period. However, India's trade with China accounts for nearly 90 per cent of India's trade with BCIM countries and most of India's trade with China is conducted through the sea route, rather than the BCIM border areas. India also has a deficit in its trade of goods with China, which perhaps accounts for the weariness of India until recently to focus on the BCIM free trade economic corridor.

Nevertheless, the potential benefits of such an economic corridor for fostering trade in these underdeveloped neighbouring areas are enormous. India's underdeveloped and relatively isolated northeastern states in particular would stand to gain from better connectivity through Bangladesh with the rest of India, as well as from trade north and eastward with China and access to Southeast Asia through Myanmar. Yet the low level of infrastructure at the borders indicates that to date the same trade and non-trade barriers which have plagued integration with ASEAN and BIMSTEC countries also remain a barrier to BCIM integration.

Another sub-regional grouping formed in 1996 with the objective of promoting trade and economic cooperation between the member countries of Bangladesh, Bhutan, India, and Nepal is the SAGQ. Here again there have been over a decade of meetings between the respective countries to discuss how to move towards greater economic integration. Yet it was not until the recent agreement by the Asian Development Bank (ADB) and the Indian government to fund the South Asia Subregional Economic Cooperation (SASEC) programme that specific actions to foster integration have been taken. Under this agreement, ADB will provide $300 million and the Indian government $58 million to build road and railway networks in the region by 2020, with much of the focus on infrastructure building at the main border crossings between the four countries as well as Myanmar (Mishra 2015). ADB funding has acted as a catalyst for addressing the infrastructure bottleneck at the borders between these countries, yet by 2016 changes on the ground were few.

In all three examples of sub-regional economic grouping between India and its eastern neighbours the potential for expanding trade is vast, but the political and infrastructure barriers to increasing trade remain significant.

India's Bilateral Free Trade Agreements with Its Eastern Neighbours

Regional economic associations have been pursued by India as a fast-track method for gaining access to established free trade zones, as well as a method for negotiating new free trade areas with several countries in one swoop. However, India has also pursued its Look East Policy and aim of fostering trade with its eastern neighbours by pursuing bilateral free trade agreements with countries that are important to India for economic as well as strategic reasons. By the beginning of 2015, India had entered into bilateral free trade agreements with six East Asian countries—Sri Lanka, Singapore, Thailand, Malaysia, Japan, and Korea—and others were under negotiation with Indonesia, New Zealand, and Australia.

India–Sri Lanka Free Trade Agreement

One of the more important bilateral free trade agreements that India has entered into with an immediate neighbour is the one with Sri Lanka. Sri Lanka and India have been trading partners for centuries. In 2014–15, India was Sri Lanka's third largest trading partner, while Sri Lanka was one of India's largest trading partners in the South Asia region. In addition to both countries being members of BIMSTEC, both have also signed the bilateral India–Sri Lanka Free Trade Agreement which went into effect in 2000, with all trade barriers being removed by 2008. The bilateral trade agreement enables duty-free trading on a wide range of products between the two countries. Indo-Sri Lankan total trade, which had hovered around U.S.$700 million in 2000, jumped to over $1 billion after the signing of the free trade agreement in 2002 and had increased five-fold to over U.S.$ 5.2 billion in 2013–14 (Government of India 2014). India's exports to Sri Lanka rose five-fold to over U.S.$4.5 billion between 2000–1 to 2013–14, while imports from Sri Lanka rose ten-fold to over U.S.$600 million. This has led to a significant boost for business, economic, and investment cooperation between the two countries, according to official sources.[3]

The rapid rise in trade between the two countries following the signing of the free trade agreement shows the large trade potential between these neighbouring countries. At the same time, while the trade volume between these two countries has increased, the share of their bilateral trade has not. Indo-Sri Lankan trade has hovered around 0.7 per cent of India's overall trade from 1997–8 through 2013–14. Thus the increases in India's trade with Sri Lanka have reflected the overall increase in India's trade volume over the past decade and a half. In a ranking of India's largest trading partners, Sri Lanka in 2014–15 still ranked as the 30th largest trading partner, compared to its 29th place before the free trade agreement was signed in 2000–1.

There have, however, been significant political changes in the bilateral Indo-Sri Lankan relationship since 2014 which auger well for increased bilateral trade. In 2014, elections brought new governments to power in both countries. India viewed the previous Sri Lankan government as having turned away from India towards China. Under the ten-years of rule of the previous president Rajapaksa, China became the largest investor in Sri Lanka, with contracts to build the Hambantota port, another 500-acre port city outside of Sri Lanka's capital Colombo, a now defunct international airport in the previous president's hometown, and many other infrastructure projects. All of this was viewed with great trepidation by India and as another example of the tussle with China for supremacy in the Indian Ocean region, particularly when two Chinese submarines were allowed to dock in Sri Lankan ports in 2014.

The Sri Lankan government of President Sirisena, who was elected in 2015, however, rebalanced the relationship with China, putting the U.S.$1.4 billion Colombo City port project, which would have effectively given ninety-nine year ownership of the port to China, on hold. It has instead refocused on its relationship with India. These actions of the Sirisena and Modi governments in both countries have led to increased cooperation in trade and investments already in 2016.

Singapore

Similarly, India is in a regional free trade agreement with Singapore through ASEAN and nevertheless signed a separate India–Singapore Comprehensive Economic Cooperation Agreement (CECA) in 2005. This agreement was signed with the purpose of increasing bilateral trade, investments, and economic cooperation as well as military and strategic cooperation, and has eliminated many tariff and non-tariff barriers. Given Singapore's strategic location at the Strait of Malacca, which is India's maritime access to the Far East, India's Look East Policy reached out specifically to Singapore in the 1990s. This focus on a closer trade relationship has paid off. Singapore's bilateral trade volume and value with India has grown since the 1990s, from U.S.$1.8 billion in 1999–2000 to U.S.$25.3 billion in 2011–12, before falling slightly to U.S.$19.3 billion in 2013–14. Singapore has also moved up in the rankings of India's largest trading partners from being the 14th largest trading partner in 1997–8 to the 10th largest in 2013–14 (see Figure 6.2). Singapore is also India's 8th largest source of foreign investments and the largest amongst the ASEAN countries.

Yet Singapore is the exception rather than the rule with regards to increased trade benefits with an eastern neighbour after the signing of a free trade agreement. In most cases India's signing of such bilateral trade agreements have not led to a greater presence of India in the markets of the countries with which they have signed such an agreement. Comparing the share of India's merchandise exports to its regional neighbours with whom it has signed bilateral trade agreements versus its total trade overall from the turn of the century to 2013–14, India's exports to these countries have on average stagnated around 35 per cent during this time period (Dhar 2014).[1] Bilateral trade agreements have generally increased the volume of share between India and the respective country, but not the ranking of the country in India's overall trade.

Facilitating Eastward Trade through Development Cooperation

In addition to free trade agreements and other agreements to facilitate eastward trade, India has also used its increasingly significant development cooperation budget to engage with its eastern neighbours, thereby potentially opening markets for India. Between 2006 and 2013, grants and loans to India's eastern neighbours increased eight-fold and expanded to cover most Southeast Asian countries. While in 2006–7 India gave grants and loans totaling 7 billion rupees to five eastern neighbours, Bangladesh, Sri Lanka, Bhutan, Nepal, and Laos, by 2013–14 the volume of this form of development cooperation with its eastern neighbours had risen to 55 billion rupees with the countries of Cambodia, Myanmar, and Vietnam being added to the list of development partners.[5] Of the grants and loans, nearly 90 per cent of the development cooperation commitments made with its eastern neighbours between 2010–11 and 2014–15 were for infrastructure projects that supported eastward trade and connectivity. Moreover, in addition to grants and loans, Indian development cooperation also encompasses government-backed Lines of Credit (LOCs) provided through its Export Import Bank. Between 2010 and 2015 India provided U.S.$ 3.7 billion in LOCs to six eastern neighbours. Since a stipulation of these LOCs is that 75 per cent of the LOCs be used toward procuring goods and services for the respective project from India, these credit lines are another tool used by India to foster eastward trade.

What Then Are the Barriers to Enhancing India's Trade with Its Eastern Neighbours?

The plethora of regional and bilateral free trade agreements India has signed with its eastern neighbours since the turn of the century show commitment to fostering trade between these neighbouring countries. And the free trade agreements have borne fruit and resulted in greater imports as well as exports with the Trade East countries. Trade volume with these countries, including China, went from over U.S.$9 billion in 1997–8 to U.S.$157 billion by 2013–14, with bilateral trade increasing with every country.

However, free trade agreements have not changed the overall trade structures with India's eastern neighbours. Most of the increase in India's trade volume with its eastern neighbours has come from increased trade with a country with whom India does not have a free trade agreement: China. Excluding China, the share of India's trade with its other Trade East neighbours compared to its overall trade volume has not changed significantly since the turn of the century. Moreover, other indicators of India's trade openness have not improved significantly. In 2014, India still ranked low on trade freedom scores, ranking 150 out of 181 countries with India's overall level of economic freedom remaining unchanged between 2010 and 2015, and ranking below regional as well as world averages (Riley and Ambassador Miller 2014). Similarly, in 2014 India dropped two places to be ranked 142 out of 189 countries in terms of the 'ease of doing business', ranking behind its neighbours Sri Lanka, Nepal, Bhutan, and Pakistan (World Bank Group 2014). This measure of doing business in India pointed to the significant hurdles in dealing with construction contracts and the enforcement of contracts, where India ranked near the bottom at 184 and 186 respectively. Relative to the progress made in lowering trade barriers amongst India's eastern neighbours and globally, India's progress on changing the structural impediments to trade has been weak.

The main barriers to increasing India's trade eastward are therefore non-tariff barriers, lack of infrastructure, and the political resolution of lingering border issues. India's non-tariff barriers to trade are a key barrier preventing effective integration between India and its eastern neighbours, as also outlined in the chapter by Bipul Chatterjee and Prithviraj Nath. Non-tariff barriers, broadly defined to include all non-tariff, trade distorting barriers ranging from border crossing delays due to cumbersome bureaucratic procedures and additional fees levied on imports, as well as differential standards on goods, special licenses and permits, and charges on imports in the form of border taxes or other fees remain significant in India. India's trade with Bangladesh, for example, is hampered by a host of non-tariff barriers, including visa restrictions, packaging requirements, laboratory testing requirements for food and cosmetic products, and border delays and fees (Aspen Institute India 2012). India made a huge step forward by resolving the issue of 'enclaves' of land, that both India and Bangladesh own within each other's territory, during the summer of 2015 and this clarification and simplification of the border will help address other problems plaguing cross-border trade between the two countries, including security problems, lack of clear rules and transit procedures, and general corruption. All of these problems add to the financial and time costs of trade, as well as political tensions. Faced with these tariff and non-tariff barriers to trade in the 1990s, negotiating free trade agreements in many ways was the easiest step to take by the Indian government to increase eastward trade. The more difficult issue of decreasing non-tariff barriers within India's eastern borders will need significant political attention and transparency-building measures, as well as significant infrastructure investments, particularly in connecting from Bangladesh to Myanmar through India's northeastern states. Addressing the non-tariff barriers, including improving transparency, decreasing bureaucratic delays, and efficiency of infrastructure building and managing is crucial to increased eastward connectivity. The 2014 creation of the National Highways & Infrastructure Development Corporation Limited, which started in 2014 and took over several projects from the Border Roads Organization due to efficiency concerns, will thus be valuable only if it is able to address these non-tariff barriers instead of replacing one bureaucracy with another.

The lack of physical infrastructure is the most visible bottleneck to eastward connectivity. As a visit to any of India's border crossings with Bangladesh or Myanmar clarifies, the existing physical infrastructure at the border is grossly inadequate and currently incapable of enabling increased border trade. A recent study of India's 35 main border customs stations with Bangladesh found all of them to have inadequate infrastructure at the border (CUTS International 2014). Similar studies of India's border with Myanmar have also found the lack of basic trade infrastructure to be a major trade barrier at these border crossings, with truck crossing delays of up to a week at the borders (De 2013). The infrastructure and resulting capacity of Indian ports also presented a trade barrier, particularly since all Indian ports were already at full capacity in 2014 (U.S. International Trade Commission 2009; 'Ports' 2014). Airports in India's northeastern states, which are crucial to India's trade with its eastern neighbours, are also abysmal, with the airport at Guwahati being the only international airport in the eight northeastern states, including Sikkim, yet even this airport has virtually no international flights. Railroad connectivity to India's northeastern states and beyond is also poor, with railroad gauge line standards between West Bengal and Myanmar changing four times. The current state of inland water connectivity from ports in Bangladesh and Myanmar to India is also abysmal.

In order to address these infrastructure bottle necks to increased eastward trade, India will need to make significantly higher investments in border infrastructure connectivity to these border stations. It will also need to make significant investments in its eastern ports, airports, and railways, and its eastern borders generally in order to enable a structurally changed level of trade at the borders and through its ports. Moreover, the level of development of the northeastern states is important to take into account: these states are relatively poor compared to the Indian average. While India's infrastructure needs are great throughout the country, the eastern border states are crucial to increased eastward trade and have little investment resources of their own. The federal Indian government will therefore have to coordinate and finance most of the infrastructure investments in India's northeastern region. In addition, public sector investments on their own will not suffice and significant private sector investments, including international investments, will also be needed to meet the minimum investments needed to address current bottlenecks, let alone expand infrastructure to enable further increases in trade. The significant increases in the 2015 Indian budget allocations to infrastructure will make a sizeable difference toward building eastward connectivity, as will the new financing of border connectivity projects by the ADB and the Japan International Cooperation Agency (JICA). Yet even those planned investments are well short of the financing needed to meet the potential for eastward trade and further options to meet the infrastructure funding gap, including through private–public partnerships, will need to be explored.

After negotiating FTAs, channelling greater investments towards infrastructure is the next easiest step. India's 2015 budget, which has allocated an increase of 700 billion rupees (approximately U.S.$10.74 billion) for infrastructure compared to the previous year's budget, is seeking to address India's infrastructure gap. It is also taking innovative steps to leverage greater resources and investments in infrastructure through establishing a National Investment and Infrastructure Fund (NIIF) (PTI 2015). Ensuring timely, transparent, and adequate infrastructure funding in the border crossings, ports, railroads, and air transport, particularly in India's northeastern region, will remain a challenge. Yet they are prerequisites for enabling increased eastward trade.

The third major area that India will have to address in order to increase its eastward trade is the political resolution of border areas. Uncertain borders are major barriers to trade, in addition to causing political uncertainty. India's eastern borders remain plagued by boundary disputes, with China generally, and have become politically contentious at the sub-national level in border states such as Assam, where the often politicized issue of cheaper migrant labour crossing the border and taking away jobs in regions with depressed economies can also be a security concern. After four decades of little headway, the Bangladesh enclaves issue was resolved during the summer of 2015 with the 119th constitutional amendment to operationalize a new land boundary agreement with Bangladesh. Yet India's eastern border with China remains disputed as witnessed by the furore caused by a map shown in China during Prime Minister Modi's May 2015 visit to China, which showed India's state of Arunachal Pradesh as belonging to China. While the lack of a border settlement with China has not prevented the growth of Indo-Chinese trade, most of this bilateral trade does not cross through these contentious land routes, instead taking the more costly but more established sea routes and land routes through third countries.

Less known are India's ongoing boundary disputes with Nepal and Myanmar. Unlike China, Myanmar is a politically unstable and poorer country, which has led to calls for a closing of the border by parts of India's security establishment (Baruah 2015). Resisting such domestic pressures to make border crossings more difficult and finding expedient resolutions on the politically stable as well as unstable borders will be essential to enhancing eastward trade. At the same time, re-engaging on political resolutions to these eastern border disputes should be conducted parallel to efforts to address infrastructure needs and non-tariff barriers in this region. Dealing with all three bottlenecks to eastern trade—non-tariff barriers, the dearth of physical infrastructure linking India eastward, and resolving border disputes—will be necessary to an 'Act East' policy, including a policy of 'Trading East'.

Notes

1. The 15 countries that I designate as *Trade East Countries* for the purposes of this article are: Bangladesh, Bhutan, Brunei, Cambodia, China, Indonesia, Laos, Malaysia, Myanmar, Nepal, Philippines, Singapore, Sri Lanka, Thailand, and Vietnam.

2. Calculations made based on data from Government of India 2014.

3. See The Free Library. 'The Indian High Commissioner in Sri Lanka says that free trade agreement between the two countries has led to massive boost of business, economic and investment cooperation'.

4. See also data from Government of India 2014.

5. Indian foreign grants are only reported in Indian Rupees, while Indian foreign Line of Credits are reported in U.S. dollar amounts.

References

ASEAN. 2015. *ASEAN Economic Community: 12 Things to Know.* Manila: Asian Development Bank. December, available at http://www.adb.org/features/asean-economic-community-12-things-know (accessed 13 March 2016).

Aspen Institute India. 2012. 'India–Bangladesh Relations: Towards Increased Partnership—A Report'. New Delhi: Aspen Institute India. Available at http://www.anantaaspencentre.in/pdf/India_Bangladesh_Report.pdf (accessed 10 December 2015).

Banik, Nilanjan. 2014. 'India–ASEAN Free Trade Agreement: The Untapped Potential', MPRA Paper no. 57954. Hyderabad: Mahindra Ecole Centrale. Available at http://mpra.ub.uni-muenchen.de/57954/ (accessed 10 December 2015).

Baruah, Sanjib. 2015.'The Nagas of India and Myanmar', *Indian Express*, 14 May; available at http://indianexpress.com/article/opinion/columns/the-nagas-of-india-and-myanmar/ (accessed 10 December 2015).

Bhattacharjee, Rupak. 2014. *IDSA Comment: North East in BCIM–EC: Problems and Prospects*, New Delhi: Institute for Defence Studies and Analysis, 14 October. Available at http://www.idsa.in/idsacomments/NorthEast%20inBCIM-EC_RBhattacharjee_171014.html (accessed 13 March 2016).

Chandrasekhar, C.P. and Jayati Ghosh. 2012. 'Emerging Countries in World Trade', *Hindu*, 24 December.

CUTS International. 2014. *India–Bangladesh Trade Potentiality: An Assessment of Trade Facilitation Issues.* Jaipur, India: CUTS International, April. Available at http://www.cuts-citee.org/ibta-ii/pdf/india-bangladesh_trade_potentiality-an_assessment_of_trade_facilitation_issues.pdf (accessed 10 December 2015).

Dasgupta, Saibal. 2013. 'Plan for Economic Corridor Linking India to China Approved', *Times of India*, 20 December; available at http://timesofindia.indiatimes.com/world/china/Plan-for-economic-corridor-linking-India-to-China-approved/articleshow/27669821.cms.

De, Prabir. 2013.'Challenges to India–Myanmar Trade and Connectivity'. New Delhi: Research and Information System for Developing Countries (RIS), 4 February. Available at http://ris.org.in/images/RIS_images/pdf/India-Myanmar%20Meeting%204%20feb%202013%20PPT/PrabirDe.pdf (accessed 10 December 2015).

———. 2011. 'ASEAN–India Connectivity: An Indian Perspective', in F. and S. Umezaki (eds), *ASEAN–India Connectivity: The Comprehensive Asia Development Plan, Phase II, ERIA Research Project Report 2010–17 Kimura*, pp. 95–150. Jakarta: ERIA.

Dhar, Biswajit. 2014. 'Are Free Trade Agreements a Dead End for India?' *East Asia Forum*, 10 October; available at http://www.eastasiaforum.org/2014/10/10/are-free-trade-agreements-a-dead-end-for-india/ (accessed 13 March 2016).

Dun and Bradstreet India (D&B). 2014. 'Ports', *India's Leading Infrastructure Companies 2014*; available at http://www.dnb.co.in/India%27s_Leading_Infrastructure_Companies_2014/Ports.asp (accessed 10 December 2015).

Government of India. 2014. 'Export–Import Data Bank', Ministry of Commerce and Industry, Department of Commerce. Version 7.2 Tradestat, May; available at http://commerce.nic.in/eidb/default.asp (accessed 1 October 2015).

Haokip, Thongkholal. 2011. 'India's Look East Policy: Its Evolution and Approach', *South Asian Survey*, 18(2): 248.

International Monetary Fund. 2014. World Economic Outlook Database.

Jain, T.R., Mukesh Trehan, and Ranju Trehan. 2009–10. *Indian Economy*. New Delhi: V.K. Publications.

Kellogg Brown & Root Pty Ltd. 2008. 'Bay of Bengal Initiatives for Multi-Sectoral Technical and Economic Cooperation (BIMSTEC) Transport Infrastructure and Logistics Study (BTILS)—Final Report', *ADB (Asian Development Bank) Technical Assistance Consultant's Report*, Australia. Available at http://www.adb.org/sites/default/files/project-document/65311/38396-01-reg-tacr.pdf (accessed 10 December 2015).

Moore, Malcolm. 2009. 'China and South East Asia Create Huge Free Trade Zone', *The Daily Telegraph*, 30 December; available at www.telegraph.co.uk/finance/china-business/6911721/China-and-South-East-Asia-create-huge-free-trade-zone.html (accessed 12 March 2016).

Mehra, Puja. 2014. 'India Inks Free Trade Agreement with ASEAN', *Hindu*, 9 September; available at http://www.thehindu.com/news/national/india-inks-free-trade-agreement- with-asean/article6391947.ece.

Mishra, Asit Ranjan. 2015. 'New Deal to Link South Asian Nations in Pipeline: India, Nepal, Bhutan and Bangladesh Working on a Deal to Boost Regional Trade and Cultural Exchange', *Live Mint*, 3 February; available at http://www.livemint.com/Politics/FbxQ6pxFClNFfwY5JEyMzK/New-deal-to-link-South-Asian-nations-in-pipeline.html (accessed 16 March 2016).

Osius, Ted and C. Raja Mohan. 2013. *Enhancing India–ASEAN Connectivity: A Report of the CSIS Sumitro Chair for Southeast Asia Studies and the Wadhwani Chair for U.S.–India Policy Studies*. Washington DC: CSIS.

Philip, Snehesh Alex. 2014. 'Time for "Act East Policy" and Not Just "Look East": Swaraj', *Outlook* (Hanoi), 14 August; available at http://www.outlookindia.com/news/article/time-for-act-east-policy-and-not-just-look-east-swaraj/856878 (accessed 9 December 2015).

Reserve Bank of India. 2014.'Foreign Direct Investment Flows to India: Country-wise and Industry-wise', *Annual Report 2013–14*. Mumbai: Reserve Bank of India.

PTI. 2015. 'Budget 2015: Government Gives Lion's Share to Infrastructure to Spur Economic Growth', *Economic Times*, 28 February; available at http://articles.economictimes.indiatimes.com/2015-02- 28/news/59612692_1_infrastructure-projects-infrastructure-fund-finance-minister-arun-jaitley (accessed 10 December 2015).

Riley, Bryan and Ambassador Terry Miller. 2014. 'Why Trade Matters and How to Unleash It: Trade Rankings from the 2015 Index of Economic Freedom', Special Report #161, *Economic Matters*. Washington DC: Heritage Foundation, 6 November. Available at http://www.heritage.org/research/reports/2014/11/2015-index-of-economic-freedom-why-trade-matters-and-how-to-unleash-it (accessed 13 March 2016).

Sikdar, Chandrima and Biswajit Nag. 2011.'Impact of India–ASEAN Free Trade Agreement: A Cross-Country Analysis Using Applied General Equilibrium Modeling', Working Paper Series no. 107, *Asia–Pacific Research and Training Network on Trade*, November.

The Free Library. 2014. 'India, Sri Lanka: HIGH COMMISSIONER—FTA Provides Massive Boost to Cooperation between India and Sri Lanka', available at http://www.thefreelibrary.com/India%2cSri+Lanka+%3a+HIGH+COMMISSIONER+-+FTA+provides+massive+boost+to...-a0377466256 (accessed 9 December 2015).

U.S. International Trade Commission. 2009. *India: Effect of Tariff and Nontariff Measures on U.S. Agricultural Exports, Investigation#332–504*. Washington DC: USITC Publication 4107, November. Available at http://www.usitc.gov/publications/332/pub4107.pdf (accessed 10 December 2015).

World Bank Group. 2014.'Economy Rankings', (Ease of Doing Business Rankings 2014); available at http://www.doingbusiness.org/rankings.

7 India and RCEP

Challenges and Opportunities of Opening Up the Farm/Food Sector

SURUPA GUPTA

INDIA JOINED THE REGIONAL COMPREHENSIVE ECONOMIC PARTNERSHIP (RCEP) in 2012 in an attempt to better integrate with the Asian economy. However, that intent contradicts India's largely defensive posture in agriculture and manufacturing at the RCEP negotiations. This poses an apparent contradiction and this chapter seeks to understand what shapes it. Identifying India's defensive and aggressive interests in agriculture and food processing, the chapter argues that domestic infrastructural deficits and policy reform bottlenecks need to be addressed if India is to fully exploit its opportunities from its trade connectivity to the east. There is, therefore, an urgent need to re-examine the defensive interests, focus on the export interests, and carry out domestic reforms that strengthen the farm sector as well as its linkages to manufacturing.

During the last decade, Indian trade policymakers have supplemented their focus on multilateralism by pursuing bilateral and regional free trade agreements (FTAs). While multilateralism—in trade and elsewhere—continues to be important for India, various political and economic considerations have driven India to seek out trade partnerships with regional actors such as the European Union (EU) and the Association of Southeast Asian Nations (ASEAN) as well as several bilateral agreements with single states.[1] India's decision to join the RCEP is consistent with this trend. Despite this spate of regional partnerships, India remains cautious and defensive when it comes to making binding commitments on market opening. The resulting trade agreements have, therefore, remained limited in scope and ambition. What then drives India's decision to join regional trade agreements such as RCEP? What calculations of costs and benefits underlie such decisions? This chapter argues that although regional FTAs offer up opportunities for some Indian producers, India's largely defensive position on agriculture and manufacturing severely restricts the extent to which many sectors can be opened up, and thus also restricts the overall benefit to the Indian economy. Though broad economic developmental goals such as employment and income generation among the poor as well as specific political goals such as strengthening cooperation in other issue areas and preventing isolation in a fast-evolving global trade architecture drive India's decision to join regional trade agreements such as the RCEP, the research for this chapter indicates that longer term political goals seem to outweigh economic goals in shaping India's decisions. Taking the case of agriculture, this chapter goes on to argue that there is an urgent need to focus on India's export interests and carry out domestic reforms that strengthen the sector as well as its linkages to manufacturing—focusing mostly on India's defensive interests in the farm sector has the benefit of buying policymakers time for reforms, but in the end, that strategy will likely be self-defeating in the broader context of India's developmental goals.

The chapter begins by providing a brief background to the emergence of RCEP. It then goes on to identify the opportunities and challenges that the RCEP offers to the Indian economy, particularly, to India's farm sector. The third section focuses on the political and economic compulsions that have shaped India's overall negotiating position on agriculture in trade agreements. Given that incomplete reforms are a part of this explanation, a brief account of the government's reform responses follows. The chapter ends with some conclusions and policy prescriptions.

The Emergence of RCEP

The proliferation of FTAs involving India is mirrored by the proliferation of FTAs in Asia overall.[2] Broadly, the proliferation of FTAs is a function of path dependence—earlier decisions by East and Southeast Asian states to embrace an export-led growth model, and the resultant growth, have created a large constituency and a compelling logic for further trade liberalization. That said, there is no denying that strategic and security interests also play an important role in the creation of at least some of the FTAs. The rise of large, fast-growing Asian economies such as China, India, and Indonesia add further impetus to pushing regionalism in Asia. The push for a broad regional agreement emerged within this context and was driven by ASEAN. Several factors were behind this push. First, according to the Asian Development Bank (ADB), the economies of Asia are expected to constitute about half of the global economy by the middle of the 21st century (Hill and Gochoco-Bautista 2013). Their share of global gross domestic product (GDP), trade, and investment are rising fast. Second, the region is also emerging as one of the fastest growing markets in the world—an Organisation for Economic Co-operation and Development (OECD) study projects that 80 per cent of the middle class in 2050 would reside in Asian countries (Kharas 2010). Third, the members of ASEAN are part of fragmented production processes that make up global supply chains. The dependence of members of ASEAN states on these fragmented production networks is higher than that of other countries (Athukorala 2008). Seamless trade rules are crucial for the functioning of this type of production processes. Consequently, the ASEAN had done two things: one, it initiated steps to achieve greater economic integration among member states and two, it entered into several ASEAN+1 FTAs involving major regional economies.[3] Increasingly, however, ASEAN members felt that the FTAs were not delivering promised benefits, in part, because they were creating layers of complex and inconsistent rules that firms found difficult to work with. Instead of the promise of lowering cost, these rules may have increased the cost of doing business. For example, multiple rules of origin associated with the various FTAs made FTA compliance a complicated process (Das 2013). Last but not least, the United States' effort to negotiate the Trans Pacific Partnership (TPP), a twelve-member FTA that includes some ASEAN and other Asia–Pacific states, added the political push for such an Asia-wide FTA. That large and growing Asian economies such as China, India, and Indonesia were not part of the TPP certainly factored into the decision to move ahead with it.

Consequently, the RCEP was conceptualized in 2011 and was formally launched at the East Asia summit in Phnom Penh, Cambodia, in November 2012. India formally joined the partnership at this meeting. The RCEP Trade Negotiations Committee was set up as the apex negotiating body and took over the negotiations in 2013. Once completed, this regional trade agreement is likely to cover an area with a population of 3.5 billion (48 per cent of the world total) and a nominal GDP of 26.1 trillion, which makes up 32 per cent of the global GDP (Das 2013: 4). Member countries collectively contribute to 27 per cent of world trade in goods and services and account for 24.4 per cent of foreign direct investment (FDI) inflow globally (Wignaraja 2014: 98). A recent study suggests that global income gains from concluding the RCEP negotiations will likely amount to $260 billion (Wignaraja 2014: 99).

RCEP: Opportunities and Challenges for India

The RCEP offers several opportunities to the Indian economy. First, according to ADB's calculations, liberalization under RCEP will likely produce a 2.6 per cent income gain for India (Wignaraja 2014). While this number is not huge and pales in comparison to the gains that other smaller economies will likely secure, it is well-known that continental-sized economies rely on both domestic and external markets for income growth. Moreover, membership in the grouping has other benefits.

A related second benefit is that Indian producers will potentially get access to a large market. Economists see particular advantages for service sectors such as information technology, telecom, business process outsourcing and knowledge process outsourcing, and other skilled services such as banking, nursing, teaching, and accounting as well as for manufacturing sectors such as pharmaceuticals, automotive, food processing, and textiles (Palit 2014; Sidhartha 2012a; Wignaraja 2014: 101). Although India's manufacturing sector has been wary of joining such FTAs, the RCEP offers opportunities to Indian firms for insertion into regional and global value chains and access to markets, foreign direct investment, and technology. A recent study identifies the sectors where such integration with RCEP members already exists and sectors where potential for further integration exists (Palit 2014). This study identifies existing comparative advantage in several manufacturing groups such as jewellery, furniture, musical instruments, sporting goods as well as possibilities of deeper integration in textile and textile products, leather and footwear, and food products. It is important to recognize in this context that participation in value chains not only expands India's potential market to RCEP members but also to the U.S. and Europe.

Third, membership in RCEP is particularly significant in the context of emerging trends towards mega-regional trade agreements that have increasingly been taking up more attention in the developed world. The possibility of a multilateral trade deal under the World Trade Organization (WTO) appears far less likely. It is important to evaluate India's RCEP membership within the context of a changing global institutional architecture for trade: these include the U.S.-led effort to negotiate the TPP involving other Asia-Pacific states as well as the Transatlantic Trade and Investment Partnership (TTIP) with Europe. As of this writing the first group came to an agreement—the final deal is contingent on legislative ratification in the member countries (Nakamura 2015). That this change is very much a driving force becomes clear from the Ministry of Commerce's brief on RCEP which states that the RCEP membership 'should not be seen in isolation but in the context of other comprehensive FTAs that are emerging...'(Department of Commerce 2015b). In 2012, India's decision to join the RCEP was, in part, shaped also by its concern that a further delay in entry would involve paying a higher price and being denied the opportunity to shape the contours of the agreement (Sidhartha 2012a). It is necessary to point out that India is not a member of groups such as Asia-Pacific Economic Cooperation. India is also located in a neighbourhood where intra-regional trade, while growing, has been slow to catch up with other areas (Moinuddin 2013). Even within the WTO, the recent trend has skewed towards plurilateral sector-specific agreements rather than a 'single undertaking' comprehensive trade agreement. Equally importantly, one must note that China is already the largest trading partner for all the countries in the region and India may increasingly be isolated and left behind (Hsu 2013: 44). Look East and Act East become more important in that context and RCEP is very much a piece of that policy (Salze-Lozac'h et. al. 2013). Other authors in this volume have made this connection as well.

Several policy analysts have suggested that India should get ready to join the TPP (Bergsten 2015; Singh 2014). While one recent study has suggested that India will potentially gain much from joining the TPP and lose substantially if it does not, most of the calculations are predicated on the assumption that the TPP is enlarged to include China (Bergsten 2015). Other studies suggest that there are potentially modest sectoral losses, in textiles for example, associated with staying out of the TPP and that joining the TPP provides substantial investment opportunities (Banga and

Sahu 2015). However, policymakers point out that the higher standards, particularly in intellectual property and dispute settlement, built into the TPP would impose substantial costs on India and that, at the moment, India is neither ready nor willing to join the TPP and subject itself to some of the higher standards.[4] They perceive the RCEP to be a relatively more favourable environment for engaging in trade liberalization.

Fourth, for India, signing the RCEP would mean establishing FTAs with Australia, China, and New Zealand, countries with which it currently does not have FTAs.[5] Das argues that being ASEAN-centred, the RCEP is likely to follow 'the ASEAN way' (Das 2013).[6] She suggests that following the ASEAN way will likely translate into a more accommodative approach to development differences of the member countries and provide more flexibility, something that is high on India's priority. Other countries such as Indonesia likely share some of India's concerns in the agriculture and other sectors.

Fifth, RCEP seeks to 'cement ASEAN's central role in the emerging regional economic architecture and seeks to harmonize the "noodle bowl" of differences between the various ASEAN FTAs' (Hiebert and Hanlon 2012). In doing so, it will likely simplify trade procedures and bring down the cost of trade in the region.

Finally, the discussion above points toward broad benefits for the Indian economy. What do we know about the likely impact on the farm sector? No published calculations of specific benefits or costs to India's farm sector exist. However, one could point to the gains some agricultural and allied sectors have made from earlier opening up due to FTAs with ASEAN, Japan, and South Korea. Additionally, potential benefits to the food sector portends well for the farm sector overall.

While the RCEP poses obvious opportunities, it poses considerable challenges as well. First, there is discomfort with the idea of signing, in effect, a bilateral FTA with China—a prospect that India considered and abandoned last decade. In deciding whether or not to join the RCEP, one of the government's chief concerns was whether such integration would flood Indian markets with cheap imports from China. A related fear was that it would worsen India's trade deficit with China—a deficit that touched $39 billion and constituted one-fifth of India's total trade deficit in 2012 (Sidhartha 2012a). The trade deficit with China remained a concern at the RCEP meeting in New Delhi in December 2014 (Seth 2014). Indian private sector has little enthusiasm for such a deal.

Second, the flexibility associated with 'the ASEAN way' can cut both ways: on the one hand, it offers countries the opportunity to liberalize at their own pace, keeping their sensitive sectors protected. This attracts less developed countries and offers wider membership. On the other, minimal liberalization and its flexibility caveats have a negative side: meaningful liberalization is slow and differential treatment allows countries to postpone necessary domestic reforms and sensitive industries to hide from increased competition. At the RCEP talks in December 2014, India, with some surprising support from China and South Korea, was able negotiate that only 42 per cent of its product lines would be subject to tariff elimination (Seth 2014).

Third, joining the RCEP would require that India brings down its tariffs further. While economists would argue that this is the positive and indeed, intended outcome of an FTA, the political challenges to tariff liberalization in India remain high. This is particularly true in the farm sector. It is important to note further that not all the ASEAN+1 agreements share a common level of ambition, similar tariff concessions, and cover every area of trade. Particularly for our purposes, it is important to note that the agricultural market access granted under the ASEAN–Australia–New Zealand FTA far exceeds that found in the ASEAN–India FTA. Tariff liberalization in the farm sector might be politically feasible only when there are some built in safeguards that can be used to protect against import surges.

While countries sign FTAs with the express intention of bringing down tariffs, Indian FTAs have managed to maintain higher average tariffs and longer exclusion lists than many in the region. For example, under the existing ASEAN–India Trade in Goods agreement, India has committed to eliminating tariffs on 78.8 per cent tariff lines. India initially anticipated that under RCEP, this threshold will need to be much higher (Hsu 2013: 49).[7] Further, the ASEAN–India FTA had 489 tariff lines in the negative list, out of which 302 were in farm products (Raju 2010).

The different agreements are also at different stages of negotiations—the ASEAN–India services agreement was adopted in September 2014 and will be effective from July 2015. This means that there is little data on gains from this agreement—something that would have provided a valuable argument to make a compelling economic and political case for further liberalization. The schedule for completion of the ASEAN Economic Community Blueprint, with an original deadline of December

2015, seems to have fallen behind (Balboa and Wignaraja 2014). This blueprint seeks to create an integrated economic region and its progress will likely determine the pace of RCEP negotiations (Das 2013: 8). Though apparently a negative, this might actually provide India more time to get ready to open up its economy further.

Fourth, there is widespread perception that while India offers a huge market, it is also a player whose demands are difficult to accommodate within an FTA framework. Wignaraja has singled out India as a possible 'stumbling block' to the RCEP negotiations on account of its hesitation to liberalize further (Wignaraja 2014: 94).[8] While all negotiators do their best to push national interest and Indian negotiators are no different, it poses an additional, if only perceptional, challenge for them.

Finally, and not least, RCEP poses some obvious political challenges for India's executive. For more than a decade now, Indian leaders have known that India needs to integrate further into the global economy if it were to develop faster, capitalize on its demographic dividend, and join the ranks of great powers. As a result, India's integration with the global economy has continued to increase: in 2013, the share of merchandise trade stood at 51 per cent of India's GDP (World Bank 2015). At the same time, Indian leaders have been keenly aware of the challenges of opening up, given an agricultural sector that is burdened with low productivity and numerous policy-related problems, a manufacturing sector that has not shown the kind of growth that catapulted China into an economic powerhouse and absorbed rural labour, and the numerous policy bottlenecks and political forces that made reform extremely difficult.

It is this last issue that this chapter primarily seeks to address. Based on India's past engagement with bilateral, regional, and multilateral trade negotiations, it would not be a stretch to assert that both agricultural and manufacturing sectors have been protectionist throughout the last couple of decades. While agriculture has been protectionist throughout, the manufacturing sector has, on occasion, put its support behind trade initiatives such as the India–EU FTA (during its initial phase), the Trade Facilitation Agreement, and so on. These positions, combined with India's federal system, successive coalition governments, and weak and divided leadership, have thwarted necessary reforms and slowed down the pace of trade liberalization. Is the past a good template for the future? The following section addresses the challenges and opportunities that will potentially shape India's position on liberalization in the farm sector and food processing. This, in turn, is likely going to play an important role in facilitating an ambitious liberalization agenda in RCEP since negotiations are all about trade-offs in different sectors. I argue that India's negotiating position in agriculture has been largely shaped by multiple problems faced by the farm sector throughout the 1990s and early 2000s, as well as by the political factors discussed above. Some of these problems persist to this day. And yet, in recent years, there are indications that India is emerging as a major exporter of agricultural commodities and has huge potential for exporting processed food. Given these changes, how should India's position on trade liberalization in the farm sector respond in the context of the RCEP negotiations?

Political Economy of India's Negotiating Position in the Farm Sector

We begin this section with an account of the economic and political factors that have, thus far, shaped India's negotiating position on trade in agriculture. India's position on trade liberalization in farm goods has not changed very much in the last ten years. Regardless of negotiations, the focus has been on limiting market access for others' farm product. While at the multilateral level, India has joined other developing countries in fighting farm subsidies in developed countries, protecting its resource-poor farmers has been one of the cornerstones of its negotiating position at that level—indeed, India has been at the receiving end of severe opprobrium on account of its strong stand on this issue (Gupta and Ganguly 2014). That remains the key negotiating position at the regional and bilateral levels as well. This section elaborates the reasons behind such a position.

During the 1990s, certain broad trends in the farm sector emerged. First, the growth of the sector slowed down after the initial spurt of growth in the 1980s as a result of the Green Revolution. Overall annual growth in production in the sector declined from 3.72 per cent in the 1980s to 2.29 per cent in the 1990s. Annual growth in food grain production declined more precipitously from 3.54 per cent during the 1980s to 1.92 per cent during the 1990s. Annual productivity growth declined as well: overall growth in farm productivity declined from 2.99 per cent to 1.21 per cent while that in food grain fell from 3.33 per cent to 1.32 per cent during the same period. The Tenth Five Year plan identified several problems that afflicted the farm sector in India. Chief among them were low public investment in creating and maintaining infrastructure for the sector, supplying necessary inputs, supplying credit to the sector, and reforming the policy framework on marketing, processing, and exporting agricultural products (Planning Commission 2002: 514–24).

Second, rural incomes remained stagnant during the 1990s. In part, this was due to the decelerating growth in agriculture—agriculture plays a significant role in reducing poverty in rural India (Planning Commission 2002: 524). The government was apprehensive that it would face pressure from the Doha Round negotiations to open its markets and that 'without speedy domestic market reforms, an opportunity to capture world markets would be converted into a threat to the future growth of Indian agriculture' (Planning Commission 2002). The specific domestic reforms that were identified as necessary were those on 'movement, marketing, credit, stock and export' of agricultural products because these affected the latter's profitability.

Third, the problems above need be seen in the context of the composition of the Indian agricultural sector at the time. The 2001 census found 127 million farming units in India. Of these, over 80 per cent were small and marginal farms. A majority of these farms operate at the level of subsistence but they also generate an income for themselves by selling surpluses in the market place when the harvest is good. Policymakers encountered a further problem: a large section of the workforce was employed in agriculture but its share of contribution to the GDP continued to fall faster than the shrinkage in the farm workforce. This story was consistent with declining productivity and income.

The 1990s' experiences as well as scholarly commentary left policymakers with a few take aways: one, the growth in the rice–wheat agriculture model associated with the Green Revolution had plateaued. Growth along with farm incomes had fallen sharply. Two, future growth in Indian agriculture would depend on diversification of agricultural production, processing, and marketing of food. The latter also promised increases in farmers' incomes. Policymakers were also aware that this change in focus would require policy reforms in several issue areas and their execution would be full of challenges. The third take away was that employment in the farm sector needed to shrink faster and that the rural economy needed more non-farm jobs. It was also inevitable that some rural–urban migration would take place if manufacturing opportunities increased. Finally, all this would have to happen without dismantling the production system and the institutional framework put in place during and after the Green Revolution to ensure food security, since India has over 1 billion mouths to feed. Although poverty has declined during the last couple of decades, the number of people living under the poverty line has remained large. According to World Bank figures, the number of people who lived in poverty was over 420 million in 2004 and declined to over 285 million in 2011.[9]

While the central government in New Delhi had to take these constraints into consideration when formulating its policy position, the overall direction of the trade negotiation brief emerged as a result of inputs, threats, and negotiating tactics of state-level bureaucracies and politicians with regional support bases. Despite rapid urbanization over the past decade, a majority of the Indian population continues to be rural. Farming provides the backbone of this rural economy—no Indian politician wants to be perceived as anti-farmer. State bureaucrats also claim to represent the interests of small and marginal farmers, who, as a result of collective action problems, have no real spokesperson.[10] Large plantation-based sectors, however, have established channels through which they express their interests. In case of the ASEAN–India FTA, farm interests representing the plantation sector were the most vocal opponents of liberalization— tea, pepper, coffee, and crude and refined palm oil remained in the special product category designated for lower tariff cuts. Potential imports from China, Vietnam, Indonesia, and Malaysia were the sources of fear. Even as talks on RCEP have begun, opposition from farmers' groups have re-emerged (IANS 2014). But the overall focus on protection has as much to do with politicians' and bureaucrats' world-views and interests as those of interest groups. The focus on protecting small farmers on the one hand and the pressure of protecting specific crops or sectors on the other have fused into a negotiating position that is overwhelmingly protectionist.

Central Government Responses: Protection and Policy Reform

As a result of these political and economic factors, the Government of India responded in two ways—at the international level, policymakers crafted a negotiating brief that focused on protecting poor farmers, and at the domestic level, they tried to encourage states to adopt a more liberal and updated policy regime in any area that affected the farm sector. Such a negotiating position was initially articulated during the Indo-Sri Lanka

FTA negotiations and then at the negotiations on agriculture at the WTO. Even though policymakers recognized potential exporting interests in the farm sector, these were never placed front and centre. The main goal of Indian negotiators has been to minimize tariff reduction in farm products and to minimize market opening so that India's small farmers could be protected from fluctuations in global commodity prices or from import surges. The operating philosophy is that unless a product is unavailable in India and is of importance to consumers, India will not import it.[11] Not only was India's negotiating position in the WTO defensive, even while negotiating a free trade agreement with Singapore, which has no agriculture sector of its own, a large number of farm products were kept in the exclusion or negative list. In the ASEAN–India FTA, several products were placed under a 'sensitive' and a 'highly sensitive' track, several were designated as special products, and over 300 were kept in the negative list. It was clear to policymakers that with crop diversification and forward linkages to organized retail and processing facilities, farmers could earn higher incomes. However, for farmers to earn higher incomes, the government needed to carry out reforms and such reforms needed time. Until such reforms were put in place, the farmers had to be protected.

At the domestic level, the government tried to encourage updating and liberalizing policy regimes on agricultural marketing, food retail, land acquisition, input access, and related areas. Though it has been clear for some time that the grain cultivation model had plateaued, concern for food security and the existing incentive structure for farmers prevented any real change in this part of the farm sector. The farmers in the main agricultural states such as Punjab and Haryana have stuck to grain cultivation because the government offers minimum support prices and procures directly from them.[12] During the last decade, farmers have responded to higher prices in other commodities by shifting cultivation to cotton, fruits, and vegetables but the latter do not enjoy the same level of safety net and incentive as grain cultivation does. When cotton and other crops fail or prices fall, news reports of farmers' suicides lay bare the rather precarious existence of the Indian farm community. Although moving away from the rice–wheat cultivation system is perceived as necessary, the process of abandoning it has not been smooth.

In order to facilitate the process, the central government's attention shifted to bringing reforms in agriculture and related areas such as marketing, land acquisition, and so on. Although these reforms began at different points in time during the last decade, most of them remain incomplete. To take the example of agricultural marketing, reforming marketing laws has been a challenge since under Indian federal structure, the central government's power to change marketing policies and infrastructure is limited to knowledge dissemination, persuasion, and providing incentives through national schemes. The real jurisdiction for policy change remains with state governments. The central government reached out to the latter with a model marketing act in 2003 and the states subsequently responded by picking the parts of the model that were consistent with their interests as well as that of their main farming constituency. Therefore, Punjab, where regulated markets bring large revenue to the state exchequer, refused to dilute the power of its market boards. Other states restricted contract farming. The result was a patchwork of marketing reforms across state borders that continued to offer an uncertain and discontinuous policy regime for movement, distribution, marketing, and contract farming across state borders for food processors and retailers.

This variation and unpredictability in marketing frameworks, coupled with restrictions on foreign direct investment in the retail sector, limited the opportunity for growth for the farm and food processing sector. Domestic private players were extremely cautious about making necessary large investments such as setting up farm-to-fork cold–chains that would facilitate the diversification of the rice–wheat system into fruits, vegetables, and other products. A cold chain would maintain quality and freshness and increase shelf-life and enable food processing. Many domestic business houses that went into agricultural marketing soon folded their ventures. Some such as Reliance Fresh, Spencers, and others soldiered on and continue to occupy pockets in urban areas.

Finally, the government had invited large players in the food processing and retail sectors, with the expectation that larger private investments would help transform the sector rapidly. Such structural transformation would also absorb excess labour from the farms into manufacturing (food processing) and service (food retail) sectors. Historically, in western countries, small farmers, sharecroppers, and agricultural labourers have found employment in the manufacturing sector as well as in infrastructure construction as traditional, farm-based economies have transformed into industrial economies. Such transformations have usually taken place during periods when the manufacturing sector has grown rapidly, creating employment opportunities for those who have been displaced from the farm sector. In India, manufacturing growth remained anaemic during the last decade (Ministry of Commerce and Industry 2011). The National Manufacturing Policy posits that while India has not been able to fully leverage the opportunities provided by globalization, this low growth 'also has attendant socio economic manifestations in terms of over dependence of a large section of the population on agriculture for its livelihood, disguised unemployment and urban unemployment' (Ministry of Commerce and Industry 2011: 2). The low growth in manufacturing is a product of lack of necessary reforms in the manufacturing and service sectors. One example of absence of timely reform is the attempt to increase FDI in multi-brand retail to more than 51 per cent. After an attempt in 2011 that failed as a result of coalition politics, the Congress-led United Progressive Alliance government was able to change the rules on this issue in 2012 (ET Bureau 2012). However, the central government left the implementation of the rule on states, which again decided to play to their respective constituencies.

Insufficient Transformation

Despite the uneven, halting, and problem-ridden reform and structural transformation process, some indicators have begun to show change. Although the farm sector continued to employ 54.6 per cent of the workforce, the total number of farmers started to show a decline—from 127.3 million in 2001 to 118.7 million in 2011. At the same time, the contribution of the sector to India's GDP continued to fall as well—from 15.2 per cent during the 11th Plan (2007–8 to 2011–12) to 13.9 per cent in 2013–14 (Department of Economic Affairs 2014).

During the last decade, the agricultural sector has indeed been going through faster diversification of products. India's export basket has been changing rapidly. Rice, corn, cotton, meat, and guar gum have replaced traditional exports such as tea and spices. Farm exports grew by 5.1 per cent between 2012–13 and 2013–14. Farm exports as a percentage of GDP have increased from 1.6 per cent in 2007–8 to 2.2 per cent in 2011–12 (Department of Agriculture and Cooperation 2014: 113). Marine product export increased by 44.8 per cent during the same period (Department of Economic Affairs 2014: 154). India has emerged as the seventh largest agricultural exporter globally and its farm exports have

grown from $5 billion in 2003 to $39 billion in 2013 (USDA 2014).
Indian agricultural producers have found markets for their products in
some ASEAN countries. Buffalo meat exports to ASEAN have increased
from 276 thousand metric tons in 2010–11 to 872.5 thousand metric
tons in 2013–14 (more than 200 per cent growth) as its value has gone
up 250 per cent. Rice—both Basmati and non-Basmati—exports have
gone up as well but the increase does not show a steady pattern—rice
is exported only after domestic demand is met (APEDA 2015). On
the other hand, despite being on a list of products that were to undergo
modest liberalization, pepper and palm oil imports from ASEAN states
have increased remarkably (Department of Agriculture and Cooperation
2015).

The government has taken initiative for setting up food-related
infrastructure such as food parks and cold chains.[13] Although food parks
have also demonstrated some teething trouble, the current government
has sought to establish seventeen new parks in an effort to encourage and
attract private players in food processing and marketing (PTI 2015). The
food processing sector has been growing at an average annual rate of 8.4
per cent. However, the industry started from a low base—the level of
processing in India still remains low as a result of inadequate post-harvest
infrastructure and the lack of technology (Ministry of Food Processing
Industries 2014). The sector also faces challenges posed by a new and
evolving regulatory regime. The discussion in this section shows that
while there have been sectoral and episodic improvements in the farm
sector, the transformation discussed in the previous section remains far
from complete. There are still too many vulnerable, low-income, resource-
poor farmers in India for policymakers to promise opening up without
some protection against sudden import surges and without opportunities
in the manufacturing and services sectors for absorbing excess labour.

Conclusion and Policy Prescriptions

India's negotiating position on farm trade has remained defensive during
the past fifteen years. A farm sector made up of a large number of small,
subsistence farmers, systemic policy and infrastructure problems, and
political hurdles that stand in the way of change have all contributed to this
position. Marketing and other reforms in agriculture have been episodic,
fitful, and incomplete, creating a mosaic of rules across the country and

not the barrier-free national market that the Committee on Agricultural Reforms recommended in 2013. While reform has remained a challenge, the sector has been going through a quiet transformation, if only sporadically. It is clear that given the size of population living in poverty, self-sufficiency in grain production and focus on agriculture as a source of livelihood security for farmers will remain a priority for decades to come. However, at the same time, a large number of farmers have been switching to other crops and both production and exports have been diversifying. How can trade policy reflect the interests of both these sets of farmers? In order to speed up this partial transformation, this chapter recommends reforms in issue areas that affect agriculture—namely land rights, marketing, insurance, distribution, credit—which need to be completed to facilitate higher incomes generation in the farm sector. Given the poverty and the uncertainty, the safety net for farmers needs to be strengthened so that the human and social cost of this transformation is minimal. At the same time, as more farmers and their offsprings leave the farm, reforms that likely have a positive impact on manufacturing and services will need to be speeded up as well. These reforms are also necessary so that agriculture can be linked in the front end to processing and retail and that will lead to lower wastage, higher incomes, and higher exports. The processing sector needs technology, infrastructure, as well as new India-wide norms.

While the environment that produced India's initial bargaining position in the agricultural negotiations has not changed substantially, it is necessary that policymakers recognize these problems and re-examine the earlier negotiating positions in the light of export growth in the farm sector. The government should evaluate earlier negotiating positions and see where India might have more flexibility. There is a need to re-examine every crop sector and also the assumptions under which the government eases imports and exports.

There is an urgent need for the government to build infrastructure such as cold chain, roads, ports, and airports that would enable the movement of farm products and food so that farmers are better integrated into a market economy that allows them to earn higher incomes. While pursuing higher incomes is a worthwhile goal, it is necessary to recognize that farmers will need support to navigate this transformation. The above cannot happen without help from the government to set up better crop insurance and other tools for remediation, should prices and/or output fluctuate.

It is necessary to reformulate India's negotiating position on agriculture weighing its defensive and aggressive interests more evenly. This can be done by evaluating the impact of previous FTAs on farm trade and identifying where Indian producers have built or discovered a comparative advantage and what specific tariff and non-tariff hurdles they have faced. There needs to be greater focus on finding interim measures to help farmers and their families go through this structural transformation. Instead of imposing blanket bans in importing farm products, the focus should be on better monitoring of prices so that in case of price drops and import surges, the government can undertake measures to protect its most vulnerable. The government should negotiate such safeguard mechanisms in trade agreements.

Finally, policymakers should give due consideration to the evolving architecture in trade. While the TPP has yet to be ratified and the TTIP negotiations are not yet complete, these negotiations are influencing India's partners in RCEP both directly and otherwise. How the regional and global trade architecture will evolve depends much on China's willingness to join the TPP and the U.S.'s enthusiasm for its entrance. But both have shown interest in creating a Free Trade Area of the Asia–Pacific. While most of these milestones are some years away, Indian policymakers and trade stakeholders might want to consider using the RCEP as a stepping stone for gradual yet meaningful integration into the region's economy.

Notes

1. For a full list, see Department of Commerce 2015a.

2. According to the Asian Regional Integration Centre's FTA database, the total number of free trade agreements, either completed or under negotiation, involving at least one Asian country has increased from 51 in 2000 to 215 in 2015.

3. These include Australia, China, India, Japan, New Zealand and South Korea. In addition, individual ASEAN states have entered into numerous bilateral trade agreements.

4. Interviews with government officials, members of business associations, and academia in New Delhi, August–September 2015.

5. It is negotiating FTAs with Australia and New Zealand but the resistance to one with China is very high.

6. The 'ASEAN way' is seen as an approach to regionalism: it places an emphasis on the principle of consultation, seeking consensus and harmony, non-confrontation and agreeability. See, for example, Narine (1997).

7. However, during negotiations India has pushed for a smaller opening against China.

8. These sentiments have been echoed by other Washington DC-based policy analysts who work in the area of Asian integration.

9. These figures are approximate, based on World Bank Indicators. The author calculated these poverty numbers using Indian population figures from 2001 and 2011 and the World Bank's poverty headcount ratio at $1.25/day (Purchasing Power Parity). The source data on population was taken from the Ministry of Finance, Government of India, http://indiabudget.nic.in/budget2013-2014/es2012-13/estat1.pdf and the data on poverty rate (poverty headcount ratio at $1.25 a day) was taken from World Bank, India, http://data.worldbank.org/country/india#cp_wdi.

10. Interest articulation in the Indian farm sector is shared by several stakeholders. For more details, see Gupta 2011: 58–60.

11. Interview with official in Department of Agriculture, New Delhi, March 2015.

12. Interview with senior bureaucrat in the Ministry of Agriculture, Punjab, in Chandigarh, July 2012.

13. Food parks provide the infrastructure such as warehouses, cold chain, research, and processing facilities in one location. The goal is to bring together farmers, processors, and retailers and link agricultural production to the market so as to maximize value addition, minimize wastage, and improve farm income. See, for example, Ministry of Food Processing Industries 2014: 37.

References

Agricultural and Processed Food Products Export Development Authority (APEDA). 2015. 'AgriExchange'; available at http://agriexchange.apeda.gov.in/indexp/genReport_combined.aspx (accessed 14 December 2015).

Asian Regional Integration Centre. 2015. FTA Database. Available at http://aric.adb.org/fta (accessed 11 May 2015).

Athukorala, Prema-chandra. 2008. 'Singapore and ASEAN in the New Regional Division of Labor', *The Singapore Economic Review*, 53(3): 479–508.

Balboa, Jenny D. and Ganeshan Wignaraja. 2014. 'ASEAN Economic Community 2015: What is next?'; available at http://www.asiapathways-adbi.org/2014/12/asean-economic-community-2015-what-is-next/ (accessed 11 May 2015).

Banga, Rashmi and Pritish Kumar Sahu. 2015. 'Trans Pacific Partnership Agreement (TPPA): Implications for India's Trade and Investment', Working Paper, New Delhi: Centre for WTO Studies. Available at http://wtocentre.iift.ac.in/workingpaper/Trans%20Pacific%20Partnership%20Agreement_Implications%20for%20India.pdf (accessed 15 October 2015).

Bergsten, C. Fred. 2015. *India's Rise: A Strategy for Trade-Led Growth*. Washington, D.C.: Peterson Institute for International Economics. Available at http://www.piie.com/publications/briefings/piieb15-4.pdf (accessed 2 October 2015).

Das, Sanchita Basu. 2013. 'RCEP and TPP: Comparisons and Concerns', *ISEAS Perspective*; available at http://www.iseas.edu.sg/documents/publication/ISEAS%20Perspective%202013_2.pdf (accessed 11 May 2015).

Department of Agriculture and Cooperation, Government of India. 2013. *State of Indian Agriculture 2012–2013*; available at http://agricoop.nic.in/Annual%20report2012-13/ARE2012-13.pdf (accessed 11 May 2015).

———. 2015. *India's Agriculture Trade Policy and Status Under Trade Agreements*. Available at http://agricoop.nic.in/imagedefault/trade/trade1922014.pdf (accessed 11 May 2015).

Department of Commerce, Government of India. 2015a. *Trade Agreements*. Available at http://commerce.nic.in/MOC/international_trade_agreements.asp (accessed 11 May 2015).

———. 2015b. *Brief on Regional Comprehensive Economic Partnership*. Available at http://commerce.nic.in/trade/international_ta_current_details.asp (accessed 11 May 2015).

Department of Economic Affairs, Government of India. 2014. *Economic Survey, 2013–14*. Available at http://indiabudget.nic.in/es2013-14/echap-08.pdf (accessed 11 May 2015).

ET Bureau. 2012. 'UPA Unleashes Big-Ticket Economic Reforms: India Inc Cheers FDI in Retail, Aviation and Power Exchanges', *The Economic Times*, 15 September; available at http://articles.economictimes.indiatimes.com/2012-09-15/news/33862902_1_multi-brand-policy-paralysis-single-brand (accessed 11 May 2015).

Foreign Agricultural Service, United States Department of Agriculture (USDA). 2014. *India Sees Surge in Agricultural Exports to Least Developed Countries*. Available at http://www.fas.usda.gov/data/india-sees-surge-agriculturalexports-least-developed-countries.

Hiebert, Murray and Liam Hanlon. 2012. *ASEAN and Partners Launch Regional Comprehensive Economic Partnership*. Center for Strategic and International Studies. Available at http://csis.org/publication/asean-and-partners-launch-regional-comprehensive-economic-partnership (accessed 11 May 2015).

Gupta, Surupa. 2011. 'The Politics of Fertilizer Supply to Agriculture: Analysis of Political Actors, Discourses and Strategies' in Regina Birner, Surupa Gupta, and Neeru Sharma (eds), *The Political Economy of Agricultural Policy Reforms in India: Fertilizers and Electricity for Irrigation*. Washington DC: International Food Processing Research Institute.

Gupta, Surupa and Sumit Ganguly. 2014. 'Modi Bets the Farm', *Foreign Affairs*, 12 August; available at https://www.foreignaffairs.com/articles/india/2014-08-12/modi-bets-farm (accessed on 11 May 2015).

Hill, Hal and Maria Socorro Gochoco-Bautista. 2013. 'Perspectives and Issues', in Hal Hill and Maria Socorro Gochoco-Bautista (eds), *Asia Rising: Growth and Resilience in an Uncertain Global Economy*, pp. 3–47. Cheltenham: Edward Elgar/Asian Development Bank.

Hsu, Kristy. 2013. 'The RCEP: Integrating India into the Asian Economy', *Indian Foreign Affairs Journal*, 8(1): 41–51.

Indo-Asian News Service (IANS). 2014. 'Farmers, Trade Unions Urge Government to Halt RCEP Negotiations', *Business Standard*, 29 November; available at http://www.business-standard.com/article/news-ians/farmers-trade-unions-urge-government-to-halt-rcep-negotiations-114112900592_1.html (accessed 11 May 2015).

Kharas, Homi. 2010. 'The Emerging Middle Class in Developing Countries', Working Paper 285, Paris: OECD Development Centre. Available at http://www.oecd.org/dev/44457738.pdf (accessed 11 May 2015).

Ministry of Commerce and Industry, Government of India. 2015. *National Manufacturing Policy*. New Delhi. Available at http://www.dipp.nic.in/English/policies/National_Manufacturing_Policy_25October2011.pdf (accessed 11 May 2015).

Ministry of Food Processing Industries, Government of India. 2014. *Annual Report, 2013–2014*. Available at http://mofpi.nic.in/H_Dwld.aspx?KYEwmOL+HGpoo8DlNeKVV3fE4aW5+awTGdnZC9kP6Bhp7nsZwxLmTQ== (accessed 11 May 2015) .

Mishra, Rahul. 2013. 'RCEP: Challenges and Opportunities for India', RSIS Commentaries no. 140, 25 July. Available at http://www.rsis.edu.sg/wp-content/uploads/2014/07/CO13140.pdf (accessed 11 May 2015).

Moinuddin, Mustafa. 2013. 'Economic Integration and Trade Liberalization in South Asia', *Asia Pathways*, 27 August. Available at http://www.asiapathways-adbi.org/2013/08/economic-integration-and-trade-liberalization-in-south-asia/ (accessed 11 May 2015).

Nakamura, David. 2015. 'Deal Reached on Pacific Rim Trade Pact in Boost for Obama Economic Agenda', *Washington Post*, 6 October. Available at http://www.washingtonpost.com/business/economy/deal-reached-on-pacific-

rim-trade-pact/2015/10/05/7c567f00-6b56-11e5-b31c-d80d62b53e28_
story.html (accessed 27 October 2015).

Narine, Shaun. 1997.'ASEAN and the ARF: The Limits of the "ASEAN Way"',
Asian Survey, 37(10): 961–78.

Palit, Amitendu. 2014. 'Regional Supply Chains in Asia: Examining India's
Presence and Possibilities in the RCEP', working paper, New Delhi: Centre
for WTO Studies.

Planning Commission. 2002. *Tenth Five Year Plan*. Available at http://planning
commission.gov.in/plans/planrel/fiveyr/10th/volume2/v2_ch5_1.pdf
(accessed 11 May 2015).

Press Trust of India (PTI). 2015.'Narendra Modi Govt. Allocates 17 Mega Food
Parks to States, Pvt. Firms', *Financial Express*, 24 March; available at http://
www.financialexpress.com/article/economy/narendra-modi-govt-allocates-
17-mega-food-parks-to-states-pvt-firms/56918/ (accessed 11 May 2015).

Raju, Sunitha. 2010. 'ASEAN–India FTA: Emerging Issues for Trade in
Agriculture', Working Paper, New Delhi: Indian Institute of Foreign Trade.
Available at http://agritrade.iift.ac.in/html/Training/ASEAN%20%E2%
80%93%20India%20FTA%20%20Emerging%20Issues%20for%20
Trade%20in%20Agriculture/Sunita%20Raju%20mam.pdf (accessed 11
May 2015).

Salze-Lozac'h, Véronique, Nina Merchant-Vega, Katherine Loh, and Sarah
Alexander. 2013. 'Regional Integration: Asia's New Frontier in 2013', *Asia
Foundation*; available at http://asiafoundation.org/in-asia/2013/01/09/
regional-integration-asias-new-frontier-in-2013/ (accessed 11 May 2015).

Seth, Dilasha. 2014.'India Offers to Remove Duty on 40% of Product Lines for
15 Countries at RCEP', *Economic Times*, 8 December; available at http://
articles.economictimes.indiatimes.com/2014-12-08/news/56839571_1_
rcep-10-asean-countries-trade-pact (accessed 11 May 2015).

Sidhartha. 2012a. 'India Gets China Jitters at ASEAN', *The Times of India*, 1
November; available at http://timesofindia.indiatimes.com/business/
india-business/India-gets-China-jitters-at-Asean/articleshow/17027594.
cms (accessed 11 May 2015).

Sidhartha. 2012b. 'India set to Join Talks for Largest Trade Bloc', *The Times of
India*, 9 November; accessed via Factiva.

Singh, Harsha V. 2014. *Trans–Pacific Partnership Agreement: Its Impact on India
and Other Developing Nations*. Manitoba, Canada: International Institute
for Sustainable Development, 12 July. Available at https://www.iisd.org/
publications/trans-pacific-partnership-agreement-its-impact-india-and-
other-developing-nations (accessed 2 October 2015).

Wignaraja, Ganeshan. 2014. 'The Regional Comprehensive Economic Partnership: an Initial Assessment', in Tang Guoqiang and Peter A. Petri (eds), *New Directions in Asia Pacific Economic Integration*, pp. 93–105. Honolulu, HI: East–West Center.

World Bank. 2015. *Data: Merchandise Trade*. Available at http://data.worldbank. org/indicator/TG.VAL.TOTL.GD.ZS.

8 Motor Vehicle Movement and Standards between Bangladesh and India

Regional Connectivity and Trade

Bipul Chatterjee and Prithviraj Nath

India and Bangladesh are two important economies of South Asia and have been growing rapidly. As a small country with a large population, Bangladesh is largely dependent on goods and services from other countries. India on the other hand is a hefty producer and possesses a greater possibility for trade with Bangladesh. Current bilateral trade between both countries is U.S.$5.5 billion (2012–13) of which Bangladesh majorly exports apparel, textile fibre, and fruits and nuts. India majorly exports raw cotton, cereals, vehicles, and machinery boilers.

Though India and Bangladesh are closely associated with each other, trade volume between the two countries forms only a small part of their total trade. It is well known that various non-tariff barriers have increased the cost of doing trade between both countries, affecting the feasibility of trade in many high potential products. Trade is held back by restrictive domestic policies, lack of intra-regional cooperation, and inefficient procedures for trade documentation and clearance. Out of these issues, the major constraints leading to lesser bilateral trade and competitiveness are the problems of logistics, trade practices, lack of a cross-border transport and transit agreement, and infrastructure.

Both countries have considered trade and transport facilitation measures aiming to reduce current physical and non-physical barriers to transportation and transit; however, the costs of intra-regional movement of goods between the two countries are increasingly becoming critical. Various studies exist on this issue and they have argued that while poor quality of physical infrastructure is an issue, trade competitiveness and growth are also majorly affected by high transaction costs caused by non-tariff policy and institutional constraints, such as red tape, inadequate enforcement of contracts, poor definition and enforcement of rules of engagement, asymmetry in standards, delays in customs, ports, and border crossings, pilferage (stealing of goods in small quantities) in transit, corruption, and highly restrictive protocols on movement of cargo. These factors also contribute to the very high amount of informal trade between India and Bangladesh.

The present chapter discusses the rationale for a motor vehicle and standards related agreement between India and Bangladesh in the context of broader regional connectivity and trade. It starts with a rationale for these agreements, discusses their policy implications, practical issues with their implementation, and finally includes recommendations towards pushing for change in the bilateral as well as regional context.

Need for Motor Vehicle Agreement

India and Bangladesh do not have a provision for motor vehicles to move across their border in order to transport goods. Presently the arrangement at the border points is that of transhipment, under which trucks of either country can only venture up to an agreed upon distance within the other's territory to unload goods. Issues like procedural delays, infrastructure bottlenecks (particularly parking and warehousing facilities, and the security of the cargo in such facilities), corruption, and governance issues are compounded and complicated by the fact that major transhipment activities happen at the border points. The infrastructure and operations machinery required under such arrangements are complicated and fraught with pitfalls, thereby enhancing the delays and cost to trade. Replacing the large scale transhipment operations with easy movement of vehicles across the borders via a motor vehicle agreement between the countries can help in effectively bypassing many of these hurdles.

Free movement of vehicles across the border and hence an agreement to this end is very important from the point of trade and connectivity between India and Bangladesh. The countries share a 2,429 km land border through which road and rail connectivity can take place and can play an important role in the trade scenario. Approximately 70 per cent of trade between the two countries happens through land routes. If cross-border vehicle movement is facilitated through a bilateral/regional Motor Vehicle Agreement, it would lead to substantial reduction in cost and time taken to complete the transaction, enhancing trade and competitiveness of firms.

The total length of the Kolkata–Dhaka corridor through Petrapole/Benapole and Jessore is 350 km. Petrapole, which is about 95 km from Kolkata, is the final transhipment area for commodities coming from across the country that are carried over to Bangladesh. At the Petrapole land customs station, which is the busiest border trade point between the countries, an average of 250 to 300 trucks per day carry Indian exports to Bangladesh, comprising rice, fertilizers, raw materials for chemical and apparel industries, and manufactured goods including tires and iron and steel articles. Only 40 to 50 trucks handle imports from Bangladesh to India, which is mostly comprised of jute products, betel nut, and fish. Even on poor roads, the distance can be covered by a truck in about 10 hours if there are no barriers or any other hindrance. The average time taken to complete the transaction including processing and crossing over at the border point varies from 5–7 days to 15–20 days. While perishable commodities like fish can complete the entire transaction in less than eight hours (Benapole/Petrapole border crossing to Kolkata markets), some others take a lot more time. Delays are caused not only by documentation and infrastructure related issues at the border crossing, but also by a lack of local political buy-in for speedy release of cargo vehicles given that the local border economy partly thrives on rent seeking, which these delays foster. Additionally, there are bottlenecks all along the corridor due to high congestion and encroachments on the road. Overall, corridor efficiency is quite low.

A Motor Vehicles Agreement has the potential to become a key policy instrument enabling a higher volume of cross-border trade between Bangladesh and India. This would improve corridor efficiency and provide incentives and opportunities for the transportation industry to invest more. It would also lead to greater containerization of the corridor. Along with the adoption of scanning, risk management, and documentary automation by customs, this could greatly increase corridor efficiency.

A number of regional cooperation organizations, including the Association of Southeast Asian Nations (ASEAN), the Andean

Community, and the Southern African Development Community (SADC), have transit or transport agreements among the member countries. Similar regional agreements could be particularly beneficial for countries like India and Bangladesh as they provide a comprehensive framework of harmonized procedures through which countries can gain access to transit facilities. The Greater Mekong Subregional Cross-Border Transport Agreement (GMS CBTA) is one good example, as it includes many elements of international instruments in the field of transport and transit facilitation and is a single comprehensive legal instrument that includes all of the non-physical measures for cross-border land transport. The main CBTA agreement has been ratified by all six GMS nations.

Furthermore, considering other regional and sub-regional economic and political negotiations, such an agreement will prove to be an enabler for greater connectivity in Eastern South Asia and further with the ASEAN group of countries. In the more recent times, given the changed political scenario in many countries of South Asia, a higher buy-in and push for greater trade and investment connectivity in the region is palpable. Ongoing negotiations between Bangladesh, Bhutan, India, and Nepal (BBIN) for a sub-regional motor vehicles agreement, between India, Myanmar, and Thailand for another sub-regional motor vehicles agreement, the emergence of the Regional Comprehensive Economic Partnership (RCEP) negotiations, and sixteen countries of Asia and the Pacific (the 10-member group of the ASEAN plus Australia, China, India, Japan, New Zealand, and South Korea) have created a positive space for better connectivity and integration of the region. Higher connectivity between India and Bangladesh will be a key and crucial enabler towards the larger regional integration negotiations and plans. Better connectivity between these two countries is also expected to help the sub-region to link itself to other regional connectivity projects like the ASEAN Master Plan for Connectivity (AMPC) project, Kaladan Multimodal Transit Transport Project, and the Bangladesh–China – India–Myanmar (BCIM) Economic Corridor project. A more connected and integrated sub-region will mean access to incremental economic benefits via connecting with other blocs and regions/sub-regions like the Bay of Bengal Initiative for Multi-Sectoral Technical and Economic Cooperation (BIMSTEC), BCIM, and ASEAN, which in turn is expected to have positive spill-over effects on other areas of cooperation leading to greater peace, security, and stability in the greater Indo-Pacific region.

Need for Bilateral Agreement on Standards

The trade baskets of India and Bangladesh mostly contain agricultural and primary products which require testing and verification for the safety and protection of human beings, plants, and animals. Such standards, required to safeguard consumer interest, have often resulted in hindrances to bilateral trade between India and Bangladesh. Various sanitary and phyto-sanitary (SPS) measures which may act as non-tariff barriers (NTBs) include plant quarantine requirements, bio-security testing, and hygiene and sanitary permits among other things. Such testing and certification requirements are further complicated by the fact that testing facilities are mostly unavailable at the border points. Instead, they are found at major cities, a considerable distance away from the border points. This in turn causes the stranding of vehicles at the borders to fulfil certification and testing norms, and further contributes to congestion and safety issues for the cargo in question.

SPS concerns are of high importance from the perspective of promoting and facilitating trade in the agriculture sector and from the point of food safety and security in both India and Bangladesh. In the case of Bangladeshi agricultural exports to India, there are SPS and bio-security requirements for getting import permits. Imports of almost all livestock, agriculture, and food products require some kind of SPS certificate and import permit under the general supervision of the Indian Ministry of Agriculture. Secondly, while exporting processed foods to India, Bangladeshi exporters have to comply with the Indian Food Safety and Standards Act 2006.

Raihan (2011) found that Bangladeshi exporters require submitting a pre-shipment inspection (PSI) certificate from a textiles testing laboratory accredited to the National Accreditation Agency of the country of origin (Bangladesh) in the case of export of textiles and textile products to India. If exporters are unable to provide a certificate then it requires testing from the notified agencies in India for each and every consignment. There have been instances of Bangladeshi traders complaining of complicated testing and certification issues. Reportedly, consignments consisting of items that are exported by Bangladeshi exporters to other markets like the EU have received certifications from laboratories accredited by EU agencies, but still they had to undergo testing at the border points for Indian markets. While such instances are not always substantiated by exact specifics of the particular circumstances, it is true that in the absence of harmonized standards, a testing regime, or a mutual recognition arrangement between India and Bangladesh, items that have implications on the safety of human, plant, and animal health have to be tested and certified before entry into India. In addition, the Textile (Consumer Protection) Regulation of 1988 imposes some strict marking requirements for yarns, fibres, and fabrics imported into India.

In the case of pharmaceutical products exported to India, for example, there are strict requirements of drug registration with the Central Drugs Standard Control Organization, which involves difficult and time consuming procedures. Foreign manufactures must register and subject their premises to inspection along the line of rules prepared by the Bureau of Indian Standards.

In the case of imports of animal products into India, sanitary import permits must be issued by the Department of Animal Husbandry, Dairying, and Fisheries. Permits must be obtained prior to shipping from the country of origin. Imports of plants and plant materials are regulated under the Destructive Insects and Pests Act 1914, the Plant Quarantine (PQ) (Regulation of Import into India) Order 2003, [1] and international conventions. All plant and plant material consignments must be accompanied by a phyto-sanitary certificate issued by the national plant protection organization of the exporting country and an import permit issued by the officer in charge of the plant quarantine station. Indian guidelines on standards do not consider certificates on standardization from the country of origin (unless there are specific agreements or policies to that end), therefore samples of the goods must be tested in Indian laboratories.

Similarly, some past studies show that Bangladesh is banning imports from India for some products. According to Trade Insights (SAWTEE 2012), Bangladesh is continuously banning imports of poultry products from India despite India having regained avian influenza free status. Under the Bangladesh Import Control Order (2009–12), some twenty-five products under four-digit Harmonized System (HS) code fall under the Control List. While Bangladesh has reduced its restricted list appreciably, this has been replaced by a text that lays down a host of conditions that need to be fulfilled before imports can be cleared by customs.

Notwithstanding the seemingly protectionist intent behind the application of such measures, there is room for much improvement in the quality of products supplied by Bangladesh. In general, Bangladesh faces problems in ensuring the quality of products and services to consumers not only in the domestic market but also in international markets. There is a lack of effective national quality policy and adequate support systems providing assistance to all enterprises to understand the principles of quality and to develop quality consciousness in business behaviour.

The National Standards and Testing Institution of Bangladesh lacks adequate infrastructure and technical facilities, and there are also problems related to administration and implementation. Because of a lack of reliability of national policy and enforcement mechanisms, there is a need for industry-specific initiatives to set up their own standards as per international requirements, and their own testing and compliance procedures. Bangladesh also needs to build its capacity to monitor the development and implications of SPS measures and other NTBs in association with other countries to ensure that rules are developed with the full participation of the concerned countries and do not impose excessive costs for unlikely risks. Under the World Trade Organization's (WTO) Aid for Trade Initiative, Bangladesh may seek aid to develop the necessary infrastructures and build the necessary capacities.

Potentially, accreditation bodies or agencies of India could set up accreditation centres in Dhaka in collaboration with a designated national agency of Bangladesh to facilitate mutual cooperation with necessary capacity-building and mutual technical and financial assistance. Non-acceptability of conformity assessment certificates of any particular product, if and when these issues arise, should be resolved by mutual cooperation programmes without restricting its trade.

In this direction, the upcoming South Asian Regional Standards Organization (SARSO) meeting in Dhaka is a very welcome step. The Agreement on the Establishment of SARSO entered into force with effect from 25 August 2011 after ratification by all member States of South Asian Association for Regional Countries (SAARC). Following this, SARSO started its operations, effective 3 April 2014. SARSO has been established to achieve and enhance coordination and cooperation among SAARC member states in the fields of standardization and conformity assessment and is aimed to develop harmonized standards for the region to facilitate intra-regional trade and to have access in the global market.

Its objectives include, among others, harmonization of national standards of the SAARC Member States, developing SAARC standards on the products of regional/sub-regional interest, promoting cooperation with the relevant international and regional organizations, facilitating exchange of information, expertise, and capacity-building among the Member States in the fields of Standardization and Conformity Assessment, promoting Mutual Recognition Arrangements (MRAs) on Conformity Assessment Procedures among the Member States, and exploring the possibility of having a common mark of conformity among the Member States (SARSO 2015).

It is hoped that SARSO will help address many of the issues faced by traders in both countries owing to lack of border infrastructure, inadequate cross-border banking facilities, and lack of mutual recognition of standards and accreditation of testing laboratories. SARSO also has nine Sectoral Technical Committees catering to nine different sectors for which regional standards are being developed. So far thirty products have been identified by SARSO for harmonization of standards. The SAARC Agreement on Multilateral Arrangement on Recognition of Conformity Assessment, and the SAARC Agreement on Implementation of the Regional Standards, have been finalized and were later signed during the 17th SAARC Summit held in Maldives on 10–11 November 2011. Both of these agreements will come into effect after ratification by all member nations. So far five member nations have done so. Under the agreement on recognition of conformity assessment it has been proposed that test certificates issued by all laboratories that are accredited by internationally accepted accreditation agencies will also be accepted by member nations. Such recognition after appropriate accreditation needs to be expedited along with enhancing the ambit of SARSO's work. It is important to look at standards from a more regional point of view that takes into account the needs and aspirations of South Asia as a region. India and Bangladesh should choose to adopt international standards or regionally accepted standards, which in turn will create equal opportunities for all importers.

Policy Implications and Concerns: Transport and Transit Facilitation

Transport and transit facilitation between India and Bangladesh continues to be a debated and important issue. The progress of negotiations has been rather slow, given the political sensitivity surrounding the issue. Much of the negotiation between India and Bangladesh is conditional upon issues that are politically sensitive to both countries. In many cases such political sensitivity holds economic sense in ransom and indefinitely delays perfectly logical cooperative measures. The most persistent and talked about political tension between the countries is arguably around the sharing of water resources of common rivers, particularly the Ganga (Padma on the Bangladesh side) and Teesta. Unless mutually agreeable solutions are reached on water sharing, possible cooperation on other issues like transit through each others' territories is far fetched. The countries have been negotiating on the draft of the bilateral motor vehicle agreement for a long period. A SAARC regional motor vehicle agreement was drafted and expected to be signed during the 17th SAARC Summit which concluded in November 2014. Unfortunately, unanimous agreement could not be reached among the SAARC member nations and the agreement was not signed. Bangladesh's concerns chiefly revolve around the transit protocols, the investment needs for upgrading its infrastructure, and the political preparedness of the country.

Transit through Bangladesh is an issue not only vital for India, but also the land-locked countries of Nepal and Bhutan. Nepal and Bhutan have been lobbying for quite some time to enable sea port access for their countries through Bangladesh, and Bangladesh has also been pushing for access to Nepal and Bhutan via India for access to a larger market in these countries. Following the non-signing of the SAARC motor vehicle agreement at the recent SAARC summit, the four countries of Nepal, Bhutan, India, and Bangladesh have been looking at a sub-regional route for higher cooperation on transport and transit facilitation. It is likely that an agreement amongst these four countries could occur. Recently there has been a lot of traction on this proposed agreement and progress has been rather good,considering the earlier pace of such talks. These are probably a consequence of the higher political buy-in around issues of regional cooperation in the very recent times, much of which emerged from positive developments surrounding India–Bangladesh bilateral issues like the Land Border Agreement and the proposed Teesta Treaty. The present government in India has indicated that it is serious about pursuing its neighbourhood policy towards a higher cooperation in the region. India's Look East Policy, which has been in existence since the nineties, has recently garnered much attention with a makeover that is being referred to as 'Act East'. It is also argued that India is trying to push for cooperation at the sub-regional level since it does not want the entire regional cooperation agenda to be derailed due to geopolitics in one of the borders. However, for such agreements to be fruitful, it will be imperative to bring clarity on many issues, including how those issues influence domestic policies in each country and how those can be dealt with. Some of the issues where further clarity and work is needed include agreement on transit protocols, documents, and charges; earmarks on specific routes and locations (for parking, loading–unloading, and so on) in each country; agreement on the vehicular standards, makes, and so forth (there have been concerns that Bangladeshi roads are not ready to carry vehicles beyond a certain size/weight); development of required infrastructure and its financing; assurance of guarantee/insurance for transit cargo; and generation of local political buy-in and ownership of the entire process.

One of the most important concerns regarding transport and transit facilitation between India and Bangladesh is that it will be crucial to have agreed upon transit protocols in place before any transport facilitation can be achieved. While a motor vehicle agreement can be a tool, the transit protocols will actually provide the push for materializing such agreements. There are concerns in Bangladesh regarding road conditions, financing infrastructure needed for transport/transit facilitation, and the relevant charges that need to be in place before transit starts happening. Transit to India is a political issue in Bangladesh and unless it is clear how Bangladesh will gain from such an arrangement, it will be difficult to move political will. Careful dialogues and deliberations need to be done to put the transit protocols in place before the countries can go ahead with transport and transit facilitation.

Second, once the transit protocols are agreed upon and put in place, it will be important to understand how they interact with domestic policies and governance structures so as to ensure that domestic policies do not hinder such an agreement and its intent by putting in place domestic/local regulations (for example, local taxes, toll collection, checking points, and so on), that negate the enabling environment for promoting easy movement of international cargo and passengers. Given that the existing draft of the motor vehicle agreement specifies that vehicles from other countries will be allowed to ply along specified routes only, major planning exercises will be required to earmark the exact routes, locations, and other such details, and to ensure that such earmarking has local political buy-in and ownership. Enabling domestic policies will also be needed and they will need to be attuned to the transit arrangements. For example, Bangladesh doesn't have a parking policy and vehicles are usually parked along the sides of the roads. This will create scope for rent seekers to extort international cargo carriers unless policies are diligently put in place and relevant authorities are mandated to build capacity of their staff to that end. Similarly, trucks passing through state borders in India at times complain of fees/tolls being charged by state agencies. It has also been noted that such unofficial toll collection/extortion in Bangladesh is more prevalent for vehicles from other countries, such as Nepal and India. It is crucial that there is better coherence between national, state, provincial, and district agencies in each country so that there is clarity regarding their roles, minimization of collection points, and harmonization of practices and charges across countries. Additionally, all relevant stakeholders need to be well aware of such provisions well in advance.

It may be mentioned here that many of these issues can be tackled if the countries are to accede to some of the international conventions on land transport facilitation. Acceding to such conventions will help to harmonize relevant regulations. Currently, out of the seven international conventions in the field of international land transport, India has signed only two—the Convention on Road Traffic and the Convention on Road Signs and Signals—and Bangladesh has signed only the Convention on Road Traffic.

With transit, the issue of containerization is expected to follow suit in due time. The existing draft of the motor vehicle agreement defines the kind of cargo vehicles that countries would allow to ply in their territories. It mentions that cargo vehicles that can carry containerized cargo will be allowed by the member countries to ply in each other's territory. Such a definition seems to limit cargo to only containerized cargo. While this is desirable for future considerations, at present the quantity of containerized cargo is not substantial when we consider trade through land route. Containerization will require investment in infrastructure and capacity of the port officials. It will require more Inland Container Depots (ICDs), better checking facilities (vehicle scanners) at ports, e-enabled data exchange between countries across the borders, enhanced capacity of customs, and other such facilities. While exporters and customs house agents are aware that containerization will solve many issues regarding delay, cost, and theft, it is still a long way off. For one thing, container providers have not been too keen to deal with Bangladesh since, reportedly, the time required for containers to come back is rather long and, at times, they have been lost or become untraceable. There are also issues regarding access of such container services by small traders since renting of containers might be prohibitively expensive for them. At the same time there aren't many third party logistics services available who could act as aggregators and book cargo from multiple small traders. Additionally, there are concerns regarding local economic impacts of containerization, and hence, political buy-in for the same. For example, Bongaon, which is the closest town on the Indian side of the Petrapole/Benapole border point, mostly thrives on an economy that is driven by trade through this corridor. There are roughly 200 local transporters, more than 2,000 labourers, more than 100 drivers/helpers, some 1,000 people working with customs house agents, local food vendors, motor repair shops, and a myriad of small-time entities who completely depend on the cargo and vehicles passing through Bongaon for their livelihood. With containerization, a large chunk of these people will be rendered jobless since there may not be any need for oading–unloading, local transport/vehicles, and the subsidiary services. This is expected to lead to political issues at the local level and such issues have been known to adversely affect trade in the past. Hence, widespread consultations need to be done to address the concern of how to integrate local economies and agents who stand to lose out in the immediate term. Additionally, much work is required on how to containerize the major part of the cargo, and the facilities required (lack of ICDs) along the routes.

In terms of transit cargo, it will be important to equip all ports with the proper infrastructure, particularly along certain routes of interest. Some of the important ports that are used for transit cargo, a point of particular interest for Bhutan, Nepal, and Bangladesh, like Banglabandha in Bangladesh (opposite Phulbari) and Panitanki/Naxalbari in India (opposite Kakkarbhita in Nepal) lack in infrastructure like parking spaces, quarantine offices and testing facilities, proper customs quarters and offices, and basic amenities. None of them have vehicle scanners which will be important if containerized cargo is to move through them. While both Indian and Bangladesh governments are upgrading the land custom stations in a phased manner, if the motor vehicle agreement is indeed signed, such development of infrastructure needs to be expedited with focus on ports and corridors most relevant for transit cargo. The Asian Development Bank (ADB) has identified ten corridors for South Asia to promote connectivity. However, efficiency for all the identified corridors will not be the same. Factors like infrastructure, local political issues, and procedural delays will influence the corridor efficiency. A recent analysis by De and Kumar (2014) argues that SAARC Corridor 1 (Lahore to Agartala) is by far the most efficient. There are good possibilities for SAARC Corridor 2 (Kathmandu to Kolkata/Haldia) to become reasonably efficient, provided that factors such as the number of documents, the cost and time to transport, the transportation standards, and the number of border-crossings, are brought down.

While planning for regional transport and transit facilitation, it is equally important to consider investment requirements and hence optimize the available resources via innovative solutions like single point border infrastructure that could be used by both countries. This will help reduce investing in similar infrastructure on both sides of the border leading to cutting of costs and streamlining of procedures. There have been instances (for example, One Stop Border Posting: Chirundu between Zambia and Zimbabwe) of such trade facilitation measures in other parts of the world with positive results.

After the transit protocols are decided and regulations are harmonized, a large scale capacity building of relevant stakeholders, including exporters, transporters, and the like will be extremely essential towards effective implementation. Presently there are substantial gaps in understanding and operationalizing procedures and regulations. In many instances, understanding of regulations and procedures vary across border points with lack of clarity on the implementation aspects. The capacity in terms of understanding protocols and processes of government officials and staff working at the ground level is problematic, with different interpretations of policies and regulations across borders and between different border points within the same country. This is creating substantial information asymmetry and further compounding the problems of delays. The capacity of private players, such as traders and customs house agents, is also a case of concern. Even access to regulations and procedures is an issue for many stakeholders. It will be important to conduct thorough and wide consultations to understand the gaps and accordingly undertake capacity building exercises.

Standards: Harmonization and Mutual-recognition

Even with a motor vehicle agreement and transit protocols in place, delays and high trade cost will continue due to non-harmonized standards in the region. With the looming reality of various mega regional agreements like the Trans Pacific Partnership (TPP), Transatlantic Trade and Investment Partnership (TTIP), and Regional Comprehensive Economic Partnership (RCEP), standards are going to be a major issue determining the trend of global trade. Many countries will face hurdles unless they buckle up to align with the high level of standards of these mega-regional trade agreements. To counter the negative impact of possible trade diversion and loss of markets, countries like India and Bangladesh have to reform their standard regimes to align with international standards, including a significant amount of capacity building, institutional strengthening, and consolidating of bilateral and intra-regional trade via harmonization or MRAs on conformity assessment procedures. Unless this happens, their share in global trade will be negatively affected over time.

The SARSO is also in need of capacity building and of a greater awareness of the organization itself. There have been agreements and Memoranda of Understanding (MoUs) between Indian and Bangladeshi standards organizations, but changing regulations and safety concerns have affected such negotiations. With the advent of SARSO, there is much hope to consolidate and bring such agencies in the respective nations to agree on standards in the region. However, not much awareness exists about SARSO.[2] It will be important to create awareness and buy-in for SARSO among all relevant stakeholders. Equally important is to look at policy directives from the countries in terms of acceptability of SARSO certifications across the region. While on paper SARSO certifications will hold true for the region, it might prove to be a very different scenario while implementing the same at the border points. There is already quite a bit of confusion and grievance in terms of the new food safety regulations under the new Food Safety and Standards Authority of India (FSSAI). This may become further complicated for practitioners once an additional authority (SARSO) is included in the equation. Unless there are specific government policies or directives in place and widespread capacity-building of officials and staff on such provisions, implementation will be a challenge.

SARSO has been working on developing regional standards and presently twenty-nine products have been identified that are of interest in the context of regional trade. Significant work on harmonization of standards in the identified products has been completed and Draft SAARC Standards have been formulated by the respective Sectoral Technical Committees of SARSO (SAARC 2015). However, given the high trade complementarities between India and Bangladesh, and also among other countries in the SAARC region, the scope and ambit of SARSO needs to be substantially enhanced. This needs to be done via increasing the number of product lines for which SARSO is developing regional standards and also by pushing for MRAs between countries on specific product categories of regional interest, using the SARSO platform.

Additionally, there is a need for internationally recognized accreditation bodies in both countries. For example, the Bangladesh Accreditation Board has yet to become a full member of agencies such as the International Laboratory Accreditation Cooperation (ILAC), though it has recently become a full member of Asia Pacific Laboratory Accreditation Cooperation (APLAC). India already has the National Accreditation Board for Testing and Calibration Laboratories (NABL) which has full membership in both ILAC and APLAC. India also has the National Accreditation Board for Certification Bodies (NABCB) which is a constituent of the Quality Council of India (QCI). NABCB is a member of the Pacific Accreditation Cooperation, which is an association of accreditation bodies in the Asia-Pacific region, and International Accreditation Forum, a worldwide association of accreditation bodies. NABCB is also a signatory to the IAF Multi-lateral Arrangement (MLA) for Mutual Recognition. Once such internationally recognized bodies are operational in all relevant countries in the region, it will be easier to put in place testing laboratories and hence certifications that are internationally and, therefore, regionally accepted.

It is important that South Asian countries are actively participating in the standards setting processes at international platforms such as Codex Alimentarius, International Plant Protection Convention (IPPC), and OIE (World Organization for Animal Health), so that the needs and aspirations peculiar to South Asia and its neighbouring countries are reflected and represented in international standards and regulations formulation processes. It is important to look at regional standards without necessarily following the assumption that the south is always a producer and the north the consumer. With increasing South–South trade, such notions are changing and regional standards in South Asia could be more southern oriented for trading within the South.

* * *

There exists a lot of positive will towards a higher regional integration in the region across different stakeholder categories. It is important to harness this will through appropriate policy and practice changes. While there are concerns, the potential is real and quite high. In the backdrop of the recently concluded SAARC Summit, it is also becoming increasingly evident that Eastern South Asia is the region to look at in the present political context. While things may take some more time to move in Western South Asia, the eastern part seems ripe for interventions. The present governments on both sides of the border seem keen on pursuing enhanced cooperation and integration and with the right policies, results can materialize in the near future. The hurdles seem mostly in terms of effective political negotiations, financing, and streamlining domestic and foreign policies. With very recent developments along the eastern sides in terms of the land swap deal between India and Bangladesh, the political will seems to be gearing up for a conducive environment to pitch for higher cooperation and integration. While there is traction and positive political will for cooperation on both transport–transit facilitation and standards, immediate results can be expected in terms of at least putting in place a framework which could be followed by protocols and implementation strategies that are to be developed and fine-tuned through further negotiations and dialogues. Cooperation on standards might take more time given the present capacity of national institutions, private players, and related government agencies. Also, standards being technical in nature, ratification of regional standards or MRAs between countries in the region will take time. Nonetheless, there is a definite positive political will towards both at present.

It is probably equally important to think of bilateral and sub-regional connectivity in the backdrop of larger regional connectivity and as an enabler for linkages to other regions and blocs. In the emerging geo-political scenario, connectivity, integration, and stability of the larger Indo-Pacific region is increasingly becoming dependent on economic, political, and social dividends from connectivity and integration among its various smaller regions/sub-regions. With the emergence of RCEP, TPP, and such mega regional trade treaties, it is important that sub-regional developments factor in the impact and possible linkages with such external yet linked developments. The incremental economic gain that can accrue to the sub-region by being infrastructure-ready (both hard and soft) for linkages to the larger regional connectivity initiatives needs to be flagged and advocated. Better infrastructure and agreements on seamless vehicular movement across borders between India and Bangladesh have definite scope for further gains from linking to other regional projects like the Kaladan Multimodal Transit Transport project, the Master Plan on ASEAN Connectivity, the Asian Highway Network, and the like. Of these, the ASEAN is of particular interest due to the fact that the member nations have been able to achieve a reasonable level of integration that is commendable when compared to the rest of Asia, and also due to geopolitical reasons, including peace, security, and stability.

Key Recommendations

Transit protocols that are mutually beneficial and enabling. Along with transport facilitation, transit protocols need to be in place. It is important to develop road infrastructure and also transit protocols through consultation, joint deliberation, and visits involving all country representatives. There needs to be a multi-modal approach for transport connectivity, and railways should be given importance. This will help in transit and trade between Nepal, Bhutan, India, and Bangladesh. Hence, such dialogues and deliberations should essentially involve all four countries.

 Ensure insurance and guarantee for goods across the sub-region. There is a need for well-defined clauses for comprehensive insurance covering the entire region, routes, and security for any motor vehicle agreement in the region. This will ensure that traders across borders have higher reliability on the system and are effectively covered for loss due to theft, quality issues, and so on. Acceding to international conventions on transport and transit facilitation may help a lot in this direction

 Common Integrated Check posts at border crossings. A higher number of Integrated Check Posts (ICPs) needs to be put in place. Countries also need to explore the idea of having single or common ICPs at the border trade points that can be utilized by both countries. This will help minimize costs by not replicating the building of high cost facilities in both countries. Similarly, certain procedures can be done on only one side of the border instead of repeating on both sides, for example, the weighing of the cargo. To this end, procedures and documentation requirements on both sides of the border need to be harmonized as far as practicable. Also, advance documentation through pre-arrival processing needs to be promoted to speed up processes.

Promoting containerization and related infrastructure. The promotion of containerization through the development of more ICDs and installing scanners at the ports/customs stations, and also ensuring that movement of containers is smooth with no unnecessary delays in returning the containers.

Enhancing coordination and cooperation between domestic stakeholders at national and state levels. A higher level of coordination is needed between Central and State agencies towards streamlining and synergizing international agreements and domestic policies for smooth implementation. Allowing the local bureaucrats to use their administrative power in a better way to resolve localized issues, such as unauthorized toll collections, extortion, and so forth.

Institutional arrangements for exchange and regular dialogues at border points. Border agency cooperation needs to be encouraged by putting in place institutional arrangements and platforms for interaction and coordination at the working level to discuss and sort out micro issues, and also conducting trade facilitation meetings with all relevant stakeholders at ports on a regular basis. This will majorly help in minimizing the information asymmetry amongst players.

Promoting harmonization on standards and MRAs. Harmonization of Standards and MRAs on Conformity Assessment Procedures between countries across the region will help a lot in enhancing regional integration. It may help to start with agreement between national accreditation and certification institutions, which can pave the way for more comprehensive governmental agreements. It will be helpful to learn from other examples, like Africa and Southeast Asia.

Harmonization of relevant domestic regulations across countries. Harmonization of transport, trade, and travel related regulations will be crucial. Also, harmonization needs to go beyond regulations covering goods to also include services. It is equally important to establish an easy, flexible, and uniform VISA regime for the region and promote soft connectivity like people to people, think tank to think tank, and so on.

Representation at international standard setting platforms and forums. Developing countries need to have greater influence on development of standards through more proactive participation in platforms like CODEX.

Policy push for sub-regional integration as precursor to larger regional integration. Sub-regional integration may help pave the way for larger regional integration, and the countries need to push for such sub-regional cooperation to start with. In the present political context it may be more pertinent to focus on Eastern South Asia to push for early results.

Learning from international experience on transit facilitation, adopting conventions. It will be good to look at international experience on transit facilitation and particularly to look at how adopting some of the international conventions on trade, transport, and transit has helped other countries and regions.

Highlight possibilities and advocate for further linkages to other regional initiatives on connectivity. It is important for India, Bangladesh, and the sub-region more generally to look at how enhancing connectivity among themselves can help them reap additional benefits by linking such connectivity with other initiatives that are external to the sub-region, but enabling in terms of creating avenues for further economic gains. The two countries and the sub-region need to be ready with enabling infrastructure (hard and soft), connected institutions, and people to be able to dove-tail with connectivity initiatives that are happening in its neighbourhood, particularly BIMSTEC, BCIM, and ASEAN.

Notes

1. The Plant Quarantine Order 2003 is the import regulation operative in India, (pertaining to plants and plant materials) issued under the Destructive Insects and Pests Act, 1914. The commodities are categorized into various schedules based on the risk posed by associated pests of concern to India. The process is based on Pest Risk Analysis.

2. This was apparent during several consultations that CUTS has undertaken among private players, officials, and other relevant stakeholders.

References

Acharya, L. and A. Marwaha. 2012. *India–Bangladesh Economic Relations.* India: Federation of Indian Chamber of Commerce and Industry (FICCI).

Asian Development Bank (ADB) and United Nations Conference of Trade and Development (UNCTAD). 2008. *Quantification of Benefits from Economic Cooperation in South Asia.*

Asian Productivity Organization (APO). 2002. 'Seminar on Sanitary and Phyto-Sanitary Measures', Conference of the APO, Japan.

Afghanistan–Pakistan Transit Trade Agreement (APTTA). 2011. 12 June.

Agreement on Road Transport between the Government of the Republic of Belarus and the Government of the Kingdom of Belgium. 1995. 7 March.

ASEAN Framework Agreement on the Facilitation of Goods in Transit. 1998. 16 December.

Basher, M.A. 2013. *Indo-Bangla Trade: Composition, Trends and Way Forward.* London: Commonwealth Secretariat.

Bhattacharjee, J. 2013. *India–Bangladesh Border Management: The Challenge of Cattle Smuggling.* New Delhi: Observer Research Foundation.

Bhuyan, A.R. 2006. 'Bangladesh–India Trade Relations: Prospects of a Bilateral FTA', *Thoughts on Economics*, 18(2): 7–34.

CUTS International. 2013. *Reforming Non-Tariff Barriers: Case for a Participatory Approach in South Asia.* India: CUTS International.

Das, S. and S. Pohit. 2005. *Quantifying Transport, Regulatory and Other Costs of India–Bangladesh Trade.* New Delhi: National Council of Applied Economic Research (NCAER).

De Mel, D. 2011. *Trade Facilitation Issues in South Asia.* Kathmandu: South Asia Centre for Policy Studies (SACEPS).

De, Prabir. 2013. *Connectivity, Trade Facilitation and Regional Cooperation in South Asia.* London: Commonwealth Secretariat.

———. 2011. *Why is Trade at Borders a Costly Affair in South Asia? An Empirical Investigation.* India: Research and Information System for Developing Countries (RIS).

De, Prabir and Arvind Kumar. 2014. *Regional Transit Agreement in South Asia: An Empirical Investigation.* Discussion Paper, South Asia Watch on Trade, Economics and Environment. Available at http://www.sawtee.org/publications/DiscussionPaper_20.pdf (accessed 17 March 2016).

De, Prabir and B. Ghosh. 2009. 'Reassessing Transaction Costs of Trade at the India–Bangladesh Border', *Economic and Political Weekly*, 43(29): 69–79.

De, Prabir, S. Chaturvedi and A.R. Khan. 2010. *Transit and Border Trade Barriers in South Asia.* World Bank2010.

———. 2008. 'Transit and Trade Barriers in Eastern South Asia: A Review of the Transit Regime and Performance of Strategic Border-Crossings', *Working Paper Series*, no. 56.

De, Prabhir, S. Raihan, and S. Kathuria. 2012. 'Unlocking Bangladesh–India Trade: Emerging Potential and the Way Forward', *Policy Research Working Paper* no. 6155.

Debate: India and Bangladesh—A New Phase in Bilateral Relations. 2011. *Indian Foreign Affairs Journal*, 6(4).

Dutta, P. 2010. *India–Bangladesh Relations: Issues, Problems and Recent Developments*. India: Institute of Peace and Conflict Studies (IPCS).

Economic and Social Commission for Asia and the Pacific (ESCAP). 2013. *Regional Cooperation for Inclusive Sustainable Development*. South and South–West Asia Development Report: 2012/2013.

———. 2001. *Monograph Series on Facilitation of International Road Transportation: Asia and the Pacific.*

Gazi, M.I.A., M.M.H. Sarker, and M. Hossain. 2014. 'Bangladesh and International Trade: a Case Study on Bangladesh–India Bilateral Business' *Banglavision*, 13(1).

Henry, L. 2008. *India's International Trade Policy*. Centre Asie: IFRI.

Henson, S. and R. Loader. 2001. 'Barriers to Agricultural Exports from Developing Countries: the Role of Sanitary and Phytosanitary Requirements', *World Development*, 29(1): 85–102.

Henson, Spencer and Edward Olale. 2011. 'What do Border Rejections tell us about Trade Standards Compliance of Developing Countries? Analysis of EU and US Data 2002–2008', *UNIDO Working Paper*, August.

Government of India, Ministry of External Affairs. 2011. 'Joint Statement on the Occasion of the Visit of the PM of India to Bangladesh', Dhaka, 7 September; available at http://mea.gov.in/bilateral-documents.htm?dtl/5147/Joint+Statement+on+the+occassion+of+the+visit+of+the+PM+of+India+to+Bangladesh (accessed 14 December 2015).

Keane, J. 2010. *Impediments to Intra-Regional Trade in Sub-Saharan Africa*. London: Overseas Development Institute.

Limau, Nuno and Anthony J. Venables. 2001. 'Infrastructure, Geographical Disadvantage, Transport Cost, and Trade', *The World Bank Economic Review*, 15(3): 451–79.

Meyer, Nico., Tamas Fenyes, Martin Breitenbach, and Ernst Idsardi. 2010. 'Bilateral and Regional Trade Agreements and Technical Barriers to Trade: An African Perspective', *OECD Trade Policy Working Papers*, no. 96.

Peetman, S. 2013. 'Standards Harmonisation in ASEAN: Progress, Challenges and Moving Beyond 2015', *ERIA Discussion Paper Series*.

Pohit, S. and N. Taneja. 2003. 'India's Informal Trade with Bangladesh: A Qualitative Assessment', *The World Economy*, 26(8): 1187–214.

Prevost, D. 2010. *Sanitary, Phytosanitary and Technical Barriers to Trade in the Economic Partnership Agreements between the European Union and the ACP Countries*. Switzerland: International Centre for Trade and Sustainable Development (ICTSD).

Press Trust of India (PTI). 'Ranbaxy now under Australia, Europe Regulators' Scanner', *The Hindu Business Line*, 22 September; available at http://www.thehindubusinessline.com/companies/ranbaxy-now-under-australia-europe-regulators-scanner/article5156542.ece (accessed 10 December 2015).

Rahman, M. 2013. *Addressing Non-Tariff Barriers to Trade in South Asia*. Bangladesh: Centre for Policy Dialogue (CPD).

———. 2010. *Advancing Bangladesh–India Economic Cooperation: Modalities and Challenges*. Bangladesh: CPD.

Rahman, M., T.I. Khan, A. Nabi, and T.K. Paul. 2010. *Bangladesh's Export Opportunities in the Indian Market: Addressing Barriers and Strategies for Future*. Bangladesh: CPD.

Raihan, S. 2011. *Economic Corridors in South Asia: Exploring the Benefits of Market Access and Trade Facilitation*. Bangladesh: South Asian Network on Economic Modelling (SANEM).

Redrado, M. 2011. *Use of International Standards in Regional Harmonization of Technical Regulations: The MERCOSUR Experience*. UK: International Standards Organization.

South Asian Association for Regional Cooperation (SAARC). 2015. 'Cooperation in Standards'; available at http://saarc-sec.org/areaofcooperation/detail.php?activity_id=47 (accessed February 2015).

South Asian Regional Standards Organization (SARSO). 2015. 'Aims and Objectives'; available at http://sarso.org.bd/site/page/8a5cb7b3-2f16-4a02-9e11- 6b7834d48329 (accessed 10 December 2015).

South Asia Watch on Trade, Economics and Environment (SAWTEE). 2012. '*Growing Maze of Non-Tariff Barriers*', *Trade Insight*, 8(3): 1–39.

Schwersensky, Sven. 1997. *The Maseru Protocol on Trade*. Johannesburg: Friedrich Ebert Stiftung.

Sengupta, J. 2010. *Time to Boost India–Bangladesh Trade and Economic Relations*. India: Observer Research Foundation.

Stoler, L. 2009. *TBT and SPS Provisions in Regional Trading Agreements*. Australia: Institute for International Trade, University of Adelaide.

Subramanian, Uma and John Arnold. 2001. *Forging Subregional Links in Transportation and Logistics in South Asia*. Washington D.C.: The World Bank, January. Available at http://dx.doi.org/10.1596/0-8213-4885-X (accessed on 5 April 2015).

Summary Record of India-Bangladesh Meeting of the Joint Working Group on Trade. 2013. Joint Statement. New Delhi.

Taneja, Nisha. 2004. 'Trade Facilitation in the WTO: Implications for India', Working Paper no. 128. India: Indian Council for Research on International Economic Relations (ICRIER).

———. 2004. 'Informal Trade in the SAARC Region: Implications for FTAs', *Economic and Political Weekly*, 39(51): 5367–71.

Thapliyal, Sangeeta. 1999. 'India–Bangladesh Transportation Links: A Move for Closer Cooperation', *Strategic Analysis: a Monthly Journal of the IDSA*, 22(12) (March): 1921–31; available at http://www.idsa-india.org/an-mar9-8.html (accessed 11 December 2015).

United Nations Conference on Trade and Development (UNCTAD) Secretariat. 2007. *Regional Cooperation in Transit Transport: Solutions for Landlocked and Transit Developing Countries*, 10 July; available at http://unctad.org/en/Docs/c3em30d2_en.pdf (accessed 11 December 2015).

———. 2013. *Transport and Logistics Innovation Towards the Review of the Almaty Programme of Action in 2014*, 13 August; available at http://unctad.org/meetings/en/SessionalDocuments/cimem7d2_en.pdf (accessed 11 December 2015).

World Bank. 2006. 'India–Bangladesh Bilateral Trade and Potential Free Trade Agreement', Bangladesh Development Series Paper, no. 13 (December). Available at http://web.worldbank.org/WBSITE/EXTERNAL/COU-NTRIES/SOUTHASIAEXT/0,,contentMDK:21177520~pagePK:146736~piPK:146830~theSitePK:223547,00.html (accessed 14 December 2015).

———. 2010. *World Bank South Asia Economic Update 2010: Moving Up Looking East*. Washington D.C. DOI: 10.1596/978-0-8213-8388-9.

———. 2012. 'Consolidating and Accelerating Exports in Bangladesh', Bangladesh Development Series, no. 29 (June). Available at http://siteresources.worldbank.org/SOUTHASIAEXT/Resources/223546-1328913542665/8436738-1341159724797/Accelerating-Consolidating-Exports-Bangladesh.pdf (accessed 14 December 2015).

III

Environment

9 Regional Integration and Its Discontents

The Case of Transboundary Water Sharing

Douglas P. Hill

All the major river systems of the Himalayas, including the Brahmaputra, Ganges, Yellow, Mekong, and Irrawaddy have many large and medium scale hydropower projects either already under construction or proposed to be constructed in the near future. A dominant view about this infrastructure-led mode of development is that a massive increase in hydropower can be used to link together different parts of the region whilst also providing a cheap and clean source of electricity that can fire economic growth and so reduce poverty in Himalayan Asia. This chapter argues that caution is needed in placing too much faith in such ambitions, since the further integration of India with its neighbours through hydropower development is likely to be highly challenging, contested, and ultimately problematic for a number of reasons. Thus there is no inevitability about whether the harnessing of these resources will substantially increase the well-being of many people and foster greater regional cooperation, or will instead become a source for new division and enmity.

Undoubtedly, in an area characterized by challenges of uneven development and energy security, the integration of the different parts of South and Southeast Asian regions could deliver significant benefits for a great number of people. At the same time, there are already a great many challenges associated with the just and sustainable distribution of transboundary waters in the borderlands of Asia, and arguably these challenges are intensified in the context of regional integration. This is particularly because of considerable power asymmetries between and within the countries of the region. As transboundary water resources are increasingly seen as a national security issue, there is a tendency amongst some commentators to de-emphasize the range of environmental, social, and economic issues related to how hydropower development is planned and implemented, even though there are potentially many adverse impacts for those living in the borderlands of Himalayan Asia. Without transparent and participatory institutions constituted at a range of scales, the potential for cooperation and mutual benefits may be undermined by the lack of legitimacy of these integrating processes.

The harnessing of transboundary water resources has a long and troubled history in Himalayan Asia, both in Southeast and South Asia.[1] However, the recent period has arguably changed the geostrategic parameters in which such interconnectivity might take place, and these changes are important to consider if we are to appreciate the role of hydropower development. In addition to India's drawing closer to its neighbours, there has been a notable rise in new energy and infrastructure partnerships (including natural gas, oil, and hydropower) between many countries such as India, Nepal, Bangladesh, China, Bhutan, and Myanmar. The increased engagement of China in South Asia has reoriented the possibilities for hydropower development for smaller countries in that region beyond the usual allies of India, the western donors, and the multilateral banks (Hill 2013). Similarly, the opening up of Myanmar is central to realizing the increased links between South and Southeast Asia, although the political, economic, and environmental framework in which this may happen remains opaque. All these challenges give fresh impetus for policymakers to think about the region in a new and open fashion, and to consider the lessons that can be gleaned from the many decades of contentious hydropower development.

In assessing how the economic, political, and environmental landscape for transboundary water has changed in recent years, the chapter argues that we need to analyse the costs and benefits of increasing interconnectivity and energy trading at multiple scales since there are significant analytical elisions stemming from the naturalization of the nation-state as the only appropriate scale through which to examine these issues (Bakker 1999; Furlong 2006). Instead, a multi-scalar analysis that examines the consequences and tensions of hydropower from local to regional scales allows us to think through the possibilities of the kinds of institutions and initiatives that are necessary to achieve a just and sustainable regional integration in Himalayan Asia. While the obstacles seem formidable, the latter part of the chapter demonstrates that there are many examples throughout the region of transboundary cooperation over water resources at a variety of scales and by different kinds of agents. Importantly, whilst governments can and must take the lead in initiating and sustaining these kinds of initiatives, this section demonstrates the considerable gains that can be made by non-governmental organization (NGO) cooperation, multi-track diplomacy, and similar kind of initiatives. Indeed, there are a number of already existing initiatives throughout the region that can be usefully drawn upon to consider how such processes might work.

Framing the Challenges of Regional Integration and Water Cooperation

Overwhelmingly, the promise and limitations of different parts of Asia becoming more closely entwined is presented in terms that emphasize large-scale infrastructure projects as the mechanism by which markets can function more effectively and economic growth can be achieved by linking fast-growing areas to slower growing ones. In this sense, the questions pertaining to the interconnectivity of different parts of Asia are not new. Indeed, India's 'Look East' policy has had a clearly articulated strategy of linking with the large and fast growing economies of North and Southeast Asia since at least 1996. Similarly, China's 'Go Out' policy has been in place since 1999. In turn, more recently India has become an attractive destination for investors from Southeast Asia and China. Many agencies within the donor community have been actively supporting such inter-linking for many years and an array of regional associations have arisen that have sought to find ways to turn the promise of inter-Asia connectivity into a tangible reality, particularly through the stronger coordination between already existing sub-regional bodies such as the Greater Mekong Subregion (GMS) and the South Asia Subregional Economic Cooperation (SASEC).

The benefits of such regional integration have been effectively spelt out in many studies that argue that such interconnectivity increases the mobility of people, goods, and services and so lowers the costs of trade, and increases the economic opportunities for economically marginalized people living in remote and land-locked areas. Increased investment will increase the probability of the transfer of efficient and sustainable technologies. It is also frequently asserted that such trade facilitation measures have the benefits of reducing poverty and the likelihood of conflict (Thuzar *et al.* 2014). In order to facilitate such interconnectivity, there is a clear emphasis on enhancing trade by the building of trans-Asian highways, the creation of regional energy grids, the upgrading of ports, and the harnessing of water resources (Das and Pohit 2006; Subramanian and Arnold 2001; Wilson and Otsuki 2007).

However, as a recent Asian Development Bank Institute and Asian Development Bank report (2013) notes, the creation of such infrastructure for interconnectivity is far from straightforward. Indeed, when discussing connecting South and Southeast Asia and the role of hydropower in energy trading, the report notes technical barriers, political resistance to energy trading, asymmetry in the power of negotiators, differing security concerns, regulatory barriers, distorted prices, and significant environmental impacts including 'disruption of riverine fauna, and displacement of human settlements and agriculture' (Asian Development Bank Institute and Asian Development Bank report 2013: 35). Unfortunately, while this report is slightly unusual in mentioning the technical as well as the political and environmental issues involved in hydropower development and energy trading, there is no further elaboration on the political and environmental issues, and ultimately the overall tone of the report suggests that it is the technical issues that are the most significant obstacles to overcome. A similar pattern is repeated in the bourgeoning literature on the potential of, and obstacles to, energy trading within Asia, such that there is often very little mention of the people who live in these areas to be linked, except in terms of the potential of this infrastructure to unlock their entrepreneurial capacities and to give them new opportunities.

While the local scale implications of transboundary water sharing might not be gaining much traction in the literature on energy sharing, there is certainly a growing literature that examines energy security challenges within the changing geopolitics of Himalayan Asia (Chellaney 2011; Christopher 2013). Indeed, at this scale we find a range of commentators that are now analysing transboundary water sharing as a matter of considerable national significance, and increasingly the modification of rivers is linked with matters of sovereignty and national security. In such an environment, there is a gap in data-sharing between countries, which makes full analysis of the mutual costs and benefits of any action problematic (Alley, Hile, and Mitra 2014). We can see the securitization of discourses around water most alarmingly in the debates over the harnessing of the Tsangpo–Brahmaputra, where many of India's anxieties over China's activities on its side of the disputed border are played out in ways that now figure highly in commentaries on the relationship between the two countries (Wirsing *et al.* 2013). Certainly, the modification of the tributaries and the mainstream of the Lancang–Mekong is another such example, and the debates over the Irrawaddy and the Salween will only intensify in coming years for exactly the same reasons.

In such an environment, the rush to harness shared rivers has the potential to inflame relations between countries where the existing terms of transboundary water sharing are often seen as unjust. Thus, India's renewed plans to pursue the Himalayan components of its river-linking project are likely to strain its relations inside Nepal and Bangladesh, as well as unsettle its own domestic politics (Alley 2012). Even a country such as Myanmar, which does not have the same enduring politics of grievance over international and intra-national water sharing that we see in Nepal, India, or Bangladesh, has witnessed significant protests against power-cuts, with much of the anger directed at the selling of gas to Thailand and hydroelectricity to China.

At the same time, there continues to be significant issues *within* many countries that must also be accounted for when considering the integration of the region. Indeed, many of these projects are projected to take place in regions which are politically troubled and where water sharing is contentious both between and within countries. It is highly likely that if these projects are not executed in a way that considers all of these different interests, they will exacerbate pre-existing tensions and perhaps create new ones. Such an outcome would be extremely unfortunate given the significant potential for mutual benefit. For example, in Northeast India, there is little indication that the kind of development agenda promoted by New Delhi has any broad legitimacy amongst the many and often conflicting stakeholders of this peripheral part of the country. This is a longstanding challenge that the Indian government has thus far been unable to overcome and which stands as an impediment to the realization of its hydropower ambitions.

Arguably similar obstacles of uneven development confront many countries in the region whose borderland regions are home to marginalized peoples, many of whose suspicions have been sharpened by years of coercive displacements, adverse environmental impacts, and unfulfilled promises—all done in the name of development. For example, the emerging issues over the shape of federalism in the 'New Nepal' means that debates over hydropower in that country frequently spill over into a range of other larger political issues, including its relationship with India (Shresta 2010). The experiences throughout the region demonstrate that if these projects are undertaken in a way that is opaque and lacks adequate consultation, they will more than likely suffer from a lack of legitimacy and will erode the potential for cooperation between and within these nations.

Clearly then, significant tension with regards to regional integration stems from the singularity of the development vision presented, such that the mode of development and the benefits that this is supposed to entail are almost always imposed from above, whether this means national governments or multilateral donors (Molle, Foran, and Kakonen 2009). Whether it is in eastern South Asia or in the Mekong, there has been an overwhelming focus on supply-side management. Certainly, when one considers the relative lack of existing storage capacity and the vast potential of the harnessing of these rivers in a variety of ways, one can see why this has been the case.

Arguably, the perspective of transboundary waters as only a potential energy source for regional markets that can be transformed through infrastructure development and trade facilitation misses much of what is actually occurring in terms of the range of ecosystem services and cultural values (Drew 2012, 2014). Indeed, if we cast our view away from the region only in terms of its capacity to be harnessed for energy, and explore instead the function of rivers as important in the livelihoods of a great number of people and as a provider of ecosystem services, then a very different picture of the costs and benefits of harnessing transboundary water resources emerges. Indeed, while certainly energy poor, people living in the Himalayas face a great number of challenges that are intrinsically tied up with their capacity to access and utilize water that extends beyond just concerns with energy. While studies of energy markets portray communities as isolated from each other, if we think about these communities in terms of ecosystem services we find a high dependence of downstream communities on those living upstream for the maintenance of dry-season water for irrigation and hydropower, drinking water, and soil fertility and nutrients (Rasul 2010). The range of ecosystem services provided by Himalayan rivers extend well beyond the immediate proximity of the mountains in terms of water supply, climate and wind regulation, groundwater recharge, and in sustaining wetland ecosystems.

At the same time, studies have demonstrated that people living in these mountains face increasing water vulnerability and water stress, difficulties with agriculture and food security, and poverty. Environmental degradation and expanding biotic and abiotic stress, as well as changing agro-ecological conditions and a range of demographic challenges, mark the regions that these people inhabit. For many people, high ratios of agricultural land to total land means that there is comparatively less scope for land reclamation as a way of augmenting food security. Further, there is also considerable uncertainty over the changing climate because of significant knowledge gaps, particularly at the sub-basin scale (Gawith et al. 2015; Jaitly 2009). The phrase 'too much and too little water' has been used as a short-hand for the challenges that climate change presents for the Hindu Kush Himalaya, with droughts and floods becoming more commonplace (ICIMOD 2012).

Clearly, while interconnectivity of the region through energy markets has its own technical challenges, a great deal is missing from the analysis unless we consider the environmental, social, and political aspects of water sharing as well. Rasul (2014) argues that the regional integration of upstream and downstream communities in the Himalayas is an important component of security, but urges that such security be conceived in such a way that incorporates a nexus of food, water, and energy. In his view, we must seek to achieve integration across the many ecosystems of the Hindu Kush Himalaya, and in doing so, pay equal attention to the region's watersheds, catchments, and headwaters.

To Build or Not to Build? Debates Around Hydropower Development

The extent to which any country should be embarking upon a new round of dam building is highly contentious across the region. Part of the opposition stems from the fact that the processes involved in the development of large scale hydro projects anywhere in the region are rarely done in a way that matches international best practice. Indeed, whether one looks at large scale hydro developments in Nepal, Pakistan, or Northeast India, a common theme is that Environmental Impact Assessments (EIA) and Social Impact Assessments (SIA) are rarely transparent or publically available (Dharmadhikary 2008; Menon and Kohli 2009; Panigrahi and Amirapu 2012). Civil society is preoccupied with donor related developmentalism as in Bangladesh and Nepal (Dahal 2001), or is constrained in the extent to which it can express dissent. In all cases the level of genuine public participation is low and all too often consultation with community groups is essentially manufactured as a compliance measure rather than entering into the process in the way that is supposed to be ensured by guidelines established by the World Commission on Dams or donor agencies. While Transboundary EIA is a growing field in other parts of the world (Bruch *et al.* 2007), there is little evidence that such processes are carried out in South Asia or Southeast Asia.

While controversies over the shape and role of hydropower for energy, irrigation, and flood protection will likely increase in the future throughout the region, the debate is perhaps most complex and divisive in India. In that country many policymakers and investors feel frustrated by the slow rate of project approval and completion in comparison to the pace and scale of equivalent projects in China, even if opposition to hydropower projects is much more extensive and important in decision-making in the latter country than is generally acknowledged within India (Brown *et al.* 2008; Magee 2006; Magee and McDonald 2009 [2006]; Mertha 2008). For the advocates of large-scale dams in the Indian Himalayas, NGOs and people's movements are an unfortunate impediment to India reaching its potential (Chellaney 2012). To them, these groups are 'anti-development' and there have even been suggestions in recent years that the funding by Western agencies of such groups is a deliberate attempt to slow down India's economic progress and thus should be treated as profoundly anti-patriotic (Mazoomdaar 2014). Unfortunately, such portrayals rarely, if ever, acknowledge that there are significant issues of governance and due process in the way that the Government of India has gone about constructing dams in the past. To the critics of the extension of large-scale dams, the lack of consultation and absence of subsequent benefit sharing means that there are few guarantees that those who are substantially disadvantaged by the building of hydropower infrastructure will be acknowledged, much less substantially compensated.

We can see vividly how these disagreements play out in many parts of Northeast India, which is the region of the country that is likely to have the greatest hydropower development in the future, and as such this area is likely to play an important role in any future regional grid or other mechanism for energy sharing across Asia. Certainly, the potential in the region is immense, with Arunachal Pradesh alone having 132 projects allocated by the state government that will have an installed capacity of more than 40,000 MW (Vagholikar and Das 2010). However, there are significant institutional issues in this region, typified by a recent World Bank Strategy Report, which suggested that the greatest obstacle to the development of water resources in the Northeast is 'the paternalism of central-level bureaucrats, coercive top-down planning, and little support or feedback from locals' (as cited in Baruah 2008).

In such an environment, debate has all too often been stifled and the same lack of procedure that we see in ostensibly less democratic regimes has prevented any effective opposition. At the 1,500 MW Tipaimukh dam site in Manipur, for example, consultation with the public, and indigenous groups in particular, has been largely absent and entry roads to the dam site have been militarized in the past (Buhril 2009). Not only have these developments further widened the culture of distrust that has continued in much of Manipur and elsewhere in the Northeast since the enactment of the Armed Forces Special Powers Act in 1958 (McDuie-Ra 2009), they have also been the catalyst for what activists in the region view as arbitrary arrests. The building of the Tipaimukh dam has also inflamed domestic politics within Bangladesh, since critics argue that the harnessing of the Barak River will reduce the essential flows of water to the Sylhet region of Bangladesh.

As well as fuelling already existing grievances from insurgent groups in places like Manipur, the building of large-scale hydro projects has also exacerbated tensions between states in Northeast India, such as with the controversial and recently delayed 2,000 MW Lower Subansiri project, which has caused division between Arunachal Pradesh and Assam (Hill 2013). Perhaps even more controversial is the series of projects proposed on the Teesta river, which begin in Sikkim before flowing into Paschimbanga (the erstwhile West Bengal), and then into Bangladesh (Ahmed 2012). These two Indian states have very different perspectives and interests, with indigenous people in Sikkim placing significant cultural value on the river and arguing that it will have significant impacts upon the

Khangchendzonga Biosphere Reserve, while those within Paschimbanga have a greater interest in the river as a source of irrigation.

With regard to Bangladesh, the opposition to the Teesta projects is based on a concern about the reduction in dry season flow to the heavily populated northwestern part of the country. The way that this opposition is articulated, however, alerts us to the ongoing relevance of historical memory in shaping water sharing discourses, since there is a considerable trust deficit still existing within Bangladesh because of the ongoing legacy of the Farakka barrage even though the opening of this occurred almost forty years ago. Teesta is also evidence of the influence of domestic politics on how India deals with its neighbours, since the completion of a water sharing deal between India and Bangladesh was scuppered in 2011 by the intervention of West Bengal Chief Minister Mamata Banerjee, who argued that any such deal would be to the detriment of farmers living in North Bengal. In the contemporary period, there are suggestions that the current National Democratic Alliance (NDA) government is putting off signing any agreement with Bangladesh until the Bharatiya Janata Party is able to gain a stronger foothold in the eastern state.

Regional Cooperation Beyond the River: Sharing Knowledge, Sharing Benefits

The preceding section has demonstrated the tremendous costs associated with the current trajectory of badly conceived and implemented initiatives that do not allow the effective voice or participation of affected stakeholders. Clearly, there are a great many political, economic, environmental, and social challenges that problematize any suggestion that a technocratic worldview can adequately account for the task of increasing Asian interconnectivity and achieving energy security through regional integration. However, it is also the case that many parts of the world, including elsewhere in the global South, demonstrate that regional cooperation and integration need not necessarily precede in this manner. Indeed, if water resource management is approached in a way which considers the many different stakeholders involved, takes seriously their different interests and worldviews, and attempts to ensure that there are mechanisms for the distribution of both costs and benefits, then transboundary rivers have the potential to foster dialogue and bring a whole range of benefits beyond the river (Sadoff and Grey 2002; Yu 2008). Considerable scholarly attention has in recent years been devoted to documenting and theorizing the potential benefits of cooperation around transboundary water resources. Sadoff and Grey (2005) suggest that there are four types of benefits, and that as one moves up in scale, from increasing benefits to the river (type I) all the way to increasing benefits beyond the river (type IV) there are environmental, developmental, and political benefits to be had. As they demonstrate, such cooperation has the potential to move water sharing from the cause of environmental degradation, human underdevelopment, and political distrust, to a source of increased sustainability, benefit sharing, human security, and greater regional harmony. While there are basins in both the global North (such as the Rhine) and the global South (such as the Orange) that have managed to move a considerable way forward in harnessing these potential benefits, it is clear that the basins in Asia, and in South Asia in particular, are still a long way short of achieving such productive cooperation.

In considering why this might be the case, we might begin by noting that water-sharing negotiations are conspicuously absent from discussions at the South Asian Association for Regional Cooperation (SAARC), the regional body that would otherwise have seemed an obvious forum for such multilateral coordination. Certainly each of the major transboundary regions have commissions set up to try and consider the perspectives of each country involved: Mahakali Commission (India–Nepal) and the Joint Rivers Commission (Bangladesh–India). While there are few studies that have examined the functioning of these bodies, there are substantial differences of opinion about their effectiveness. Some commentators have argued that they operate reasonably effectively even if some people within these countries feel aggrieved. Others, however, suggest that the relationship is essentially marred by India's dominance, which in the case of Bangladesh is reinforced by the fact that it is the upper riparian, while in the case of Nepal the historic dependence of the Himalayan country leaves little room for manoeuvre in negotiations. This is particularly significant because historically India has consistently refused to countenance multilateral discussions on the issues of transboundary water sharing (Hill 2008). In assessing the current institutional and geo-strategic framework of transboundary water cooperation, then, a wide range of commentators have argued that the current institutional frameworks are insufficient (Gyawali and Dixit 2001; Islam 2006; Iyer 1999, 2001).

Against this pessimism, at the intergovernmental level there are hopeful steps that suggest the potential for further cooperation in the near future. In April 2013, there were two significant moments in this regard, the first of which was the initiation of a framework for tripartite cooperation involving Bhutan–India–Bangladesh (BIB) and Nepal–India–Bangladesh (NIB) (Hill 2015). These steps towards breaking away from the pattern of bilateral negotiation between India and its smaller and less powerful neighbours do not eradicate the significant power asymmetries which exist between these countries, but it does enable the discussion of regional cooperation in a way which takes a whole of 'basin' approach. The new bodies established under these dialogues will include responsible ministers from each of the countries as well as a technical committee of experts from each country. A further hopeful step was the re-signing of an agreement between India and China on flood data. Since 2008 the two countries have had an information sharing agreement that entails China providing data to India on the Brahmaputra twice per day during the flood season between June and October. Newspaper reports suggest that India has raised the possibility of a joint mechanism to enhance this in the future.

While the increase in dialogue between countries involved in water-sharing in Himalayan Asia is undoubtedly a welcome and necessary step, the preceding parts of the chapter have demonstrated that the levels of uneven development and marginalization that exist within these countries mean that it should not only be the institutions of the state that are involved in debate about how such water-sharing takes place. Given the opaque nature of many of the bureaucracies in the region, a key component of a regional body for coordinating the Himalayan rivers must be that it goes well beyond Track I (government to government) diplomacy to create space for networks of civil society and people's movements from across the region.

In arguing for such a possibility, Crow and Singh (2009) suggest that what is needed is a more broad-ranging regional organization for himalayan authority for water services and environmental cooperation, similar to those found elsewhere in the world and perhaps modelled after the success of the Mekong River Commission (MRC). While far from a perfect body and certainly subject to ebbs and flows of regional politics, the MRC has demonstrated its capacity to mediate between competing regional interests (Schmeier 2013). Moreover, there is a significant, though constrained, space for the participation of NGOs in its deliberations and a greater attention to multi-stakeholder platforms for dialogue than can be found in South Asia (Dore 2007). Civil society groups in the Mekong have also been able to utilize data generated through the efforts of people living and working in project areas in collaboration with NGOs. This grassroots research or *Thai Baan*, as citizen science is referred to in Thailand, was influential in the reversal of the decision to dam the Pak Mun River after extensive data was collected by villagers on the potential impact on fisheries, environmental, and social impacts (Sangkhamanee 2012). The potential for a more open and transparent institution for South Asia operating on similar lines is undoubtedly something that policymakers need to consider in an era when regional connections over water-sharing are intensifying. Alley *et al.* (2014) have demonstrated how citizen science, including participatory Geographic Informations Systems (GIS), has a similar role to play in filling in information gaps in the South Asian context. Widespread adoption of such processes will not only aid policymakers by providing a more accurate understanding of the trade-offs involved in any hydropower development, they will also give the process a great deal more legitimacy.

While there are clearly significant obstacles to bringing to fruition this vision of institutions for regional cooperation, it is also notable that there are a range of multi-track initiatives already in place that have attempted to build momentum for dialogue (Sangkhamanee 2012). These include the World Bank and a number of donor countries that have attempted to foster momentum for such a regional organization through the South Asia Water Initiative (SAWI). This includes sponsorship of the 'Abu Dhabi Dialogues' (ADDs), which bring together Afghanistan, Bangladesh, Bhutan, China, India, Nepal, and Pakistan to promote dialogue. The ADDs have been convened on five occasions and they also feature small grant projects for NGOs.

Other notable examples of multi-track initiatives in recent years include the Observer Research Foundation's efforts in collaboration with external agencies to promote dialogue, such as 'Waging Peace: Water issues between India and Pakistan' (in collaboration with

Atlantic Council); 'the Intra-regional Ganga Dialogue' (in collaboration with The Asia Foundation); and 'Connecting the Drops Initiative' (in collaboration with the Stimson Centre). Similarly, the International Union for Conservation of Nature's (IUCN) recent 'Ecosystems for Life' programme has been an important mechanism by which dialogue can be stimulated between NGOs, Parliamentarians, and policymakers on both sides of the Indo-Bangladesh border. We might also note the success of pan-South Asian think tanks, as well as the development of People's SAARC and the regional intergovernmental learning and knowledge sharing centre, the International Centre for Integrated Mountain Development (ICIMOD), which is based in Kathmandu but serves the broader member countries of the Hindu Kush Himalayas, including in capacity building in the region.

Along with the difficulties associated with improving the transparency and effectiveness of institutions and increasing dialogue across national borders with regards to water-sharing, another important challenge for increasing the effectiveness and sustainability of energy-trading must be a greater emphasis on benefit sharing mechanisms. Benefit sharing may take a monetary or non-monetary form but the key idea is to craft mechanisms by which a proportion of the ongoing benefits of multi-purpose hydropower projects can be distributed to local communities, particularly those who have been adversely affected by the construction of the project in the first place (Mekong River Commission Secretariat 2014). There is a range of different ways to approach benefit sharing and many countries in the region, including in the Mekong region, India, and Nepal, already have some mechanisms in place. However, these remain only national-to-local agreements and do not include transboundary components whereby communities that are living downstream but in another country might be included. Perhaps predictably, there are a number of challenges associated with the existing benefit sharing mechanisms in Himalayan Asia, including in terms of enhancing the transparency around how funds are used; ensuring that agreements have longevity and are not just one-off agreements to ensure community consent for a project; and a tendency to ignore groups that are affected by a project but live beyond the immediate vicinity of the project area. Nevertheless, given the enormous stakes involved in the development of energy trading throughout Himalayan Asia, and the potential for this to be destabilized and even disrupted if project-affected people feel the process is lacking in legitimacy, such benefit sharing mechanisms need to be incorporated into the planning frameworks of policymakers across the region.

* * *

This chapter has outlined the tremendous potential of deepening inter-Asia connectivity to promote sustainable and prosperous use of the waters of Himalayan Asia. It has noted that large scale transformation of the great rivers of this region is already underway and that this transformation opens up the possibility of a great many benefits for people at a range of scales, from the local to the regional. On the other hand, the chapter has also documented how much of this development is occurring in a regulatory environment that is far from best practice. The increasing securitization of Asia's rivers is derived from the intense competition for energy security in a rapidly changing political, economic, and geopolitical environment involving many of the world's fastest growing economies. As the chapter has demonstrated, in such an environment, there is a danger that all sorts of actions will be authorized in the name of national security, and in doing so authorities will ignore the concerns of the people living in the peripheral regions of the Himalayas. The already existing challenges of water control and governance may be exacerbated in the future with the tremendous rush to harness these resources by the building of many medium and large scale dams.

Clearly, such infrastructure has the potential to generate electricity, enhance and augment storage, as well as increase the efficiency of irrigation, all of which could have significant benefits for people of the region. However, the way that such projects have been planned and executed is far from global best practice and as such, despite an occasional consideration towards participation, stakeholder dialogue, and consultation, it is unclear how much space will be available for people who do not share this barely reformed modernist, technocratic vision of development, or indeed those who may disagree that the costs and benefits are evenly distributed.

In contrast, in much of the world there is now an increased emphasis upon adaptive management, which is more holistic in the way that it considers ecosystem services and people's relationships toward water. In such an approach, there is often greater emphasis on developing institutions that operate in a comparatively transparent and accessible manner. Certainly, such a shift in Himalayan Asia is problematized by the fact that there is an overwhelming technocratic emphasis amongst many of the bureaucracies charged with water resource management and the need to consider a range of other values is not one that is embraced easily by such agencies. Further, the enduring suspicion between nations over each other's intentions with regards to the use of shared transboundary water resources is not something that can be overcome quickly. However, the chapter has also demonstrated that there are already a range of initiatives in place that are seeking to foster dialogue about how water resources might be more sustainably managed. Whilst significant obstacles remain, there is little question that a more open, transparent, and just distribution of Himalayan waters is needed, even if such an outcome is less likely than enmity and division.

Note

1. For a review, see Hill 2008: 59–80; Molle, Foran, and Kakonen (eds) 2009; Sneddon and Fox 2006.

References

Ahmed, Imtiaz. 2012. 'Teesta, Tipaimukh and River Linking: Danger to Bangladesh–India Relations', *Economic & Political Weekly*, 47(16): 51–3.

Alley, Kelly D. 2012. 'Water Wealth and Energy in the Indian Himalayas', *The Silk Road*, 10: 136–45; available at http://www.silk-road.com/newsletter/vol10/SilkRoad_10_2012_alley.pdf (accessed 16 September 2014).

——— . 2004. 'The Making of a River Linking Plan in India: Suppressed Science and Spheres of Expert Debate', *India Review*, 3(3): 210–38.

Alley, Kelly D., Ryan Hile, and Chandana Mitra. 2014. 'Visualising Hydropower Across the Himalayas: Mapping in a Time of Regulatory Decline', *Himalaya, the Journal of the Association of Nepal and Himalayan Studies*, 34(2): 52–66.

Asian Development Bank Institute and Asian Development Bank. 2013. *Connecting South Asia and Southeast Asia: Interim Report*. Tokyo: Asian Development Bank Institute. Available at http://hdl.handle.net/11540/170 (accessed 12 January 2015).

Bakker, Karen. 1999. 'The Politics of Hydropower: Developing the Mekong', *Political Geography*, 18(2): 209–32. doi: 10.1016/S0962-6298(98)00085-7.

Baruah, Sanjib. 2008. 'A Road, Smooth and Sleek like a Snake: Development and the Rhetoric of Vision', *Eastern Quarterly* (Publication of the Manipur Research Forum, Delhi), 5(1): 61–5.

Brichieri-Colombi, Stephen and Robert W. Bradnock. 2003. 'Geopolitics, Water and Development in South Asia: Cooperative Development in the Ganges–Brahmaputra Delta', *The Geographical Journal*, 169(1): 43–64.

Bruch, C., M. Nakayama, J. Troell, L. Goldman, and E.M. Mrema 2007. 'Assessing the Assessments: Improving Methodologies for Impact Assessment in Transboundary Watercourses', *International Journal of Water Resources Development*, 23(3): 391–410. doi: 10.1080/07900620701400161.

Buhril David. 2009. 'Enquiring Tipaimukh Dam: Development or Destruction?' Available at http://www.researchgate.net/publication/255597393_Enquiring_Tipaimukh_Dam_Development_or_Destruction (accessed 4 December 2015).

Brown, Philip, Darrin Magee, Yilin Xu. 2008. 'Socioeconomic Vulnerability in China's Hydropower Development', *China Economic Review*, 19(4): 614–27.

Chellaney, Brahma. 2012. 'From Arms Racing to 'Dam Racing' in Asia: How to Contain the Geopolitical Risks of the Dam-Building Competition', *Transatlantic Academy Paper Series*. Washington, D.C.: Transatlantic Academy.

———. 2011. *Water: Asia's New Battleground*. Washington, D.C.: Georgetown University Press.

Christopher, Mark. 2013. *Water Wars: The Brahmaputra River and Sino-Indian Relations*. CIWAG Case Study on Irregular Warfare and Armed Groups. Newport: U.S. Naval War College.

Crow, Ben and Nirvikar Singh. 2009. 'The Management of International Rivers as Demand Grows and Supplies Tighten: India, China, Nepal, Pakistan, Bangladesh', *India Review*, 8(3): 306–39.

Dahal, Dev Raj. 2001. *Civil Society in Nepal: Opening the Ground for Questions*. Kathmandu: Centre for Development and Governance.

Das, Samantak and Sanjib Pohit. 2006. 'Quantifying Transport, Regulatory and Other Costs of Indian Overland Exports to Bangladesh', *World Economy*, 29: 1227–42.

Dharmadhikary, Shripad. 2008. *Mountains of Concrete: Dam Building in the Himalayas*. Berkeley: International Rivers.

Dore, John. 2007. 'Multi-stakeholder Platforms (msps): Unfulfilled Potential', in Louis Lebel, John Dore, Rajesh Daniel, and Yang Saing Koma (eds), *Democratizing Water Governance in the Mekong Region*, pp. 197–227. Chiang Mai: Mekong Press.

Drew, Georgina. 2014. 'Developing the Himalaya: Development as if Livelihoods Mattered', *Himalaya, the Journal for the Association of Nepal and Himalayan Studies*, 34(2): 31–8.

————. 2012. 'A Retreating Goddess? Conflicting Perceptions of Ecological Change Near the Gangotri–Gaumukh Glacier', *Journal for the Study of Religion, Nature and Culture*, 6(3): 344–62.

D'Souza, Rohan. 2008a. 'Framing India's Hydraulic Crisis: the Politics of the Modern Large Dam', *Monthly Review Press*, 60(3) (July–August): 112–24.

————. 2008b. 'River-linking and its Discontents: the Final Plunge for Supply-Side Hydrology in India', in Kuntala Lahiri-Dutt and Robert J. Wasson (eds), *Water First: Issues and Challenges for Nations and Communities in South Asia*, pp. 99–121. New Delhi: Sage.

Furlong, Kathryn. 2006. 'Hidden Theories, Troubled Waters: International Relations, the "Territorial Trap", and the Southern African Development Community's Transboundary Waters', *Political Geography*, 25(4): 438–58.

Gawith, David, Douglas P. Hill, and Daniel G. Kingston. 2015. 'Reattributing Water Stress Vulnerability in the Himalayas', *Climate and Development*, 7(5).

Glassman, Jim. 2010. *Bounding the Mekong: The Asian Development Bank, China and Thailand*. Honolulu: University of Hawaii Press.

Goldman, Michael. 2005. *Imperial Nature: The World Bank and Struggles for Social Justice in the Age of Globalization*. New Haven: Yale University Press.

Gyawali, Dipak and Ajaya Dixit. 2001. 'How Not To Do a South Asian Treaty', *Himal*, April.

Hill, Douglas P. 2015. 'Where Hawks Dwell on Water and Bankers Build Power Poles: Transboundary Waters and the Frontiers of Neo-Liberalism', *Strategic Analysis*, 39(6): 729–43.

————. 2013. 'Transboundary Water Resources and Uneven Development: Crisis In and Beyond Contemporary India', *South Asia: Journal of South Asian Studies*, 36(2): 243–57.

————. 2012. 'Alternative Institutional Arrangements: Managing Transboundary Water Resources in South Asia', *Harvard Asia Quarterly*, 14(3): 61–6.

————. 2008. 'The Regional Politics of Water Sharing: Contemporary Issues in South Asia', in Kuntala Lahiri-Dutt and Robert J. Wasson (eds), *Water First: Issues and Challenges for Nations and Communities*, pp. 59–80. New Delhi: Sage.

Hossain, Ishtiaq 1998. 'Bangladesh–India Relations: The Ganges Water-Sharing Treaty and Beyond', *Asian Affairs*, 25(4): 131–50.

International Union for Conservation of Nature (IUCN). 2015. 'Ecosystems for Life: A Bangladesh–India Initiative (E4L)'; available at https://www.iucn.org/about/union/secretariat/offices/asia/asia_where_work/india_programme_office/india_programmes_and_initiatives/ecosystems_for_life__a_bangladesh_india_initiative/ (accessed 8 December 2015).

International Centre for Integrated Mountain Development (ICIMOD). 2012. *Role of Policy and Institutions in Local Adaptation to Climate Change: Case Studies on Responses to too Much and too Little Water in the Hindu Kush Himalayas*. Kathmandu: International Centre for Integrated Mountain Development.

Islam, Nazrul. 2006. 'IRLP or the Ecological Approach to Rivers?' *Economic and Political Weekly*, 41(17): 1693–702.

Iyer, Ramaswamy R. 2001. 'Delay and Drift on Mahakali', *Himal Southasian*, 14(6) (June): 40–2.

———. 1999. 'Conflict-resolution: Three River Treaties', *Economic and Political Weekly*, 34(24): 1509–18.

Jaitly, Ashok. 2009. 'South Asian Perspectives on Climate Change and Water Policy', in David Michel and Amit Pandya (eds), *Troubled Waters: Climate Change, Hydropolitics, and Transboundary Resources*, pp. 17–31. Washington D.C.: The Henry L. Stimson Center.

Magee, Darrin and Kristen McDonald. 2009 [2006]*. 'Beyond Three Gorges: Nu River Hydropower and Energy Decision Politics in China', *Asian Geographer*, 25(1–2): 39–60. (*Published in 2009 but dated 2006 in order to fit with publication cycle.)

Magee, Darrin. 2006. 'Powershed Politics: Yunnan Hydropower under Great Western Development', *The China Quarterly*, 185 (March): 23–41.

Matthews, Nathanial and K. Geheb (eds). 2015. *Hydropower Development in the Mekong Region: Political, Socio-economic and Environmental*. London: Routledge.

Mazoomdaar, J. 2014. 'Invisible Strings – The IB Report On NGOs' Tehelka, 11(26). Available at http://www.tehelka.com/2014/06/ngo-invisible-strings/ (accessed 5 January 2015).

McCully, Patrick. 2001. *Silenced Rivers: The Ecology and Politics of Large Dams*. New York: Zed Books.

McDuie-Ra, Duncan. 2009. 'Fifty-year Disturbance: the Armed Forces Special Powers Act and Exceptionalism in a South Asian Periphery', *Contemporary South Asia*, 17(3): 255–70.

Mehdudia, Sujay. 2013. 'Nepal, India & Bangladesh to Make Most of Ganga Water, Hydropower', *Hindu* (New Delhi), 15 April.

Mekong River Commission (MRC)'s Initiative on Sustainable Hydropwer. 2014. *National-to-Local Benefit Sharing Options for Hydropower on Mekong Tributaries evaluated by 2013: Draft Executive Summary*. Vientiane, Laos: Mekong River Commission Secretariat. Available at http://www.mrcmekong.org/assets/Publications/Reports/Regional-Synthesis-Draft-Executive-Summary-FINAL.pdf (accessed 3 September 2014).

Menon, Manju and Kanchi Kohli. 2009. 'From Impact Assessment to Clearance Manufacture', *Economic and Political Weekly*, 44(28): 20–3.

Mertha, Andrew C. 2008. *China's Water Warriors: Citizen Action and Policy Change*. Ithaca: Cornell University Press.

Molle, Francois. 2009. 'The "Greening of Isaan": Politics, Ideology and Irrigation Development in the Northeast of Thailand', in Francois Molle, Tira Foran, and Mira Käkönen (eds), *Contested Waterscapes in the Mekong Region: Hydropower, Livelihoods and Governance*, pp. 253–82. London: Earthscan.

Molle, Francois, Tira Foran, and Mira Kakonen (eds). 2009. *Contested Waterscapes in the Mekong Region: Hydropower, Livelihoods and Governance*. London: Earthscan.

Molle, Francois, Peter Mollinga, and Philippus Wester. 2009. 'Hydraulic Bureaucracies and the Hydraulic Mission: Flows of Water, Flows of Power', *Water Alternatives*, 2(3): 328–49.

Panigrahi, Jitendra K. and Susruta Amirapu. 2012. 'An Assessment of EIA System in India', *Environmental Impact Assessment Review*, 35 (July): 23–36.

Pomeranz, Kenneth. 2009. 'The Great Himalayan Watershed: Agrarian Crisis, Mega-Dams and the Environment', *New Left Review*, 58 (July–August): 5–39.

Rasul, Golam. 2010. 'The Role of the Himalayan Mountain Systems in Food Security and Agricultural Sustainability in South Asia', *International Journal of Rural Management*, 6(1): 95–116.

———. 2014. 'Food, Water and Energy Security in South Asia: A Nexus Perspective from the Hindu Kush Himalayan Region', *Environmental Science and Policy*, 39: 35–48.

Sadoff, Claudia and David Grey. 2002. 'Beyond the River: The Benefits of Cooperation on International Rivers', *Water Policy*, 4: 389–403.

———. 2005. 'Cooperation on International Rivers: A Continuum for Securing and Sharing Benefits', *Water International*, 30(4): 420–7.

Sangkhamanee, Jakkrit. 2012. 'Decolonising the River: Transnationalism and the Flows of Knowledge on Mekong Ecology', in Shirlena Huang, Mike Hayes, Sang Kook Lee (eds), *Managing Transnational Flows in East Asia*, pp. 173–86. Paju, Korea: Jimoondang.

Schmeier, Susanne. 2013. *Governing International Watercourses River Basin Organizations and the Sustainable Governance of Internationally Shared Rivers and Lakes*. London: Routledge.

Shresta, Ratna Sansar. 2010. 'Federalism and Water Resources in Nepal', *IUCN Policy Brief* (March). Available at https://cmsdata.iucn.org/downloads/federalism_and_water_resources_in_nepal.pdf (accessed 12 July 2011).

Smajgl, Alexander and John Ward (eds). 2013. *The Water-Food-Energy Plexus in the Mekong Region: Assessing Development Strategies Considering Cross-Sectoral and Transboundary Impact.* New York: Springer.

Sneddon, Chris and Coleen Fox. 2006. 'Rethinking Transboundary Mekong Basin', *Political Geography*, 25(2): 181–202.

Subramanian, Uma and John Arnold. 2001. *Forging Subregional Links in Transportation and Logistics in South Asia.* Washington, D.C.: World Bank.

Swain, Ashok. 2004. *Managing Water Conflict: Asia, Africa and the Middle East.* London: Routledge.

Thuzar, Moe, Rahul Mishra, Francis Hutchinson, Tin Maung Maung Than, and Termsak Chalermpalanupap. 2014. 'Connecting South and Southeast Asia: Implementation Challenges and Coordination Arrangements', *ADBI Working Paper Series* no. 501. Tokyo: Asian Development Bank Institute. Available at http://hdl.handle.net/11540/1098 (accessed 4 December 2015).

Vagholikar, Neeraj and Partha J. Das. 2010. *Damming Northeast India: Juggernaut of Hydropower Projects Threatens Social and Environmental Security of Region.* Pune; Guwahati; New Delhi: Kalpavriksh; Aaranyak; and ActionAid India. Available at https://chimalaya.files.wordpress.com/2010/12/damming-northeast-india-final.pdf (accessed 15 March 2014).

Vaidyanathan, A. 2001. *Water Resource Management: Institutions and Irrigation Development in India.* New Delhi: Oxford University Press.

Wilson, John S. and Tsunehiro Otsuki. 2007. 'Regional Integration in South Asia: What Role for Trade Facilitation?' *World Bank Policy Research Working Paper* 4423 (December). Available at http://elibrary.worldbank.org/doi/pdf/10.1596/1813-9450-4423 (accessed 15 March 2014).

Wirsing, Robert G., Christopher Jasparro, and Daniel C. Stoll. 2013. *International Conflict over Water Resources in Himalayan Asia.* Basingstoke: Palgrave Macmillan.

World Bank. 2006. *Natural Resources, Water and the Environment Nexus for Development and Growth in Northeast India.* Strategy Report. Washington D.C.: World Bank.

Yu, Winston. 2008. 'Benefit Sharing in International Rivers: Findings from the Senegal River Basin, the Columbia River Basin, and the Lesotho Highlands Water Project', *Africa Region Water Resources Unit Working Paper* no. 1. Washington, D.C.: World Bank. Available at http://documents.worldbank.org/curated/en/2008/11/10019058/benefit-sharing-international-rivers-findings-senegal-river-basin-columbia-river-basin-lesotho-highlands-water-project (accessed 15 March 2014).

10 Governance, Connectivity, and Knowledge Transparency in the Brahmaputra Basin

Kelly D. Alley

THIS CHAPTER FOCUSES on problems related to governance, infrastructure development, and knowledge transparency in the Brahmaputra river basin spanning the northeastern region of India. The Northeast generally refers to the contiguous seven states that form India's northeastern borders with China, Myanmar, and Bangladesh and also includes the state of Sikkim which lies to the west of Bhutan and to the east of Nepal. The tributaries and main streams of the Brahmaputra river system run from the mountainous regions of Tibet and Bhutan and from the Indian states of Sikkim and Arunachal Pradesh to the plains of West Bengal and Assam, and eventually to the vast delta of Bangladesh and into the Bay of Bengal. Some of the most important but also most invasive large scale activities in this basin and other basins in the Himalayas are water projects that generate hydroelectric energy and create reservoirs to store or channel water for irrigation and flood control (Bandyopadhyay and Ghosh 2009; D'Souza 2006, 2014; Grumbine and Pandit 2013; Gyawali 2003; Menon and Kohli 2005). Other large projects such as road and bridge constructions are meant to facilitate these water projects and therefore must be considered along with them.

The U.S. Department of State has recently identified governance and climate change as two of the three most important challenges for the region and for advancing the goal of Pan-Asian connectivity in South and Southeast Asia. This chapter assumes that these focus areas of governance and climate change are intertwined with and significantly impacted by infrastructure development, specifically the intensive road, water, and energy projects that mark the landscapes of northeast India. To improve connectivity, the governmental aim is to build power grids to facilitate in-country and transnational economic and cultural activity, to create roads to facilitate trade and mobility, and to expand digital communications access and technology for citizen exchanges and knowledge transparency. However well-intentioned these goals may be, there are and will continue to be environmental risks and impacts from advancing large scale water and energy projects, and these will be compounded by climatic trends that may be long term and difficult to reverse. Therefore a critical look at all the intended and unintended outcomes of projects is required in the early stages of development. To this end, the chapter offers observations on the early stages of hydropower and road development in Arunachal Pradesh and Assam, and reflects on alternate ways of thinking about connectivity in the region that may be more adaptable to the riverine environment and better meet the needs of residents living along the vast Brahmaputra floodplain.

Governance and the Clearance Process for Hydropower Projects

Problems with the enforcement and implementation of environmental laws, policies, and protocols are a subject of deep debate among activists and scientists in India today. High level government committees also consider weak implementation and non-compliance an impediment to national progress (Price 2014; Government of India 2014). Citizens use legal action and specifically the writ of mandamus to demand compliance to environmental protocols and regulations meant to protect the public good. These citizen actions extend from the unique history of public interest litigation in the Supreme Court and empower ongoing assessment and review through the National Green Tribunal. Citizens also directly enter policy debates and monitoring exercises through membership on court appointed committees. They also conduct modes of civil resistance that include opposing and boycotting public hearings, conducting demonstrations, and blocking access roads and streams to project sites.

It is useful to use Ananya Roy's notion of informality in this chapter to highlight the specific ways in which government or state agencies approach project approvals and plans. Roy and others have shown that by avoiding official mapping of current land-uses such as informal settlements, agricultural uses, and existing natural or cultural heritage, a government entity may intentionally disregard these elements and others in project plans. The intentional vagueness of project plans, protocols, and associated regulations can then be used by state actors to re-plan and re-map the urban landscape for desired development projects in the so called public interest. Roy points out that the absence of land titles, the existence of fuzzy boundaries and incomplete maps, and the vagueness of urban policies are 'the basis of state authority and serve as modes of sovereignty and discipline' (Roy 2009: 83). In this chapter these techniques are considered part of the official 'mode of informality' and this construct helps to shed light on governance behaviour related to energy projects.

In the northeastern corner of the Brahmaputra river basin, especially in Sikkim and Arunachal Pradesh, the government's aim is to add large megawatt capacity to power grids while responding, in theory, to emerging carbon reduction agreements (Alley 2011, 2012, 2014; Alley et al. 2014; Drew 2012; Menon and Kohli 2005; Vagholikar and Das 2010). In Arunachal Pradesh, hydropower development is also a direct response to construction upstream in Tibet. Dams on both sides of the Line of Actual Control (LAC) affirm each nation's territorial claims and water agendas (Chellaney 2011; Hill 2013). Indian public sector companies are also moving into Bhutan and Myanmar where environmental and social impact assessments for dam projects are not required. Private and public sector Indian and Chinese companies are tapping Nepal's hydropower potential. This is an important region for the Indian government as it looks for ways to augment its power capacity with in-country and neighbouring country projects. To do this, the Indian government is providing incentives and subsidies to enable interested companies to get the necessary clearances and land acquisitions for projects, and procure financing through evolving frameworks of public-private partnerships (Alexander 2014; Bosshard 2002; Kant 2005; Nimasow et al. 2013). Companies also have the option to sell power on a merchant basis which would reap higher profits than what is possible through government contracts for power at a fixed rate. International agencies under the United Nations Framework Convention on Climate Change (UNFCCC) have made hydropower projects eligible for Clean Development Mechanism carbon credits and some Indian companies have applied for those credits and the accompanying financing.

In India the 'license raj' continues to shape the ways in which access to water and forest resources and licenses are obtained to develop infrastructure. A trade in clearance and permit documents has also blossomed, particularly through gaming 'memoranda of understanding' (MoU), the document that establishes the early phase of a project agreement between a state entity and a public or private sector company (Rajshekhar and Sukumar 2013; Thakkar 2010). The license raj approach to project contracts and environment and forest clearances underscores the deep structure of rent seeking behavior in the Indian bureaucracy, and generates specific problems for energy and the nation (Bear 2015; Bussell 2012, 2013; Government of India 2014; Rajshekhar and Sukumar 2013). The licence raj approach and the government's mode of informality are essential to understand as problems of governance that complicate the country's development activities. The specific ways these approaches shape clearance processes for hydropower projects need to be spelled out in greater detail to make them visible and identifiable for redress.

The Central Government Ministry of Environment, Forests, and Climate Change (MoEFCC) is the regulatory industry that issues access and use rights for key resources such as rights to forest products and the conversion of forest land to other uses, rights to divert and channel rivers, and rights to re-allocate private land from citizens to other users. This Ministry issues the Forest Clearance through the Forest Advisory Committee (FAC), a committee of experts appointed by it to assist in clearance decisions. Likewise, the Ministry issues the Environment Clearance through its Expert Appraisal Committee (EAC). The EAC and the FAC assist the Ministry in assessing projects before issuing such clearances. In addition to these key clearances, a project developer must get a clearance from the Indian Board for Wildlife if wildlife is impacted and a techno-economic clearance from the Central Electricity Authority. At the state level, 'no objection certificates' must be collected from the state pollution control board, the state irrigation and public health departments, the public works, the revenue department, and fisheries. In some states, these 'no objection clearances' are being eliminated from the regulation process in order to 'expedite' project development (Narain 2014; Rajshekhar 2014).

To propose a streamlining of these clearances through a 'single window', the High Level T.S.R. Subramanian Committee recently proposed a rewriting of the country's six main environmental laws.

Their report recommended taking the clearance powers away from the MoEFCC and vesting them in a national level National Environmental Management Agency (NEMA) and a state level State Environmental Management Agency (SEMA) (Rajshekhar 2014). This would enable, in their words, 'expeditious clearances' especially in projects of national importance. The Committee's new report argues in a straightforward way to correct the MoEFCC practices which have reduced regulation and monitoring to unaccountable rent-seeking activities. The report can be read in a number of ways; however, it is worth noting that the executive offices are interested in such a move as it would empower central ministries in the clearance process. It would also facilitate a vertical deployment of rents and diminish the horizontal distribution across a swath of agencies. In this vertical integration through the SEMA and NEMA, the ruling party at the Centre could also become a key recipient. These recent initiatives to develop windows for expeditious clearances for projects connect with the larger global financing trends underway to push mega-projects on infrastructure and draw public funds to finance these endeavors (Alexander 2014). This shows that neoliberal demands for industry incentives—usually the drivers of deregulation—come second to government strategies of informality that are used to move projects through the clearance stages. In addition, the hollowing out of the regulatory framework proposed by the Subramanian report would provide a comfortable institutional context for administrative informality, as it prompts an even more vigilant response from citizen monitors.

Since this region is also an eco-sensitive, transboundary watershed, hydropower projects, connectivity infrastructure, and climatic extremes will end up transforming the hydrological cycle and in the process create the conditions for hydrohazards like those already seen across the Himalayan region (Dobhal et al. 2013; Mustafa 2013). These hydrohazards—the destruction of dams during flooding and glacial lake outbursts, the loss of life from sudden dam releases, and the siltation of riverbank property from dam muck and debris sites—are prompting citizen groups and court appointed committees to observe and monitor inert infrastructures such as dams, roads, and supporting infrastructure, and trace how rapidly changing river flows behave with dam barrages, tunnels, and debris sites. In this socio-political dynamic then, the state is acting quickly in consort with private companies while citizen monitoring groups are actively participating in corrective and even obstructive measures, as a way to assess in advance the dangers and environmental and hydrological effects of these projects.

The hydropower potential of India's northeast is concentrated in two states, Sikkim and Arunachal Pradesh. In 2001, the Central Electricity Authority (CEA) envisioned the possibility of constructing 168 large hydroelectric projects in the Brahmaputra basin that would generate over 63,000 MW of energy (See Figure 10.1).

Twenty-two projects and 15,000 MW of energy were mapped out in the Subansiri river basin (Dutta and Sarma 2012: 2953; People's Movement in Subansiri Valley and River Basin Friends n.d.). When the state government assumed the authority to write MoUs with private power companies, the identification of projects took off, creating what critics called a 'MoU virus' through the allotment of MoUs for 153 projects (Chakravartty 2011) (See Figure 10.2).

The MoU virus also reflected the struggle over project rights between the National Hydroelectric Power Corporation (NHPC) and the Arunachal Pradesh state government. From 2003 to 2006 the NHPC prepared detailed project reports (DPRs) for six projects but after 2006, the state government took five of the six projects away from the public sector corporation and awarded them—through the signing of MoUs—to private companies.

The NHPC's first project in the region, the 2,000 MW Lower Subansiri Dam, was problematic from the outset. When the company started construction in 2001, the Assam Government and the regional office of the MoEFCC recorded that the company violated the Forest Conservation Act (1980) and the EInvironment Impact Assessment Notification (1994). Several citizen groups also contested the authenticity of the company's public hearing and pointed out the inaccurate data in the EIA (Vagholikar 2005, 2009, n.d.).

In 2002, the NHPC submitted an application for project approval from the Indian Board for Wildlife since the project was to submerge part of a nearby Sanctuary (Vagholikar 2009: 72). The Wildlife Committee concluded that wildlife habitats and species within and beyond the sanctuary would be submerged in upstream and downstream areas. Riding over the objections raised by non-official members of the committee, the MoEFCC eventually got the forest and environment clearances during a meeting of the Indian Board of Wildlife Standing Committee in May 2003 (Vagholikar 2005; 2009: 72). The MoEFCC was able to do so by

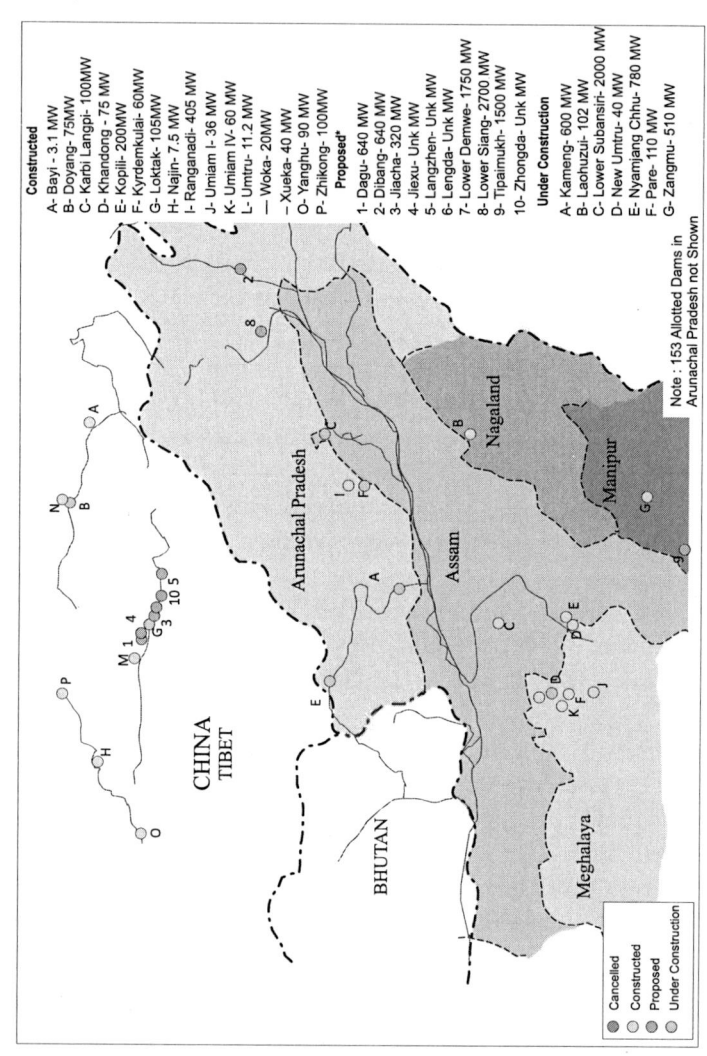

Constructed
A- Bayi - 3.1 MW
B- Doyang- 75MW
C- Karbi Langpi- 100MW
D- Khandong - 75 MW
E- Kopili- 200MW
F- Kyrdemkulai- 60MW
G- Loktak- 105MW
H- Najin- 7.5 MW
I- Ranganadi- 405 MW
J- Umiam I- 36 MW
K- Umiam IV- 60 MW
L- Umtru- 11.2 MW
– Woka- 20MW
– Xueka- 40 MW
O- Yanghu- 90 MW
P- Zhikong- 100MW

Proposed*
1- Dagu- 640 MW
2- Dibang- 640 MW
3- Jiacha- 320 MW
4- Jiexu- Unk MW
5- Langzhen- Unk MW
6- Lengda- Unk MW
7- Lower Demwe- 1750 MW
8- Lower Siang- 2700 MW
9- Tipaimukh- 1500 MW
10- Zhongda- Unk MW

Under Construction
A- Kameng- 600 MW
B- Laohuzui- 102 MW
C- Lower Subansiri- 2000 MW
D- New Umtru- 40 MW
E- Nyamjang Chhu- 780 MW
F- Pare- 110 MW
G- Zangmu- 510 MW

Note : 153 Allotted Dams in
Arunachal Pradesh not Shown

CHINA
TIBET

Arunachal Pradesh

Assam

Nagaland

Manipur

BHUTAN

Meghalaya

○ Cancelled
○ Constructed
○ Proposed
○ Under Construction

Figure 10.1 Status of Hydropower Projects in the Northeastern Brahmaputra Basin as of 2013.

Source: ESRI World Terrain map. Map by Ryan Hile.

Note: Map not to scale and does not represent authentic international boundaries.

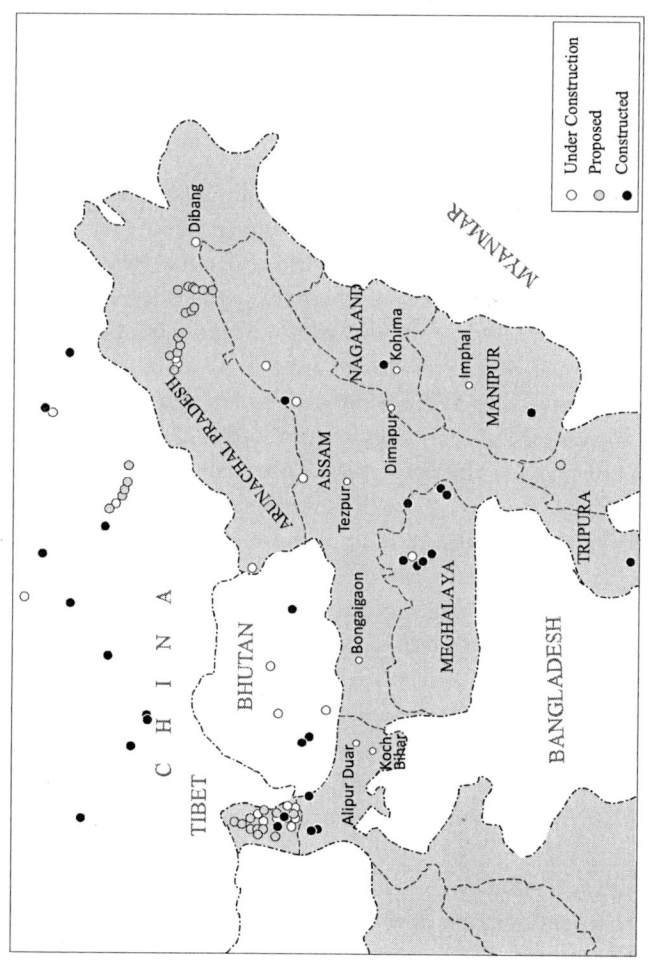

Figure 10.2. Constructed, Under Construction, and Proposed Dams in Lower Tibet, Arunachal Pradesh, and Assam as of January 2015. Map by Samriddhi Shakya.

Source: ESRI topographic map. Map by Samriddhi Shakya.

Note: Map not to scale and does not represent authentic international boundaries.

agreeing to implement certain stringent conditions in dam construction which included: 1) declaring the catchment area a Protected Area, and 2) banning construction of additional dams upstream on the Subansiri river. But in August 2003, a former member of the Wildlife Board was compelled to file a petition in the Supreme Court to show that the MoEFCC had deliberately omitted in the final clearance these two conditions imposed by the Standing Committee. In April 2004, the Supreme Court ordered that the project could go ahead only if it fulfilled all the original conditions.

In May 2005 the state government of Arunachal Pradesh approached the Supreme Court to waive or modify the two conditions required by the Wildlife Board. The state government was envisioning sixteen mega dams upstream on the same river. The NHPC was interested in developing two of them. Communities in the basin were vehemently opposed to additional dams and argued that upstream and downstream towns, settlements, and agricultural land would be extensively submerged. To solve the matter, the Supreme Court asked the Wildlife Board to review again the original conditions for the Lower Subansiri (Vagholikar 2009: 72). Several Board members said waiving these conditions would set a dangerous precedent; others argued that a cumulative impact assessment should assess the carrying capacity of the basin before additional dams could be considered.

The Wildlife Board eventually replaced the 'no dams upstream' condition with the qualifier that 'any proposal in the upstream of the Subansiri River would be considered independently on its merit by the Standing Committee as and when submitted by the proponents' (Vagholikar 2009: 73). In 2011 community members and activists gave up battling with the dominant script of permits and clearances and blocked the streets and rivers to prevent cargo from reaching the construction site.

In June 2014 the NHPC management was gearing up to restart construction of the Lower Subansiri Dam. This triggered protests in Assam and within a week state government officials in Assam announced that the project would not restart, to quiet the issue for the time being. Instead, the Central MoEFCC shifted their focus to the NHPC's proposed Dibang Multipurpose Project in the Dibang river basin. The MoEFCC quickly appointed new members to the FAC to get the clearances done for that project.

The operations of official informality in terms of unmapping, deregulation, and reconstituting conditions and committee memberships are woven through the entire history of the Subansiri project and also through the early stages of the Dibang project. The MoEFCC was mandated by the Wildlife Board and the Supreme Court to write in two main conditions for the Subansiri project. But the Ministry was able to get the conditions redefined and ultimately declawed. When the Subansiri project was stalled again by citizen occupation of territory, the Ministry shifted focus, rearranged the FAC and got that committee to award clearances for the Dibang (Dandekar 2014). These new clearances came after years of refusals by former committee members (Mazoomdar 2014).

Road Connectivity

The road building agencies of the northeast region of India experience ongoing problems and challenges in completing and maintaining a road network (See Figure 10.3).

The Brahmaputra river system complicates the linear notion of mobility where it is generally thought that the shortest possible route between two points ought to be concretized by a paved road. The riverine system expands and contracts with the monsoon season and seasonal glacial melt. Since the river system is the dominant force shaping the aquatic and terrestrial landscapes of the basin, the road plans must be adaptable to this kind of extreme waxing and waning of river flows. The roads must work around or jump over, as much as possible, the wicked streams of the monsoon, while holding up to erosion and the sediment load unleashed by wicked flows in the mountainous areas. Along the plains the great flows deposit sediment throughout the valley floor following the twists and turns of the braided streams.

These seasonal river processes interfere with road building and complicate work to sustain many of the built roads in the region.

Considerable resources are put into these continuous efforts to repair and rebuild roads and bridges every season (See Figure 10.4).

Sections of pavement must be repaved, and sections of roads must be entirely rebuilt from eroded mountainsides. In the spaces where roads or bridges are washed away or cannot be completed or repaired due to rising streams, local modes of transport develop to shuttle people, vehicles, and cargo from one side of a stream to another. Local entrepreneurs operate boats and ferries of various sizes to shuttle people, vehicles, cargo, and other assets across the many streams of the braided Brahmaputra (See

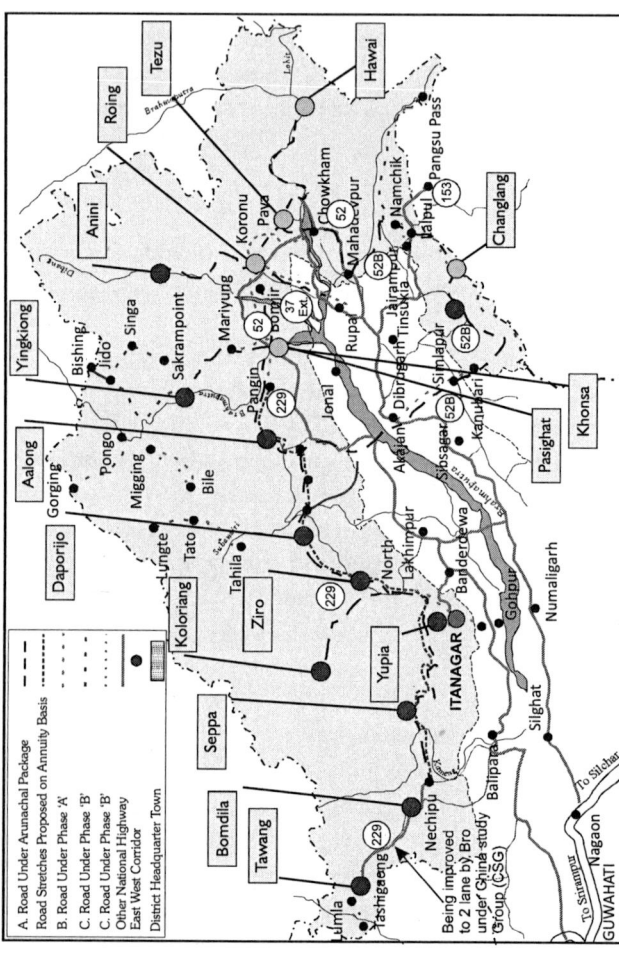

Figure 10.3 Map of Road Projects in Arunachal Pradesh and Assam.

Source: Ministry of Development of North Eastern Region, available at http://www.mdoner.gov.in/content/sardp-ne (accessed on 7 May 2015).

Note: Map not to scale and does not represent authentic international boundaries..

Figure 10.4 Sediment in the Brahmaputra River near Dibrugarh
Source: Photo by Kelly D. Alley.

Figure 10.5 Bridge Destroyed by Flooding in a Tributary of the Siang River
Source: Photo by Kelly D. Alley.

Figure 10.5). Since this local industry is unregulated, the transporters charge whatever the market will bear and this translates into significant costs for people traversing the region and when crossing the state of Assam. For example, the traverse from Pasighat on the plains of Arunachal Pradesh to Dibrugarh in Assam would require a family in a car, motorcycle, or bicycle or on foot, to cross three or four streams on a boat. The transport of the car would cost them anywhere from 500 to 1,500 rupees for each boat trip. In between these streams local tax collectors also stop traffic to collect a fee for crossing a small bridge or motoring across a section of road they claim to maintain. These are unregulated road or bridge agents that appear to maintain the infrastructure as if it were their private project, and reap a profit through a tax or crossing fee.

All of these fees place a significant burden on passengers and cost much more than a government road system would for the individual user (See Figure 10.6). When the longest bridge in India, the bridge from Dhola to Sadia in Assam, is completed, it will connect sections of the state that are now divided by many streams of the Brahmaputra

Figure 10.6 A Ferry Boat Crossing the Brahmaputra River
Source: Photo by Kelly D. Alley.

and will provide a faster travel time from Assam to Arunachal Pradesh (Mukherjee 2015). The new bridge would also undercut some of the over-charging that currently exists for shuttle and infrastructure maintenance services.

Road building in the mountainous areas of Arunachal Pradesh is also hazardous due to constant erosion and landslides, especially during the monsoon season. Where roads remain a single lane, however, the erosion is much less. Road widening is occurring in many places, especially at lower elevations, and this causes additional erosion as the roadside underbrush and forest cover are destroyed. This means that every road widening project creates new needs for sediment removal and repair and rebuilding of the road.

The widening of roads is required to truck heavy equipment and machinery to the hydropower site. The view of the government is that wider roads are needed to facilitate the transport of heavy machinery, but the consequences of widening may end up meaning more blockage from landslides and less connectivity. Road blockage also impacts citizens living in the region, as it prevents them from the mobility needed for their own subsistence. Road blockages can also lead to extreme suffering during the monsoon, when village to village connectivity is breached by rising flood waters and landslides.

Like many residents of mountainous regions, those who live on the sandy islands that form the vast floodplain of the Brahmaputra have no access to a continuous energy source through a grid and must generate their own solar sources of energy for the home and work (Hazarika 2005). They are also disconnected from news and information unless, in rare cases, they have a satellite dish. Many floodplain villages can receive information and news through radios. Radio Brahmaputra, a community participatory radio station in Dibrugarh, is the main form of regional communication for the 10 million residents of the floodplain (See Figure 10.7).

What is important about this sector of the resident population, the floodplain dwellers, and those residents living in remote mountainous regions, is that they would not benefit from a government plan to upgrade

Figure 10.7 The Staff of Brahmaputra Radio in Dibrugarh
Source: Photo by Kelly D. Alley.

and broaden access to digital technologies and connections. They cannot easily access digital worlds due to the lack of a sufficient energy supply. It is therefore important to consider ways to improve radio connectivity throughout the floodplains and mountainous regions by supporting community and participatory stations such as Radio Brahmaputra. Training for radio staff in the areas of weather forecasting, flood alert techniques, communications for disaster management, and general programming for community entertainment and education is also extremely important.

Transboundary Knowledge Transparency

One of the possible outcomes of the recent initiative to improve digital connectivity in the region is better exchange of information between people of the region and citizens and governments of the neighbouring countries of Bhutan, Myanmar, China, and Bangladesh. Better information exchange is needed so that citizens understand the plans and effects of the construction and operation of large infrastructure projects, to ensure their own safety. In this context, knowledge exchange through reliable paths such as radio transmissions for floodplain residents and digital sources for urban dwellers can help citizens remain connected as they share the benefits of the river system. But what is the current state of affairs with regard to transboundary knowledge of the operations of hydropower projects and what is needed to improve transparency? The chapter now turns to one sub-basin in the state of Arunachal Pradesh to look at how transboundary communication between India and China is progressing. This example will also point to the mode of informality in operation, and will indicate that this mode impacts residents and citizens on both sides of the LAC.

According to government reports, the Siang has the greatest hydropower potential of all the rivers in the state. The Siang River in Arunachal Pradesh is called the Yarlung Tsangpo River in Tibet. It originates at Lake Mansarovar near Mt. Kailash before traversing 2,057 km across Tibet and entering India at the Arunachal Pradesh border. The upper catchment area of the Siang is mountainous with deep and narrow valleys, bordered on the west by the Subansiri Basin and on the east by the Dibang Basin. In India the Siang River flows for 1,970 km to the confluence with the Siyom River and then travels 97 km to join the

Brahmaputra in Assam. The other major tributaries of the Siang River are the Yamne, Simang, Sigong, Ringong Asi, and Yang Sang Chhu.

In July 2007, when the state government of Arunachal Pradesh was allotting MoUs for hydropower projects, Velcan Energy Holdings, a company with hydropower projects in Brazil and Lao People's Democratic Republic (LPDR) and biomass projects in India, announced its move into India's hydropower market. After obtaining the MoUs from the state government, Velcan was able to move forward with the DPRs and then pursue the public hearings and forest and environment clearances for the three projects. In May 2013, after five years of field surveys, the DPR for Tato I was filed with the Indian CEA. The DPR for Heo was filed in July 2013. At that time the company wrote, 'Velcan Energy is optimistic that the filing will lead to a Techno-Economic Clearance (TEC) by the CEA in the second half of 2014. This clearance will then allow Velcan Energy to begin negotiations for a Power Purchasing Agreement (PPA) with possible clients. The studies detailed in the DPR show that this project can produce electricity at a competitive price for clients in India'(Reuters 2013).

The public hearing for Tato I was reported in September 2013 and the public hearings for Pauk and Heo were reported in December 2013. All three public hearings had to be cancelled on the first attempt due to unrest over land issues (Overdorf 2012). Several citizen groups asserted that the projects should not be considered until a cumulative impact study (beyond the required EIA) is prepared and reviewed by downstream communities. Shortly thereafter the company declared that the public hearings had been completed on the second attempt. It is unclear from this process, however, whether downstream residents have sufficient information on cumulative impacts to assess the costs and benefits of all these projects.

In June 2014 the Centre for Inter-Disciplinary Studies of Mountain and Hill Environment at the University of Delhi (CISMHE) completed the EIAs for the three projects. This prompted the non-government organization (NGO) South Asia Network for Dams, Rivers, and People to point out the underlying conflict of interest: the CISMHE was established as a Research and Development centre by the Power Ministry (Pradhan 2014). It is generally known by experts and citizen activists that EIAs are created to serve the purpose of clearing a project; they do not carefully and adequately document the existing biosphere and hydrosphere. Instead, these assessments tend to minimize the anticipated ecological, hydrological, and social impacts of a proposed project. Moreover, EIAs include intentionally thin data sets. Given this problematic process, the question is: why was this company awarded the clearances and not another? Other private players with proposals in various stages of clearance have been waiting as well. Specifically Jaypee Power Company has been on hold with its Lower Siang proposal and Reliance has several proposed projects for the Siang basin. Both have faced strong resistance from the local communities. It is possible that the international track record of Velcan made it a safe bet. In India, all the formal procedural steps had been taken: the MoU, the scoping and surveys, the Detailed Project Report, and the public hearings. The Velcan Company was sufficiently documented and eligible for the next level of clearances. More importantly, though, its projects were proposed in the upper Siang basin, just below the disputed border with China (Mishra 2013). Farther upstream along the Yarlung Tsangpo, the People's Republic of China (PRC) has permitted four medium sized run of the river projects; one is completed and the others are under construction (Krishnan 2013) (See Figure 10.2). Together as three medium sized project, the Velcan run of the river dams would match the scale of China's endeavours. Additionally, the EIA process, of which citizens have been highly critical, has worked in favour of the company. Citizen groups used the demand for a cumulative impact study as a measure to stall the clearances, but government and company representatives used the study to bolster their standing. After the Central Water Commission completed the cumulative impact study (R.S. Envirolink 2013), the government and company could argue for the clearances. At that point the citizen groups could only oppose the contents of the EIA but not its legitimizing functions (Tayeng 2015).

In the shadows are five other mega projects that have not yet been allotted, including the Siang Upper Stage I (6,000 MW) and the Siang Upper Stage II (3,750 MW). The latter two are in the investigation stage (Pradhan 2014). There is an attempt to delink the sanctioning of these individual projects from the cumulative impact assessment and the carrying capacity assessment of the Siang Basin, two reports that citizens have called up for their inadequate data sets and faulty analyses. Pradhan (2014) notes, '[s]uch a large-scale development which is expected to take place over a period of [the] next 10–15 years will cause huge environmental impacts and exert tremendous pressure on carrying capacity of Siang basin. Cumulative Impact Assessment and Carrying

Capacity Assessment of Siang basin which was conducted by Central Water Commission (CWC) as directed by Inter-Ministerial Group (IMG) in February 2010 on the directions of Prime Minister's Office (PMO). The study is yet to be approved through a credible participatory process. The study itself has very serious shortcomings.

It is easy for the media to stir up transboundary fears when reporting on dam building along the Yarlung Tsangpo in Tibet since the general public is apprehensive about China's border activities. The Ministry of External Affairs can then use these media presentations to bolster the exceptional status of these hydropower projects. Since the Indian army is populating the state of Arunachal Pradesh with installations, highways, and airports, energy projects are identified along with military settlements as projects that establish territorial sovereignty. Concurrently, the PRC and India assert that the run of the river projects do not divert any significant amount from the river stream, to appease downstream communities in India and Bangladesh. Indian and Chinese authorities are also holding off on any agreement or treaty regarding transboundary water sharing. All parties remain silent on the known externalities that may develop from the operation of the hydropower infrastructures: the land and riverbank changes these projects have created, and the deposition of muck, debris, and silt through the construction process. All these externalities have proven hazardous for downstream riparian residents in the other Himalayan states of Uttarakhand, Himachal Pradesh, and Sikkim, where the industry is more developed. In one of my field meetings, an industry representative working in the Siang basin hypothesized that Chinese companies had already started construction activities in the remote region around the Great Bend in Tibet and that muck and debris from the four projects on the Tsangpo were entering the river stream (see also Watts 2010). In 2014, Chinese and Indian diplomats celebrated a breakthrough when they agreed to share hydrological data on the transboundary rivers during the monsoon season (Gupta 2014). This agreement was limited to the exchange of flow data and did not include requirements to disclose information on project plans and operations, muck disposal sites, or the schedule of water releases from the storage ponds and reservoirs.

Dam construction in the Siang Basin shows that there are significant breaks in communication and compliance between hydropower companies, regulatory agencies, and the public on both sides of the international

LAC. It is clear that within India a public hearing to initiate the clearance process is an incomplete way to allow citizens' inputs into the assessment of the costs and benefits of a project and set the compensation for impacts on livelihoods. Citizens raise many complaints about compensation and government officials tend to downsize citizen needs while complaining that compensation politics mars development in the national interest. The water sharing implications and changes in the hydrograph of the basin are also significant and need skilled scientific analysis and translations for public knowledge and transparency. The lack of information exchange between China and India will continue to hinder disaster preparedness and management, to the benefit of no one.

Concluding Directions

At the global level, there is an ongoing tension between India and China over territorial integrity; it is a subtext to the energy plans of both countries in border regions where energy projects are considered a formal way of trumping territorial counter-claims. Within this hydrosphere are a myriad of river streams, all flowing into the larger braided Brahmaputra River, which swells massively during the four-month rainy season. This chapter has suggested ways to think about flood or climate friendly infrastructure; roads must not be envisioned by linear models but must be fashioned according to the meandering behaviour of river flows. Roads and bridges should be built on scales that can withstand big changes in flow volume and velocity, along with massive sediment loads. Since connectivity for floodplain residents must be augmented in a low energy environment, radios may be a more appropriate form of communication over digital technologies.

Finally, this chapter has addressed problems with the culture of governance. Citizen-led legal action has provided pathways for intervening in elite decision-making, project planning, and environmental impact assessment, and has pushed for better enforcement and implementation of environmental laws, policies, and protocols (Government of India 2014; Price 2014). The National Green Tribunal continues to push for citizen and NGO involvement on monitoring and steering committees, but the process is constantly drawn down by cooptation: court appointed committees produce reports that are either accepted or dismissed by a powerful official who may then call for a new committee and a new report.

The endless creation, dismantling, and reconstitution of committees and reports may allow for vetting approaches and solutions, but makes any remediation extremely time consuming. Efforts need to be made to appoint skilled scientists to these committees and require that they follow a vetted, formalized protocol. Environmental laws, policies, and protocols should not be diluted further through calls for expeditious clearances.

Opportunities for rent seeking and gaming in permits and clearances must be eliminated and company and government procedural compliance enforced by strict regulatory oversight and citizen monitoring. Citizen monitoring groups must be emboldened through existing democratic institutions to keep checks on powers and rights. Procedures for public hearings as they are established by the EIA Notification of 2006 should be followed and strengthened. Additional avenues for information sharing and assessing cumulative impacts should be developed for public knowledge. All basin country government departments should put data and plans for hydropower and other infrastructure development in the public domain in an expeditious manner. The science wings of basin country governments and universities can also develop climate and stream flow modeling for transboundary flood alert systems in China, India, Bhutan, Nepal, and Bangladesh. Multilateral transboundary river agreements need to be created to include disclosure of hydropower projects and related muck disposal practices and water and land uses. Finally, regulatory agencies should require hydropower companies to follow a schedule of water releases and create a protocol for crisis releases. They should also make that schedule available to the public through digital and radio communications.

References

Alexander, Nancy. 2014. *The Emerging Multi-Polar World Order: Its Unprecedented Consensus on a New Model for Financing Infrastructure Investment and Development*. Washington, D.C.: Heinrich Boll Foundation North America.

Alley, Kelly D. 2014. 'The Developments, Policies and Assessments of Hydropower in the Ganga River Basin', in Rashmi Sanghi (ed.), *Our National River Ganga: Lifeline of Millions*, pp. 285–305. Netherlands: Springer.

———. 2012. 'Water Wealth and Energy in the Indian Himalayas', *The Silk Road*, 10: 136–45.

————. 2011. 'The Disappearing Rivers of India', *Asia Pacific Memo*, 15 November; available at http://www.asiapacificmemo.ca/the-disappearing-rivers-of-india (accessed 14 May 2015).

Alley, Kelly D., Ryan Hile, and Chandana Mitra. 2014.'Visualizing Hydropower across the Himalayas: Mapping in a Time of Regulatory Decline', *Himalaya, the Journal of the Association for Nepal and Himalayan Studies*, 34(2): 52–66.

Bandyopadhyay, Jayanta and Nilanjan Ghosh. 2009. 'Holistic Engineering and Hydro–Diplomacy in the Ganges–Brahmaputra–Meghna Basin', *Economic and Political Weekly*, 44(45): 50–60.

Bear, Laura. 2015. *Navigating Austerity: Currents of Debt along a South Asian River*. Stanford: Stanford University Press.

Bosshard, Peter. 2002. *Power Finance: Financial Institutions in India's Hydropower Sector*. Berkeley: South Asia Network for Dams, Rivers and People, International Rivers Network, and Urgewald.

Bussell, Jennifer. 2012. *Corruption and Reform in India*. Cambridge: Cambridge University Press.

————. 2013. 'Varieties of Corruption: The Organization of Rent-Seeking in India', *Westminster Model of Democracy in Crisis?* Harvard University, 14 May.

Chakravartty, Anupam. 2011. '"MoU Virus" Hits Arunachal Pradesh', *Down to Earth*, 9 September; available at http://www.downtoearth.org.in/news/mou-virus-hits-arunachal-pradesh-33962 (accessed 10 December 2015).

Chellaney, Brahma. 2011. *Water: Asia's New Battleground*. Georgetown: Georgetown University Press.

Dandekar, Parineeta. 2014.'Manipulating Environment & Forest Clearances for Dibang Project: Déjà vu: LSHP History Repeated: Will it be Tragedy or Comedy?', *South Asia Network for Dams, Rivers and People*, 6 October.

Dobhal, D.P., Anil K. Gupta, Manish Mehta, and D.D. Khandelwal. 2013. 'Kedarnath Disaster: Fact and Plausible Causes', *Current Science*, 105(2): 171–4.

Drew, Georgina. 2012.'Ecological Change and the Sociocultural Consequences of the Ganges River's Decline', in B.R. Johnston (ed.), *Water, Cultural Diversity, and Global Environmental Change: Emerging Trends, Sustainable Futures?* pp. 203–18. Paris: UNESCO–IHP.

D'Souza, Rohan. 2006. *Drowned and Dammed: Colonial Capitalism and Flood Control in Eastern India*. New Delhi: Oxford University Press.

————. 2014. 'Filling Multipurpose Reservoirs with Politics: Displacing the Modern Large Dam in India', in M. Nüsser (ed.), *Large Dams in Asia: Contested Environments between Technological Hydroscapes and Social Resistance*, pp. 61–73. Netherlands: Springer.

Dutta, Ranjit and Sarada K. Sarma. 2012. 'Lower Subansiri Hydroelectric Power Project and Future of the Subansiri River Ecosystem', *Annals of Biological Research*, 3(6): 2953–7.

EIA Directorate. 2013. *Cumulative Impact and Carrying Capacity Study of Siang Sub-Basin Including Downstream Impacts*. Volume I, prepared for Central Water Commission: R.S. Envirolink Technologies Pvt. Ltd.

Government of India. 2014. *Report: High Level Committee to Review Various Acts Administered by the Ministry of Environment, Forests and Climate Change*. Available at http://www.moef.nic.in/sites/default/files/press-releases/Final_ Report_of_HLC.pdf (accessed 31 January 2016)

Grumbine, R. Edward and Maharaj K. Pandit. 2013. 'Threats from India's Himalaya Dams', *Science*, 339(6115): 36–7.

Gupta, Joydeep. 2014. 'China, India Formalise Brahmaputra Agreement', 5 July, available at Thethirdpole.net (accessed 14 March 2016).

Gyawali, Dipak. 2003. *Rivers, Technology, and Society: Learning the Lessons of Water Management in Nepal*. London: Zed Books.

Hazarika, Sanjoy. 2005. 'Waters of Despair, Waters of Hope', *Gateway to the East: A Symposium on Northeast India and the Look East Policy*.

Hill, Douglas. 2013. 'Trans-boundary Water Resources and Uneven Development: Crisis in and beyond Contemporary India', *South Asia: Journal of South Asian Studies*, 36(2): 243–57.

Kant, Promode. 'Clearance of Large Hydel Projects: Environmental Procedures and Considerations', *The Ecologist Asia*, 11(1): 34–7.

Krishnan, Ananth. 2013. 'China Gives Go-ahead for Three New Brahmaputra Dams', *The Hindu*, 30 January.

Mazoomdar, Jay. 2014. '6 Years, 2 Rejections Later, India's Largest Hydro Project Cleared', *The Indian Express*, 24 September.

Menon, Manju and Kanchi Kohli. 2005. *Large Dams for Hydropower in Northeast India: A Dossier*. New Delhi: South Asia Network on Dams, Rivers and People; Kalpavriksh.

Mishra, Deepak. 2013. 'Developing the Border: The State and the Political Economy of Development in Arunachal Pradesh', in D.N. Gellner (ed.), *Borderland Lives in Northern South Asia: Non-state Perspectives*, pp. 141–62. Durham: Duke University Press.

Mukherjee, Sharmistha. 2015. 'Longest Bridge in India Provides a Quick Link to LAC', *Indian Express*, 4 May.

Mustafa, Daanish. 2013. *Water Resource Management in a Vulnerable World: The Hydro-Hazardscapes of Climate Change*. London: I.B. Tauris.

Narain, Sunita. 2014 'Sunita Narain: Breaking the Impasse of 2013', *Business Standard*, 12 January.

Nimasow, Gibji, Reter Potom, and Tanyang Yaying. 2013. 'Environmental Impact of Siyom Hydro Project of Payum Circle West Siang District, Arunachal Pradesh', *IJCS New Liberty Group*.

Overdorf, Jason. 2012. 'India Dam Protest Update: Siang Public Hearing Canceled', *Global Post*, 16 April.

People's Movement in Subansiri Valley and River Basin Friends. n.d. 'Subansiri Hydro Electric Project', Unpublished Paper.

Pradhan, Amruta. 2014. 'Pauk, Heo, Tato-I Hydropower Projects: CISMHE's Shoddy EIAs Seven Big Hydro on Third Order Tributary of Brahmaputra!' *SANDRP Blog*, 9 July.

Price, Gareth. 2014. *Attitudes to Water in South Asia*, Chatham House Report. London: Royal Institute for International Affairs.

Rajshekhar, M. 2014. 'TSR Subramanian Panel Bats for New Green Norms', *The Economic Times*, 24 November.

Rajshekhar, M. and C.R. Sukumar. 2013. 'Hydelgate: We Get into Projects after Permits and Licenses are in Place, Says Anil Chalamalasetty, Greenko', *The Hindu*, 6 May.

Reuters. 2013. 'Velcan Energy: Successful Filing of Tato-1 HEP Techno—economic Studies (India)', Press release, 11 June.

Roy, Ananya. 2009. 'Why India Cannot Plan Its Cities: Informality, Insurgence and the Idiom of Urbanization', *Planning Theory*, 8(1): 76–87.

Tayeng, Ratna. 2015. 'Hydropower Dams and Development: Local Perspectives', *Online International Interdisciplinary Research Journal*, 5(1): 335–50.

Thakkar, Himanshu. 2010. *Indian Express Campaign for Big Hydro in North East*. Berkeley: South Asia Network for Dams, Rivers and People.

Vagholikar, Neeraj. 2005. 'Damning our Wildlife', *Sanctuary Asia*, 25(1).

———. 2009. 'The Subansiri Subversion', *Sanctuary Asia*: 72–3.

———. n.d. 'Lower Subansiri Hydel Project: Stop All Work Till Critical Issues are Resolve'. Green Heritage. Available at https://sites.google.com/site/greenheritageassam/hot-news-1/lower-subansiri-hydel-project--stop-all-work-till-critical-issues-are-resolve.

Vagholikar, Neeraj and M. Firoz Ahmed. 2003. 'Tracking a Hydel Project', *The Ecologist Asia*, 11(1): 25–32.

Vagholikar, N. and P. Das. 2010. *Damming Northeast India*. Pune; Guwahati; New Delhi: Kalpavriksh; Aaranyak; and ActionAid India.

Watts, Jonathan. 2010. 'Chinese Engineers Propose World's Biggest Hydro-Electric Project in Tibet: Mega-Dam on Yarlung Tsangpo River Would Save 200m Tonnes', *The Guardian*, 24 May.

11 Pulses against Volumes

Transboundary Rivers and Pan-Asian Connectivity

Rohan D'Souza

I N A WORLD ADDICTED TO INSTANT MESSAGING and ringed several times over with communication satellites and mobile phone networks, the term connectivity feels almost outdated. This unending quest to conquer space through time, nonetheless, is not without exasperating political and economic consequences. In recent times, however, efforts to compress geographies into ever more compact folds through large dams, roads, navigation canals, and bridges, for example, are chiefly understood as wicked challenges for managing trade-offs between the environment and the economy. More so, if one has to deal with something as voluble and temperamental as a transboundary river: which, as a wildly flowing entity, can often times disorient politico–legal boundaries and perplex painstaking claims over territory and sovereignty.[1]

Questions are therefore inevitable: how will the idea of 'connectivity' grapple with transboundary rivers, when to harness the latter requires nations and governments to play zero-sum games? That is, any benefit extracted at one point of the flow will simultaneously involve costs borne at another segment of the river's sinuous course. To understand, however, the political, economic and ecological disorderliness of the transboundary river in the context of Pan-Asian connectivity, we are required to first review, ever so briefly, the notion of connectivity itself and how it has in recent years begun to acquire an unusual conceptual bounce and wide official acceptance.

Tracing the Thread of 'Connectivity'

For the many wise heads of state who gathered at the 17th session of the Association of Southeast Asian Nations (ASEAN), the need for 'connectivity', interestingly enough, seemed uppermost on their minds. Such that, the august collection of leaders enthusiastically adopted the Ha Noi Declaration of 28 October 2010, which was unambiguously summed up as the *Master Plan on ASEAN Connectivity* (MPAC) (ASEAN 2011). As a strategic document, the MPAC is unsurprising for its neat alignment with the already agreed upon objective for mutating the ten Southeast Asian Countries[2] into a new regional vector—a cohesive 'political, economic, and cultural community' that will speed up the movement of goods, peoples, and ideas within the re-articulated economic spaces of Southeast Asia. This great effort, as spelled out in the MPAC, involves in the main trying to meaningfully achieve three significant initiatives for the immediate future:

- enhanced physical infrastructure development (physical connectivity),
- effective institutions, mechanisms, and processes (institutional connectivity), and
- empowered people (people–to–people connectivity) (ASEAN 2011).

Whilst institutional and people–to–people connectivity are relatively less problematic as goals to be defined and pursued, the drive for physical connectivity, on the other hand, can collide against various kinds and levels of opposition. In part, it is not difficult to foresee that building any giant mega-infrastructural project will invariably boil over into environmental and social anxieties and resentments; notably, because impacts brought on by deforestation, loss of biological diversity, and the displacement of communities, which many previous studies have pointed out, have inevitably bred popular disquiet, stiff resistance, and even chronic violence.[3] Put differently, as the ASEAN countries begin to link their nations through bridges, roads, railways lines, and ports or as they try to augment their energy expectations with large dams, hydroelectric projects, and coal-fired thermal plants, they will increasingly find themselves hard pressed to clear large swathes of tropical evergreen forests, divert sprawling rivers systems into a warren of underground tunnels, eliminate wildlife, and destroy a range of historically evolved livelihood strategies.

The discussion on physical connectivity, hence, cannot be restricted to dry technical debates about efficiency and logistics. Rather, building infrastructures at scales somewhat immodestly envisioned in the Ha Noi Declaration of 2010 will invariably cough out, at the very least, several wicked and vexatious political and environmental challenges. The idea of Pan–Asian connectivity, likewise—if it is to rhyme with and further amplify this current ASEAN mood—can also cause in its wake huge environmental costs, poorly understood social trade-offs and possibly long drawn out and intractable political resistance.

This stirring belief that giant infrastructural development leads to definitive economic redemption is not a small denomination of the faithful.[4] The enthusiasm for 'building' ASEAN and Pan-Asian connectivity speaks to several much wider contexts and calculations: notably, addressing the current seemingly inconsolable political and economic grief that haunts the world's economy with its origins directly traceable to the 2008 global financial meltdown.[5] Small wonder that the pursuit of 'world economic recovery' continues to consume the attention of the powerful international grouping of the G-20,[6] who in a series of summits and meetings have sought an acceptable consensus over how to fix what they perceive to be a yet sputtering global growth machine. And from their tool-kit of solutions has steadily emerged a now overwhelming understanding that pursuing mega-infrastructural projects will be the inherently virtuous path to pursue. Big infrastructure, in other words, to meet energy, transportation, and water management needs are thus expected to crank up and lift overall global economic growth. In sum, infrastructure-in-itself has become the new paradigmatic model for development and economic growth. This infrastructure—wielded literally like a giant steel and concrete shovel—is now tasked with the role of filling up the meteor-size crater of insolvency and debt caused by the hard impact of the 2008 financial crisis with heaps of institutional investments, global trade, and regional economic integration (G20 Leaders' Communiqué 2014).[7]

Can Ideology Trump Ecology?

But is this G-20 inspired solution ideologically too slanted and therefore too lopsided in terms of design and objective? Such, in fact, is the strong assessment and view of the Henrich Boll Foundation (a think tank of the

German Green Party), who in a hard hitting recent report written up by Nancy Alexander, titled *The Emerging Multi-Polar World Order*, argued that the mobilization of trillions of dollars from 'institutional investors' for mega-infrastructure through the drive for connectivity was meant to not merely herald a change in economic tempo but is actually poised to become a political 'game changer':

> [long term institutional investors]... would transform the accountability relationships between the state and its citizens, on the one hand, and the large 'pools' of financial investors, on the other. This process is called 'financialization' of infrastructure as an 'asset class'. (Alexander 2014)

The long term institutional investors who are being referred to in the above quote comprise pension funds, insurers, sovereign wealth funds, investment companies, and endowments, with estimates that suggest holding to be well over $85 trillion (2011 figures) (Alexander 2014: 5). In the opinion of the Heinrich Boll report, it will be these very same long term institutional investors who will be either dragooned or encouraged into emptying their deep pockets from huge mounds of capital to, in turn, fund much of the infrastructural connectivity. The catch here, nonetheless, will greatly depend on the abilities of the proliferating number of connectivity enthusiasts to capture and then channel this enormous gush of money through a carefully honed and calibrated financial and legal regulatory regime; involving in the main, a range of efforts to re-orient fiscal incentives, fiscal instruments, and capital markets in such a way that they end up transforming 'infrastructure' into an 'asset class'. By asset class, as Nicholas Hildyard points out, one refers to infrastructure that is turned into a financial platform of sorts for enabling 'turbo charged' profit-seeking (on an average above 30 per cent returns) in multiple markets (Hildyard 2012). In effect, for both Hilyard and the Henrich Boll Foundation, building connectivity through infrastructure as an asset class marks a profound departure from previous approaches in which infrastructure was developed principally as a public good rather than turned into a conduit to generate private sector profit.

This shift towards the 'financialization' of infrastructure as an 'asset class' has also announced in particular a stronger commitment and impetus for Public–Private Partnerships (PPP), which, increasingly the world over, have now become one of the primary modalities for financing and implementing infrastructure projects. The PPP model, crudely spelled out, is an arrangement which strives to combine state enterprises with private companies to realize public endeavours. The belief is that PPPs provide efficiency gains by saving on cost-overruns and project delays, and that they bring in resources for the project. This wholesome embrace of the PPP model has, in fact, been more than enthusiastically pursued in Asia.

India, for example, hopes to raise 40 per cent of its planned $200 billion annual expenditure on infrastructure between 2013 and 2017 from the private sector. In the energy sector alone, where the government plans to increase power generation by 68,869 MW by 2012, some 13.4 per cent of the finance is to be raised from private investors. Financial analysts predict that, by 2017, private companies will provide some 50 per cent of India's energy, as against 12 per cent in 2010. In the roads sector, too, massive spending is planned, again with major private sector participation. Announcing the world's biggest road building programme in 2009, Kamal Nath, India's then Minister for Road Transport and Highways, stated that he wanted to spend $70 billion by 2012 on building 7,000 kilometres of world-class highways; $48 billion of the investment is expected to come from the private sector, with 60 per cent of the new build taking the form of 'build–operate–transfer' toll road schemes. 'The good news', commented Venturebeat, 'is that Corporate India is stepping up to the plate to take up projects that will alleviate the country's infrastructure constraints. And it is finding willing partners among Private Equity firms to fund these vital projects' (Hildyard 2012: 8)

Making the PPP model work has, however, also involved a strong impatient commitment to implement projects by simultaneously dismantling or enervating environmental regulations/norms. In India in particular, as Kelly Alley's and Douglas Hill's essays in this volume have shown as well, the muscular drive in recent years by the Indian Government to pursue the construction of hydro-electric dams in the North-eastern Himalayas has not only fuelled protests by local communities around potentially unacceptable environmental and social impacts, but that, in great measure, the peculiar nexus between the Indian government/state and private capital has been critical in forcing the pace for the speedy clearances given to such projects in the region (also see Alley 2012, 2014; Hill 2013; Menon and Kohli 2005; and Vagholikar and Das 2010).

Whilst many activists, politicians, scholars, and experts have consumed their energies in debating the environmental and social costs against the potential benefits of these hydro projects in India, it appears increasingly to be the case that the premises and assumptions that inform these strong disagreements and differences have begun to reach some sort of conceptual quagmire. That is, the evidence marshalled by supporters on either side of the divide over how transboundary river systems should be harnessed seems unable to clinch arguments either way. In effect, neither the proponents for building dams or modern water infrastructures nor those challenging such kinds of hydraulic developments are able to convince each other. Put differently, has the debate over river development become too ideological to move forward? And does this not put the whole desire for Pan–Asian connectivity into troubling doubt and question; especially given that connectivity will involve building hydraulic infrastructure across Asia's many transboundary rivers and hydro-basins? On the other hand, could a shift towards embracing new knowledges about rivers and their ecologies hold the key to overcoming the internecine and the most likely intractable challenges for harnessing flows?

New Knowledges and Old Deadlocks

Modern river management in Asia is often characterized as being defined by reductionist engineering and comprehensive water control. In technological terms, this has meant the introduction of infrastructures such as weirs, barrages, perennial canal systems, and inevitably large dams (D'Souza 2006b). The hydraulic principle underlying these varied structural interventions, however, has remained disarmingly simple: regulate flows either through diversion or impoundment in order to then 'harness' volumes as cusecs or megawatts. Under the sobriquet 'supply-side hydrology' this strategy, moreover, is underpinned by a strong belief that water/flows/rivers lacks a historical/cultural context nor does it possess ecological qualities. The need for 'an additional quantity of water', hence, is expected to be met by simply increasing 'the available supply of water through new development projects'. The conceptual understanding of water, in such an ideological framing, is thereby simplified as being one of a culturally and ecologically unencumbered volume. Four defining ingredients are crucial to reinforcing the supply-side hydrology paradigm:

1. Technical expertise as civil engineers (Biswas and Embid 2003; D'Souza 2003).
2. Perfecting skills as quantitative hydrologists (Biswas 1970).

3. Carrying out high-modernist social planning agendas (Scott 2006).
4. Assembling giant centralized national water bureaucracies (D'Souza 2006a; Klinensmith 2007; Molle *et al.* 2009).

What appeared as a seemingly unquestionable triumph by modern structures of steel and concrete over flows has, however, been unsettled by innumerable ecological and political complications. While the politics has been sharply expressed as volatile disagreements, disputes, and conflict over water access and entitlement, the ecological has been made manifest in the form of various environmental stresses such as waterlogging, salinity, ground water depletion, irretrievable loss of fisheries, the emergence of dead zones in water bodies, and the destruction of a range of biologically rich breeding grounds such as marshes and estuarine ecologies (McCully 2001). In other words, the belief that water could simply be physically transferred to regions where it was apparently needed has become a source, especially in India, for intractable and endemic conflict (Joy *et al.* 2008).

In recent decades, however, there has been a sharp turn away from this civil engineering view of treating rivers as being simply volumes flowing down a channel. A fresh scholarly turn, since the late 1980s, has been able to compellingly argue for a paradigm shift. Notably, by focusing on the centrality of the 'flood pulse' and the inherent variability of flow, these studies and other such research exercises have pointed out that the river is made up of a collection of delicately poised fluvial webs and ecological relationships. And the stochastic nature of the river's flow regime is critical to forging nutrient rich and biotically productive interactions between floodplains, wetlands, swamps, and estuarine zones. If anything, therefore, a river is a complex biological, chemical, and geomorphological process in motion (Junk *et al.* 1989; Sedell *et al.* 1989; Tockner *et al.* 2000; and also see Gopal 2013). Messing around with the flood pulse or altering the river's flow regime in significant ways such as by dams, diversion structures, or large reservoirs will inevitably simplify the scale and scope of interactions and therefore generate several negative ecological and fluvial feedbacks.

But what could possibly be the political and social implications of moving from a volume-civil engineering perspective on rivers to a pulse-ecological processual notion of flow? And significantly as well for the purpose of this essay, can such new knowledges help resolve the many tangled tensions that have cropped up with hydro-electric projects and the construction of large dams in the Asian region? In other words, can Pan-Asian connectivity, with its many desires for harnessing transboundary rivers through hydro-infrastructures, tap into the new ecological sciences about rivers in order to then craft policies that meaningfully address social, political, and environmental concerns?

Assembling Constituencies for Development and Growth

The ongoing bitter struggle over the Indian government's decision to build the Lower Subansiri Hydroelectric Power Project (LSHPP) on the Subansiri River, at a point that nearly straddles the border of the Assam and Arunachal States of India, is instructive to us in many ways. For one, the LSHPP has been mired in several levels of conflict from its very inception and consequently it has become possibly the most debated and discussed large dam/hydro-electric project in recent years in India. Secondly, and more significant for us, however, is the fact that the LSHPP has also inspired considerable scientific and social scrutiny with many careful studies making it possible for us to weigh the issue in a more informed manner now. While rehearsing and evaluating all the claims from the various reports, documents, and published papers on the LSHPP would make for an interesting research topic in its own right, our purpose in this brief essay is served by gesturing to an insightful assessment by Sanjib Baruah, a much respected scholar on India's Northeast.

In an arresting discussion, Baruah's article published in the *Economic and Political Weekly* details for us the many findings and assessments by a slew of committees and organizations who carried out careful studies on the LSHPP (Baruah 2012). One such expert committee, set up in December of 2006, to study the impacts of the Lower Subansiri was made up of 'professors of civil engineering, environmental science, geography, geology, life sciences and zoology—all drawn from three of Assam's most prestigious academic institutions: Gauhati University, Dibrugarh University, and the Indian Institute of Technology in Guwahati'. This expert committee went on to submit its report in June 2010, in which they seemed to have stumbled onto the Brahmaputra valley's unexpected ecological realities. More specifically, the zone that comprised the sprawling flood plain that was woven into the river's sinuous braiding channel and lay just downstream of the dam. It is only fitting that the Survey's acknowledgement of the dependent and complicated nature of the relationships between people, land, and flowing water is reproduced as a long quote below:

> The survey found that people in those zones depend on the river in many different ways depending on their distance from the river. Apart from getting water and fish from the river, they harvest fuel wood, sand and pebbles as well; and depend on it for transportation.
>
> The diurnal and seasonal fluctuations in the water level of the river—the diurnal variations necessary to meet the variation of power demand during the day—says the report, 'will definitely affect the river ecosystem as well as the ecology of the connecting wetlands. Aquatic fauna and flora, and dolphin population of the Subansiri will be destroyed by the project with its existing design and operational parameters.' The fluctuations of the water level on downstream communities, the report concluded, will impact lives in the downstream areas in many other ways. For instance, it will dramatically affect the transportation infrastructure of country and motor boats that carry people as well as 'domesticated animals, crops, thatches, pottery articles, forest products.' The very low flow of the river during the day time in the dry season would restrict the movement of boats, while the sudden release of excess water from the reservoir when the rivers are in spate will make movement treacherous. (LSEG Report 2010: Chapter X: 5–10 in Baruah 2012)

This detailed information, if more fully added up and grasped, tells us that the Brahmaputra valley is largely peopled by riverine communities who have created much of their life–worlds through flood recession agriculture and subsistence fishing.[8] And, more importantly, their livelihoods and arts of living require the river to be a collection of variable pulses rather than standardized flows. Baruah, in fact, goes on to elaborate another telling point:

> A recent World Bank study calls subsistence fisheries 'a vital but largely unquantified economic activity and livelihood component of rural communities and particularly of the poor'. They 'provide vital local nutritious food and a safety net for many poor households'. It is not only an important source of nutrition for those who are fishermen in an occupational sense; fishing maybe a component of the survival strategies of many rural households with diverse occupations. Yet "because of their variety, dispersion and social complexity, small-scale fisheries are often poorly documented". (Baruah 2012)

In effect, the Brahmaputra valley is a richly productive ecosystem precisely because of its variable pulses, braided channels, and erratic flows. A river made up of muscle, cartilage, bones, and gills; a soaked highway of trundling vegetation, coils of sediment, and organic material, all thickened in nutrient-rich silted waters. This moving inland ocean is a communication network strung along by biological webs, organic nodes, and intricate fluvial connections. Put differently, the Brahmaputra river system of which the Subansiri is a tributary feeds and creates and re-creates a floodplain through a pulsing flood regime. It is upon this fairly productive ecosystem that riverine communities have built complex knowledge systems with which they harness and utilize these flows.

By seeing the Brahmaputra river system through the eyes and livelihood practices of its innumerable riverine communities who populate particular ecological niches in the vast flood plains, one is compelled to acknowledge both a different hydraulic reality and the fact that a far different development and economic growth model would be required if one wishes to build on their livelihood strengths and knowledges. And a start would necessarily require that one has to first accept that such a living–ecosystem–fluvial process must conceptually be posed as the dissimilar other to the civil engineering metaphor of treating the river as merely the sum total of standardized volumes and statistical flows.

What can be thus far considered as an important take home message from the ongoing LSHPP debates, disputes, and intense struggles, is that constructing modern hydraulic infrastructures over rivers, and more so in the case of transboundary river systems in Asia, require a clearer grasp of prevailing livelihood realities on the ground. Building dams or diversions or reservoirs in Asia will invariably mean impacting populations with deep cultural and livelihood histories, and importantly as well, these communities are in possession of a range of skills and knowledges about their section of the river. Engaging with and meeting the aspirations of these riverine communities and fisher peoples will thus be crucial to defining benefits and determining the scale and scope of projects, whether it be the urgency for hydro-electricity or flood control or connectivity through navigation.

Towards Pan-Asian Connectivity

As pointed out earlier, the idea of connectivity has been closely associated with the larger G-20 inspired effort to pursue the 'financialization' of infrastructure as an 'asset class'. That is, the attempt appears to be to inaugurate a giant push for infrastructure-led development and growth—especially in Southeast Asia and other countries in Asia—with the idea of trying to realize super profits for the private sector rather than to use the construction boom to consolidate public goods. However, as we have sought to suggest, building modern hydraulic projects such as hydro-electric schemes or large dams across rivers and especially over transboundary rivers are fraught with a range of political and environmental consequences. In part, these often troubled and sometimes tension-ridden complications arise, as we have tried to explain, from the way flows have been sought to be harnessed through narrow civil engineering perspectives rather than understanding rivers and their ecosystem as being defined by variable flood pulses and as geomorphological processes. And finally, in shifting to a pulse-ecological processual notion, the complex socio-cultural, economic, and ecological worlds of riverine communities and fisheries people can be further revealed and finally grasped. This learning, in effect, re-situates the challenge for Pan–Asian connectivity. Instead of pursuing the building of modern hydraulic infrastructure as an expert-led, top down, civil engineering, and profit driven model, the effort can be directed towards engaging with riverine communities and other river dependent constituencies in order to then arrive at what constitutes meaningful development. In sum, negotiating with the intertwined economic and ecological worlds along the flow will be central to evolving credible and participatory terms for the Pan–Asian connectivity to meet its many challenges.

Notes

1. China, for example, is home to, or more correctly, the catchment to ten major transboundary river systems which includes some of the longest river systems in the world, such as the Indus, Ganges, Brahmaputra, Irrawaddy, Salween and the Mekong.

2. The current ASEAN members list comprises Indonesia, Malaysia, Philippines, Singapore, Thailand, Brunei, Cambodia, Laos, Myanmar, and Vietnam.

3. There are a number of insightful monographs on the social, political, and environmental impacts and implications of large dams in Asia. For a sampling see D'Souza 2008; McCully 2001; Nilsen 2010; Roy 1999; and Singh 1997.

4. See the excellent theorization of the idea of infrastructure by Brian Larkin (2013).

5. There are a substantial number of monographs, articles, and assessments of the global financial crisis of 2008. Amongst the many, however, two striking

monographs for me that stand out for the non-economists would be Stiglitz 2010 and Lewis 2010. Also see Swagel 2013 for an informed list of writings on the financial crisis.

6. G-20 members are: Argentina, Australia, Brazil, Canada, China, France, Germany, India, Indonesia, Italy, Japan, Republic of Korea, Mexico, Russia, Saudi Arabia, South Africa, Turkey, the United Kingdom, the United States, and the European Union.

7. To get a sense of big infrastructure as a developmental and growth ideology see the communiqué issued as the G-20 Leaders' Communiqué Brisbane Summit, 15–16 November 2014. Available at https://g20.org/.../2014/12/brisbane_g20_leaders_summit_communique.pdf (accessed 2 May 2015).

8. For a compelling argument that links the emergence of modern flood control in the Brahmaputra valley to the British empire's quest to turn the region into a jute producing frontier, see Saikia 2015.

References

Alley, Kelly D. 2012. 'Water Wealth and Energy in the Indian Himalayas', *The Silk Road* ,10: 136–45; available at http://www.silk-road.com/newsletter/vol10/SilkRoad_10_2012_alley.pdf (accessed 12 March 2016).

———. 2014. 'The Developments, Policies and Assessments of Hydropower in the Ganga River Basin', in Rashmi Sanghi (ed.), *Our National River Ganga: Lifeline of Millions*, pp. 285–305. Netherlands: Springer.

Alley, Kelly D., Ryan Hile, and Chandana Mitra. 2014. 'Visualising Hydropower Across the Himalayas: Mapping in a Time of Regulatory Decline', *Himalaya, the Journal of the Association of Nepal and Himalayan Studies*, 34(2): 52–66.

Alexander, Nancy. 2014. *The Emerging Multi-Polar World Order: Its Unprecedented Consensus on a New Model for Financing Infrastructure Investment and Development*. Washington D.C.: Heinrich Böll Stiftung, December.

ASEAN. 2011. *Master Plan on ASEAN Connectivity*. Jakarta, Indonesia: ASEAN Secretariat, Public Outreach and Civil Society Division.

Baruah, Sanjib. 2012. 'Whose River Is It Anyway? Political Economy of Hydropower in the Eastern Himalayas', *Economic & Political Weekly*, 47(29) (July): 41–52.

Biswas, Asit K. 1970. 'Edmond Halley F.R.S. Hydrologist Extraordinaire', *Notes and Sources of the Royal Society of London*, 25(1): 47–57.

Biswas, Asit K. and Antonio Embid. 2003. 'Editorial', *International Journal of Water Resources Development*, 19(3): 351–2.

Brisbane G20 Leaders' Summit. 2014. *G20 Leaders' Communiqué Brisbane Summit*. 15–16 November; available at http://www.g20australia.org/official_

resources/g20_leaders_communique_brisbane_summit_november_2014 (accessed 9 December 2015).

D'Souza, Rohan. 2008. 'Framing India's Hydraulic Crises: Politics of the Modern Large Dam', *Monthly Review Press*, 60(3) (July–August): 112–24.

———. 2006a. *Drowned and Dammed: Colonial Capitalism and Flood Control in Eastern India*. New Delhi: Oxford University Press.

———. 2006b. 'Water in British India: The Making of a "Colonial Hydrology"', *History Compass*, 4(4) (May): 621–8.

———. 2003. 'Supply-Side Hydrology in India: The Last Gasp', *Economic and Political Weekly*, 38(36) (September): 3785–90.

Gopal, Brij. 2013. *Environmental Flows: An Introduction for Water Resources Managers*. New Delhi: National Institute of Ecology.

Hildyard, Nicholas. 2012. *More than Bricks and Mortar: Infrastructure as Asset Class: A Critical Look at Private Equity Infrastructure Funds*. United Kingdom: Corner House Publications, September.

Hill, Douglas P. 2013. 'Transboundary Water Resources and Uneven Development: Crisis In and Beyond Contemporary India', *South Asia: Journal of South Asian Studies*, 36(2): 243–57.

Joy, K.J., Biksham Gujja, Suhas Paranjape, Vinod Goud, and Shruti Vispute (eds). 2008. *Water Conflicts in India: a Million Revolts in the Making*. London: Routledge.

Junk, Wolfgang, Peter B. Bayley, and R.E. Sparks. 1989. 'The Flood Pulse Concept in the River-Floodplain Systems', in D.P. Dodge (ed.), *Proceedings of the International Large River Symposium*, pp. 110–27. Canadian Special Publications in Fisheries and Aquatic Sciences 106.

Klingensmith, Daniel. 2007. *One Valley and a Thousand: Dams, Nationalism, and Development*. New Delhi: Oxford University Press.

Larkin, Brian. 2013. 'The Politics and Poetics of Infrastructure', *Annual Review of Anthropology*, 42: 327–43.

Lewis, Michael. 2010. *The Big Short: Inside the Doomsday Machine*. New York: W. W. Norton.

Menon, Manju and Kanchi Kohli. 2005. *Large Dams for Hydropower in Northeast India: A Dossier*. New Delhi: South Asia Network on Dams, Rivers and People; Kalpavriksh.

McCully, Patrick. 2001. *Silenced Rivers: The Ecology and Politics of Large Dams*. New York: Zed Books.

Molle, Francois, Peter Mollinga, and Philippus Wester. 2009. 'Hydraulic Bureaucracies and the Hydraulic Mission: Flows of Water, Flows of Power', *Water Alternatives*, 2(3): 328–49.

Nilsen, Alf Gunvald. 2010. *Dispossession and Resistance in India: The River and the Rage*. London: Routledge.

Roy, Arundhati. 1999. *The Cost of Living*. London: Flamingo.

Saikia, Arup Jyoti. 2015. 'Jute in the Brahmaputra Valley: The Making of Flood Control in Twentieth–Century Assam', *Modern Asian Studies*, 49(5) (September): 1405–41.

Scott, James C. 2006. 'High Modernist Social Engineering: The Case of the Tennessee Valley Authority', in Lloyd I. Rudolph and John Kurt Jacobsen (eds), *Experiencing the State*, pp. 3–52. New Delhi: Oxford University Press.

Sedell J.R., J.E. Ridley, and F.J. Swanson. 1989. 'The River Continuum Concept: a Basis for the Expected Ecosystem Behaviour of Very Large Rivers?' in D.P. Dodge (ed.), *Proceedings of the International Large River Symposium*, pp. 49–55. Canadian Special Publications in Fisheries and Aquatic Sciences, 106.

Singh, Satyajit. 1997. *Taming the Waters: The Political Economy of Large Dams in India*. New Delhi: Oxford University Press.

Stiglitz, Joseph E. 2010. *Free Fall: America, Free Markets and the Sinking of the Global Economy*. New York: W.W. Norton.

Swagel, Phillip. 2015. 'Financial Crisis Reading List', *The New York Times*, 15 July; available at http://economix.blogs.nytimes.com/2013/07/15/financial-crisis-reading-list-2/?_r=0 (accessed 9 December 2015).

Tockner, K., F. Malard, and J.V. Ward. 2000. 'An Extension of the Flood Pulse Concept', *Hydrological Processes*, 14: 2861–83.

Vagholikar, Neeraj and Partha J. Das. 2010. *Damming Northeast India: Juggernaut of Hydropower Projects Threatens Social and Environmental Security of Region*. Pune; Guwahati; New Delhi: Kalpavriksh; Aaranyak; and ActionAid India, 2010. Available at https://chimalaya.files.wordpress.com/2010/12/damming-northeast-india-final.pdf (accessed 12 March 2016).

Index

Abe, Shinzo 13
Abu Dhabi Dialogues (ADDs) 207
'Act East' initiative/policy 2, 4–5, 15,
    32–3, 70, 84, 110, 117, 127–8,
    152, 179 (see also Modi, Narendra)
'Act Home', importance of 32–3
Action Committee against Unabated
    Taxation 122n10
Afghanistan 29–30, 33n4, 207
agricultural sector of India 157
    challenges faced by 5
    insufficient transformation of 6
    need to liberalize 6
    role to reduce poverty 157
agricultural uses 218
Air India 26
All-India Muslim League 34n12
All Tripura Tigers Force (ATTF)
    122n3
Al Qaeda 64
ancient Greater India 16
Andaman and Nicobar Islands 18
Andean Community 173
anti-colonial solidarity 17
anti-Islam 55
anti-ship ballistic missiles (ASBM)
    119
ARF Work Plan on Counterterrorism
    and Transnational Crime 58–9

Argentina 251n6
Armed Forces (Special Powers) Act
    (AFSPA) 119–20
Arquiza, Eileene 53
Arunachal Pradesh 99, 108–10, 118,
    123n16, 144, 203, 218, 223, 231
    MoUs for hydropower projects
        232
    road infrastructure package
        announced in 2015 123n16
    road projects in 226, 229
ASEAN+1 FTAs 150
ASEAN + 3 12
ASEAN–Australia–New Zealand
    FTA 154
ASEAN–China Free Trade Area
    (ACFTA) 128
ASEAN Comprehensive Plan of
    Action on Counter Terrorism 59
ASEAN Convention on Counter-
    Terrorism (ACCT) 55–6, 60, 64
ASEAN Convention on Counter
    Terrorism, Philippines (2007) 59
ASEAN Defence Ministers' Meeting
    + 8 forum (ADMM+8) 12
ASEAN Economic Community
    Blueprint 154–5
ASEAN+India 121
ASEAN–India Free Trade Area 128

ASEAN–India FTA 154, 158–9
ASEAN–India Joint Declaration
    for Cooperation to Combat
    International Terrorism, Bali
    (2003) 58–9
ASEAN–India Plan of Action 61
ASEAN–India summit (2002)
    14–15
ASEAN Master Plan for
    Connectivity (AMPC) project 173
7th ASEAN Ministerial Meeting on
    Transnational Crime (AMMTC),
    Cambodia (2009) 59
ASEAN Plus Three (APT) 53
ASEAN Regional Forum (ARF) 53,
    59
ASEAN Regional Forum, Phuket
    (2009) 58
ASEAN Vision 2020 55
ASEAN way approach 153–4, 165n6
Asia–Europe Meeting (ASEM)
    mechanism (2006) 12
Asia Foundation, The 208
Asian Century 64
Asian Development Bank (ADB) 137,
    143, 150–1
    identification of corridors for
        connectivity 182
Asian Development Bank Institute
    198
Asian economies 150
Asian Regional Integration Centre
    164n2
Asian Relations Conference 17
Asian solidarity 1
Asia Pacific Laboratory Accreditation
    Cooperation (APLAC) 184
Assam / Assamese 86n9, 90, 97, 117,
    144, 203, 221, 228–9, 232, 247
    constructed, under construction,
        and proposed dams in 223

division of ethnic groups 109
    maternal mortality ratio 114
    militants 97
    Myanmar raids in 103
    road projects in 223, 226
Assam Rifles 102
asset class 249
Association of Southeast Asian
    Nations (ASEAN) 3, 5, 19, 28, 33,
    117, 127, 132, 148, 188
    Commemorative Summit in New
        Delhi 2012 12–13, 31, 33n7,
        54
    car rally during 14
    Prime Minister Singh
        statement during 16
    counterterrorism policy 3–4
    and India 53
    cooperation to counter
        terrorism 58–64
    dialogue partner in 1995 2, 54
    strategic partnership 54
    trade relations between 20,
        133–4
    inter-governmental organization 60
    leadership meeting in Phnom
        Penh 13
    members list 250n2
    as a non-threatening organization
        53
    rebuffed Beijing efforts for building
        exclusivist institutions 12
    regional level action policy 3–4
    17th session of 241
    7th summit in Brunei Darussalam,
        2001 55
    transit or transport agreements
        172–3
Atlantic Council 208
Australia 29–30, 86n18, 130, 137,
    153–4, 164n3, 173, 251n6

Ayeyawady–Chao Phraya–Mekong
Economic Cooperation Strategy
27

balance of payments crisis (1991) 129
Balkanization 110
Bandung Conference of 1955 1, 17, 83
Banerjee, Mamata 204
Bangladesh 24, 27–8, 70, 96, 129
dependence on goods from other
countries 170
and India
Bangladesh handed over
wanted fugitives 112
bilateral trade between 6, 170–1
diplomatic engagement 32
free movement of vehicles
across border 171
naval facilities construction in 71
Bangladesh Accreditation Board 184
Bangladesh, Bhutan, India, and Nepal
(BBIN) 173
Bangladesh-China-India-Myanmar
(BCIM) 27, 36n40, 132–3, 173,
188
India's trade relations with 134–7
Bangladesh Import Control Order
(2009–12) 175
Bangladesh Liberation War (1971)
108
Barua, Paresh 96
Barua, Raju 96
Bay of Bengal Initiative for Multi-
Sectoral Technical and Economic
Cooperation (BIMSTEC) 2,
27–8, 127, 132, 173, 188
India's trade relations with 134–7
Belgium 101, 130
Bharatiya Janata Party (BJP) 22, 74,
82, 86n10, 204
leadership conclave in 2014 23

Bharat Mala highway project 37n47
Bhattacharyya, Rajeev 97
Bhaumik, Subir 114
Bhutan 27, 70, 97
armed groups establishment 112
India's public sector companies
movement for dam projects
218
Bhutanese Army 112
Bhutan–India–Bangladesh (BIB)
tripartite cooperation 206
bilateral agreements 4–5, 133, 148
bilateral cooperation 60–1
bilateral free trade agreements 137–9
bilateral trade 6, 20, 76, 128, 138–40,
144, 164n3, 170, 174
bloc politics 18
BN-2 Defender Islander maritime
patrol aircraft 80
border / bordering / borderlands 4–6,
70, 110, 128, 160, 171, 195–6,
199–200, 216, 233–4
agency cooperation 187
conflict between India and China
over Arunachal Pradesh 108
crossings 141, 182, 186–7
guard forces 102
home of marginalized peoples
199–200
of India
crossings with Bangladesh or
Myanmar 142
eastern 142, 144
western 113
infrastructure 143, 177
points 174–5, 182, 187
security 102
taxes 141
unrest 4–5
Border Roads Organization 142
Bose, Subhash 117

Brahmaputra river basin/valley 7–8,
108, 110, 119, 121
challenges for 216
directions to overcome challenges
and improve governance 235–6
governance and clearance process
for hydropower projects
217–25
modern flood control emergence
in 251n8
rich in productive ecosystem
248–9
road connectivity in 217–31
transboundary knowledge
transparency 231–5
Brazil 232, 251n6
Bridge on the River Kwai,
The 78
Britain/United Kingdom 71, 108,
130, 251n6
British Raj 16, 31, 70
Brunei 144n1, 250n2
bureaucratic lethargy 26
Bureau of Indian Standards 175
Burma/Burmese (Rangoon) 17,
85n8
annexation by British in 1885 109
and India, relationship between 72
Khaplang fight for freedom 113
military coup in 18
8888 Revolt 73, 81
Suu Kyi involvement with military
of 71

Caliph 63
Cambodia 24, 72
Vietnam invasion to overthrow Pol
Pot regime 2
Canada 100, 102, 251n6
capacity-building 59, 61
carbon credits 218

Carrying Capacity Assessment of
Siang basin 233–4
ceasefire / ceasefire agreement 98–
100, 103, 112–15, 120
Central Drugs Standard Control
Organization 175
Central Electricity Authority (CEA)
221, 232
Central Water Commission (CWC)
233–4
Centre for Inter-Disciplinary
Studies of Mountain and Hill
Environment (CISMHE) 232
Centre for Land Warfare Studies,
New Delhi 58
Chakmas 109
China /Chinese 12, 14, 24, 72, 83,
234, 251n6
cross-border insurgencies and role
of 95–7
dominance over Indo–Pacific 69
expansion into Myanmar 71
'Go Out' policy 197
hosted one unit from Manipur 111
involvement in Colombo port
expansion 25
and Myanmar, relationship
between 104
suspension of hydroelectric
dam project 92
trade relations 75–6
pushing of south through
Myanmar 94–5
transboundary river systems in
250n1
Chin state 102
civil society 118, 121, 202, 206–7
Clean Development Mechanism 218
climate change 201, 216–17
Clinton, Hillary Rodham 14
Coca Cola countries 18

Codex Alimentarius 184, 188
coercive displacements 200
cold–chains 160, 162–3, 165n13
Cold War 16–17, 21, 122n1, 129
  bloc politics of 18
  India's policymakers ignore
    Southeast Asian states 1
  reason for 1
Colombo Powers 17
communication satellites 240
Congress party 82, 86n11
Connecting the Drops Initiative 208
connectivity, notion of 240 (see also
    Pan-Asian connectivity)
  institutional and people–to–
    people 241
  tracing thread of 241–2
Convention on Road Signs and
  Signals 180
Convention on Road Traffic 180
Copernican revolution 37n55
Corporate India 244
counterterrorism
  ASEAN and India relations in
    3–4
  ASEAN policy on
    challenges after 9/11 55
    committed to use US led
      coalition language 57
    Declaration on Joint Action to
      Counter Terrorism 55
    Gerstl judgement 56
    Plan of Action 59–60
    post-9/11 response 54–5
  challenges and way forward 60–2
  India's policy on
    hindrances towards 58
    immediate and short-term
      response 57
    mired in systematic weakness
      58

potential cooperation between
    ASEAN and India 58–60
  under Prime Minister
    Narendra Modi 58
  rivalry with Pakistan 57
cross-border
  activities of terrorists groups 62
  banking facilities 177
  cooperative ventures 60
  drug trafficking 72
  infrastructure projects 36n45
  insurgencies 95–7
  land transport 173
  sanctuaries 90
  trade 129, 172, 258
  transport and transit agreement
    170
  vehicle movement 172
cultural development of Asia 1
cultural heritage 218
Cumulative Impact Assessment 233
customs, immigration, quarantine, and
  security issues (CIQS) 59
Cyclone Nargis 75, 81

Dalai Lama 96
dam(s) 92, 202–3, 209, 224, 240–1,
    244–7, 249–50
  barrages 220
  China ambitious plan of building
    118
  constructed, under construction,
    and proposed 223
  construction in Siang Basin 234–5
  destruction during flooding and
    glacial lake outbursts 220
  on LAC 218
Das, Gurcharan 35n19
democracy 71, 82, 86n19, 91–2
Destructive Insects and Pests Act
    1914 175, 188n1

detailed project reports (DPRs) 221,
232–3
Dibang Basin 231
Dibrugarh University 247
Directorate General of Field
Intelligence (DGFI) 113
The Discovery of India (Jawaharlal
Nehru) 17
Disturbed Areas Act 120
Doha Round 157
domestic political problems in India 4
domestic taxation regime 33
downstream communities 200–1,
232, 234, 248

East Asia 12, 94
India's engagement with 24
East Asia Summit (EAS) 12, 53
East India Company 22
East Pakistan 109, 111
ecology 242–5
Economic and Political Weekly 247
economic development 1–2, 18, 55,
77, 129, 149, 258
economic reform process of India
(1991) 21, 35n19
economic transformation 6
*Emerging Multi-Polar World Order,
The* (Nancy Alexander) 243
energy trading 196, 198, 208
Environmental Impact Assessments
(EIAs) 202, 232–3
environment clearance 219, 221, 232
Environment Impact Assessment
Notification (1994) 221
ethnic armies 98
ethnic insurgencies 29
ethnic mutinies 109
ethnic rebels 95–7, 100, 103–4
ethnic sensitivities 105
ethno-nationalist terrorism 57

European colonialism, collapse of 1
European Union (EU) 98, 148,
174–5
Expert Appraisal Committee (EAC)
219

Farakka barrage 204
federation/ federalism 101–2
Fernandes, George 30
financial inclusivity 117
financialization of infrastructure 243,
249
food parks 162, 165n13
Food Safety and Standards Authority
of India (FSSAI) 183
foreign direct investment (FDI)
RCEP member countries
contribution in world GDP
151
Singapore in India 127
foreign economic engagement of India
21
foreign grants 145n5
foreign policy of India
after BJP first government in 1998
74
bilateral counterterrorism ties with
ASEAN nations 4
under Modi 2–3
under Nehru 1
Forest Advisory Committee (FAC)
219, 224
forest clearance 219
Forest Conservation Act (1980) 221
France 24, 71, 251n6
Free trade agreements (FTAs)
5–6, 15, 133 (*see also* Regional
Comprehensive Economic
Partnership (RCEP); Trade East
policy of India)
proliferation of 149

G-20 242, 251n6
Gadkari, Nitin 123n16
Gandhi, Indira 18–19, 83
Gandhi, Rajiv 70–1, 74, 86n11
Garo National Liberation Army
   (GNLA) 112
Garos tribe 109, 112
Gauhati University 247
Geneva Accords (1954) 17
Geographic Informations Systems
   (GIS) 207
German Green Party 243
Germany 100–1, 251n6
Global Competitiveness Index 35n30
global financial crisis of 2008 250n5
Global Trade Analysis Project
   (GTAP) 134
good governance 117
governance 8, 114, 134, 216–17
Gowda, Deve 26
Greater India Society 16
Greater Mekong Subregion (GMS)
   197
Greater Mekong Subregional Cross-
   Border Transport Agreement
   (GMS CBTA) 173
great powers 53, 56, 59, 64, 155
Green Revolution 156–8
Gujral, I.K. 86n11

Haider, Salman 25
Hajongs 109
Ha Noi Declaration of 2010 242
Harmonized System (HS) code
   175
Havel, Vaclav 26
Hazarika, Sanjoy 77
Heinrich Boll report 243
Henrich Boll Foundation 242–3
High Level T.S.R. Subramanian
   Committee 219–20

High Powered Committee, Nagaland
   123n11
Hildyard, Nicholas 243
Himalayan Asia/Himalayan river/
   Himalayas 118, 195–7, 201,
   209–10
   challenges 200
   dialogue on water sharing 206
   geopolitics of 198
   river-linking project 199
Hindu Congress 34n12
Hindu Kush Himalaya 201
Hlaing, Min Aung 80, 92
Holland 71
human rights 73, 91–2, 98, 111, 120
hydrohazards 220
hydro-infrastructures 247
hydrology paradigm, supply-side
   245–6
hydropower projects development 7,
   195–6, 198, 200, 217
   clearance process for 217–25
   debate over 201–4
   infrastructure 234
   northeastern Brahmaputra Basin,
      status in 222
   regulatory agencies role in 236
   in Sikkim and Arunachal Pradesh
      218

IAF MLA (Multi-lateral
   Arrangement) for Mutual
   Recognition 184
ideology oriented terrorism 57
import-substituting industrialization
   (ISI) 1
India–ASEAN Free Trade
   Agreement (FTA) 2, 134
India–ASEAN trade accord (2009) 23
India–EU FTA 155
Indian Air Force 78, 81

Indian Army 78, 110
Indian Board for Wildlife 219, 221,
    224–5
India / New Delhi 12–14, 31, 75, 199
    approach to Southeast Asia
        15–17, 23
    and Dhaka, tensions between 27
    dispute over concession to foreign
        companies 23
    interest in Myanmar 90
    national security decision making
        institutions 31
    permission for arms sale to
        Myanmar 80
    support of Hanoi 19
Indian Institute of Technology,
    Guwahati 247
Indian National Army 117
Indian Navy 13, 30, 32
India–Singapore Comprehensive
    Economic Cooperation Agreement
    (CECA) 139
India–Sri Lanka Free Trade
    Agreement 137–9, 158–9
Indo-China conflict/war in 1962 18,
    108
Indo-Myanmar border 90, 95
Indonesia 17–18, 24, 55, 251n6
Indo-Pacific security 15
Indo-Pak war in 1965 and 1971 18,
    108
informality, notion of 217
informal settlements 218
infrastructure 195, 216–17, 219–20,
    228–9, 231, 242–4, 248, 250
    creation for interconnectivity 198
    deficit 128
    as a developmental and growth
        ideology 251n7
    hydro and hydropower 202, 234,
        247

India's 162, 165n13
    annual expenditure on 244
    border 143
    investment in Myanmar 3
    Japan planning for northeast
        118
    port 35
    seaport 25
    physical 77, 134–5, 142, 144, 171,
        241
    water 245
Inland Container Depots (ICDs)
    180–1
INS *Kirpan* 81
INS *Rana* 81
institutional investors 243
insurgencies across border 4–5
Integrated Check Posts (ICPs) 186–7
intelligence cooperation 61–2
Inter-Ministerial Group (IMG) 234
internal conflicts 57–8, 62–3, 95,
    109–11
International Centre for Integrated
    Mountain Development
    (ICIMOD) 208
International Control Commission 17
International Laboratory
    Accreditation Cooperation
    (ILAC) 184
International Plant Protection
    Convention (IPPC) 184
International Policy Digest 122n1
International Union for Conservation
    of Nature's (IUCN) 208
Inter Services Intelligence (ISI) of
    Pakistan 113
Intra-regional Ganga Dialogue 208
Iran–Pakistan–India pipeline 27
Iraq 55, 63
irrigation 200, 202, 204, 209, 216,
    219

Islam 63
Islamic State of Iraq and al-Sham
    (ISIS) 62–4

Jammu and Kashmir 118
Janata Dal 86n11
Jane's Defence Weekly 95
Japan 12, 30, 69, 83, 104, 251n6
Japan International Cooperation
    Agency (JICA) 143
Jawaharlal Nehru Award 74
Jaypee Power Company 233
Joint Rivers Commission
    (Bangladesh–India) 205
Joint Working Group on Counter-
    Terrorism 61–2

Kachin Independence Army (KIA)
    95, 98–9, 102, 104, 106n10
Kachins ethnic group 101, 104
Kachin state 104
Kaladan Multi-Modal Transit
    Transport Project 78, 86n15, 173
Kamatapur Liberation Organization
    (KLO) 122n4
Kanwal, Gurmeet 58
Karen National Union 98
Karen Peace Council 98
Kashmir 57, 74
Khaplang, Shangwang Shanyung
    103
Khasis 109
Ki-moon, Ban 98
Kishida, Fumio 117
kisan bazars (farmer's markets) 23
knowledge transparency 216
Kokang Chinese 104
Kolkata–Dhaka corridor 172
Korean War 17
Kyaw, Htin 104
Kyi, Khin 71

Land Border Agreement 178
land titles 218
Laos 13, 27, 72, 140, 144n1, 250n2
leadership indifference 26
license raj approach 219
Lin, Bonny 85n1
Line of Actual Control (LAC) 218,
    231, 235
lines of credit (LOCs) 140
Lok Sabha 84
'Look East' policy (LEP of India (2002)
    2, 4–5, 12, 19–26, 28, 31, 36n34, 69,
    73, 83–4, 86n11, 90, 103, 105, 110,
    117–18, 128–9, 152, 178–9 (*see
    also* Association of Southeast Asian
    Nations (ASEAN))
    3.0 119
    Barack Obama administration
        support for 93–4
    focus on political front 132
    formulation of 122n1
    impact on trade relations with
        Singapore 139
    strategies of linking with growing
        economies 197
Lower Subansiri Hydroelectric Power
    Project (LSHPP) 203, 221, 224–
    5, 247, 249

Mahakali Commission (India–Nepal)
    205
'Make in India' campaign 33
Malaysia 18–19, 55, 250n2
Maldives 19, 70, 177
Manipur 77, 79, 86n9, 99, 102, 109,
    203
man-portable air defence systems
    (MANPADS) 94–5
Maoist China 73
Master Plan on ASEAN Connectivity
    (MPAC) 241

Meghalaya 109–10, 123n16
Meghen, Rajkumar (Sana Yaima) 97
Mekong–Ganga Cooperation
  Initiative 2, 27
Mekong-India Economic Corridor 13
Mekong River Commission (MRC)
  206–7
Mexico 251n6
Middle East 63
Ministry of Agriculture, India 174
Ministry of Commerce 15
Ministry of Environment, Forests,
  and Climate Change (MoEFCC),
  India 219–22, 224
Misra, Udayon 112
Mizo National Front 111
Mizoram 109, 111
Mizos/Mizo rebels 95–6, 109
mobile phone networks 240
Modi, Narendra 2–3, 15, 22, 32–3,
  58, 94, 120, 139
  commitment to improve railway
    system 27
  prioritized relationship with East
    Asian neighbours 127
  relationship with ASEAN 53
Monroe Doctrine 71
Mon state 102
Moroney, Jennifer D.P. 85n1
Morung Express 115
motor vehicle agreement
  BBIN negotiations for sub-
    regional 173
  between India and Bangladesh,
    need for 171–4, 183
MoU virus 221
Mt. Kailash 231
Mukherjee, Pranab 28
multilateral initiatives by India 2
Mutual Recognition Arrangements
  (MRAs) on Conformity

Assessment Procedures 177,
  184–5, 187
Myanmar 3, 13, 27–8, 32, 110, 121,
  129, 250n2
  arms sales to 84, 86n19
  attain independence in 1948 85n2
  civil war in 97–103
  Coco Island leased to China 105n2
  flawed peace process policy 105
  general election in 2010 91
  increasing links with between
    South and Southeast Asia 196
  and India, relationship between 69
  cooperation to counter
    terrorism 61
  economic cooperation 75–9
  future scenario 103–5
  interest in border security 79
  Myanmar reliance on China
    and its impact on 81–3
  public sector companies
    movement for dam projects
    218
  reasons for deviation 72–5
  security cooperation 79–81
  support for military junta 4
  military heavy dependence on
    China 91
  as a near neighbour in Southeast
    Asia 70–2
  new reforms process in 2011 92
  political prisoners release in 2011
    90–1
  present scenario of peace process
    in 97–103
  turning to ASEAN and India for
    support 92–4
Myanmar Peace Center 98
Myilvaganan, M. 122n1

Naga insurgency 119

Nagaland 77, 79, 86n16, 99, 102, 109,
111, 114–16, 123n16
Naga model 99
Naga Political Groups (NPGs) 115
Naga rebel/Nagas 99, 103, 109–10,
111, 112, 116
Naga Semi-Autonomous Area 121
Nath, Kamal 23, 244
National Accreditation Board for
Certification Bodies (NABCB)
184
National Accreditation Board
for Testing and Calibration
Laboratories (NABL) 184
national cause 115
National Democratic Alliance (NDA)
government 204
National Democratic Front of
Bodoland (NDFB) 112, 122n3
National Environmental Management
Agency (NEMA) 220
National Green Tribunal 217, 235
National Highways & Infrastructure
Development Corporation Limited
142
National Hydroelectric Power
Corporation (NHPC) 221, 224
National Investment and
Infrastructure Fund (NIIF) 143
nationalist movement, Indian 16
Nationalist Socialist Council of
Nagaland (NSCN) 79, 99, 114, 121
Nationalist Socialist Council of
Nagalim-Isaac and Muivah
(NSCN-IM) 96, 99
National League for Democracy
(NLD) 104
National Liberation Front of Tripura
(NLFT) 122n3
National Socialist Council of Nagalim
(NSCN) 112

National Standards and Testing
Institution of Bangladesh 176
Nationwide Ceasefire Agreement
(NCA), Myanmar 97–8, 100, 104
natural heritage 218
NDFB-S 112
Nehru, Jawaharlal 1, 11, 34n12
dream of non-alignment 82
economic and military assistance
to Burma 17
sentiments about bloc politics of
Cold War 18
support for RCEP negotiations
23–4
Nepal 19, 27, 70, 97, 134, 137, 140–1,
144n1, 178, 180, 186, 196, 199,
216, 218, 236
boundary dispute with India 144
earthquakes in 118
hydro developments in 202
Neutral Nations Repatriation
Commission 17
New Nepal 200
New York Herald Tribune 17
New York Times 17
Non-Aligned Movement 17
Non-Aligned states 73
nonalignment principle 1
non-governmental organizations
(NGOs) 197, 207–8, 232, 235
non-interference 60
non-tariff barriers (NTBs) 5, 134–5,
139, 141–2, 144, 170, 174, 176
northeast region (NER), India 3, 5,
7–8, 79, 216
borders connectivity with other
countries 108
challenges of connectivity 26–9
China's support for ethnic rebels
in 96
closing of Chinese door 111–17

cross-border linkages 26
disturbed region 119–20
export peace building 121–2
geo-strategic architecture initiative
  of 110
hydropower projects potential in
  221, 244
rail and road connectivity
  117–19
seizure of arms 96
North Korea 85n7, 91–2
North Vietnamese aggression 19
NSCN-Khaplang 103
Nu, U 73

Obama, Barack 14, 33n4
  Asian pivot 94
  support for India's Look East
    policy 93
Obama–Modi summit 2015 35n25
Observer Research Foundation 207
One Stop Border Posting 182
open economy 22
Operation Golden Bird 86n9
Operation Sahayata 81
Organisation for Economic Co-
  operation and Development
  (OECD) 150

Pakistan 18, 27, 34n13, 35n30, 57, 62,
  77, 108, 111, 113, 141, 202, 207
  assistance to NER rebels 110
  role stems from dispute over
    Kashmir 57
  as source of terrorism 57–8
Palaung state 104
Pan-Asian connectivity 8, 117, 216,
  240, 249–50
  assembling constituencies for
    development and growth
    247–9

new knowledges and old deadlocks
    245–7
  tracing connectivity thread 241–2
pan-Asian regional solidarity 16
Panetta, Leon 33n4
Panglong Agreement (1947) 103
Pant, Harsh V. 58
parliamentary democracy 85n2
Partition of India 5
  uniquely disadvantaged by 108–11
peacemaking 98
People's Revolutionary Party of
  Kangleipak 79
Philippines 18, 55, 250n2
  and India, relationship between
    18, 55
  cooperation for
    counterterrorism 61
Pitsuwan, Surin 121
Plant Quarantine (PQ) (Regulation
  of Import into India) Order 2003
  175, 188n1
Pol Pot regime 2
Portugal 71
poverty 157–8, 163, 165n9, 195, 198,
  201
Power Purchasing Agreement (PPA)
  232
pre-shipment inspection (PSI)
  certificate 174
Prime Minister's Office (PMO) 234
Public–Private Partnerships (PPP)
  243–4

Quality Council of India (QCI) 184

Rabasa, Angel 85n1
Rabhas 109
Radcliffe, Cyril 109
Radio Brahmaputra 230–1
railroad connectivity 142, 171–2

railway system/networks/projects in
India 23, 27, 77, 78, 137, 171–2
Rajiv Doctrine 70–1, 85n4
Rajkhowa, Arabinda 96
Rakhine state 102
Rao, Narasimha P. V. 2, 21, 25–6, 29,
36n36, 73, 83–4, 86n9, 86n11,
129
Rao, Nirupama 85n3
RCEP Trade Negotiations
Committee 150
Reangs 109
Reddy Committee Report 120
regional agreement 5, 63
regional autonomy 102
Regional Comprehensive Economic
Partnership (RCEP) 6, 20, 173,
183, 186
emergence of 149–51
and India
Central government response
through reforms 158–61
insufficient transformation in
agriculture sector of India
161–2
opportunities and challenges
for India 151–6
policy prescriptions 162–4
political economy for
negotiation in farm sector
156–8
purpose of joining 148
regional cooperation 4, 34n8, 60, 109
knowledge and benefits, sharing of
204–9
regional economies 150
regional energy grids 198
regional integration 173, 185, 187–8,
195
benefits of 197
challenges of 197–201

regional leadership 16
regional peace 30
regional security 19, 30–1, 33
in Asia, a two-way struggle 69
religious terrorism 57
Rhodes, Ben 94
Right of Secession 102
river systems 241 (see also
Brahmaputra river basin/
valley; Transboundary waters/
transboundary water sharing)
hydropower projects 195
road(s) 235
back-breaking 117
in Bangladesh, conditions of
179–80
blockages 229–30
construction in Burmese highlands
77
India's 116
ADB grant to build 137
building programmes in 2009
244
connectivity in northeastern
part 225–31
package announced by
Nitin Gadkari for road
infrastructure 123n16
infrastructure 186
Rohingyas 85n7
Roy, Ananya 217–18
Russia 83, 86n19, 251n6

SAARC Agreement on
Implementation of the Regional
Standards 177
SAARC Agreement on Multilateral
Arrangement on Recognition of
Conformity Assessment 177
SAARC Corridor 1 (Lahore to
Agartala) 182

SAARC Corridor 2 (Kathmandu to
Kolkata/Haldia) 182
Saffron Revolution of 2007 71, 74–5
San, Aung 34n12, 92
sanitary and phyto-sanitary (SPS)
174, 176
Saran, Shyam 36n33
Saudi Arabia 251n6
seaport infrastructure in India 25
Second World War 117
securitization 64n2, 199, 209
Sein, Thein 72, 76, 85n7, 90–1, 94
self-governance 109
Sema, K.H. 115
Shan *sawbwas* (local princes) 101
Shans ethnic group 101, 104
Shan State Armed Police Force 102
Shan State Army 102
Shan State Restoration Council 98
Shariah 63
Sharma, Mihir S. 34n17
Sharmila, Irom 120
Shekhar, Chandra 86n11
Shwe, Than 75
Siang River, Arunachal Pradesh 228,
231–2
Sikkim 110, 119, 142, 203–4, 216,
218, 221, 234
Siliguri corridor 28
Singapore 12, 19–20, 25–6, 30,
35n31, 72, 83, 92, 127, 250n2
and India, free trade agreement
between 139
Singapore Airlines (SIA) 26
Singh, Manmohan 2, 13, 15–16,
21–2, 33n5, 74–6
Singh, Rajnath 23
Sinha, Jawant 34n18
Sinha, Yashwant 23, 29
Sirisena 139
Siyom River 231

Social Impact Assessments (SIA) 202
South Africa 251n6
South Asian Association for Regional
Cooperation (SAARC) 118, 127,
176–7, 184–5, 208
South Asia Network for Dams,
Rivers, and People 232
South Asian Growth Quadrangle
(SAGQ) 133
India's trade relations with 134–7
regional motor vehicle agreement
178
South Asian Regional Standards
Organization (SARSO)
addressing of issues faced by
traders 177
aim of 176
certifications 183
developing regional standards 184
need of capacity building 183
South Asia Subregional Economic
Cooperation (SASEC) 137, 197
South Asia Water Initiative (SAWI)
207
South China Sea 30, 32
South Commission 21
Southeast Asia (SEA) 2, 14, 69, 76–7,
83, 105, 117, 119, 122n1, 250
active involvement in standards
promotion 184
association of India with 70
communist penetration in 1
as 'Greater India' 17
India's cultural colonies in 16
India's foreign economic policies
impact on relations with 1–3
MPAC 241
and New Delhi, relationship
during Cold war era 16
northeast India cross-border
linkages with 26

security issue in 29–32
security role of India in 31
Southeast Asia Treaty Organization
(SEATO) 1, 17–19
Southern African Development
Community (SADC) 173
South Korea 12, 25, 83
South–South trade 185
Soviet blocs 73
Spain 71
Special Partnership for the Era of the
Indo–Pacific 123n17
Sri Lanka / Sri Lankan 25, 27, 35n30,
133–4, 137, 144n1, 144n3
civil war 19
grants and loan by India in 2006-7
to 140
naval facilities construction in 71
Rajiv Gandhi sent Indian
peacekeeping force to 70, 83
Standardization and Conformity
Assessment 177
standards, need for bilateral
agreement between India and
Bangladesh
ban on imports of poultry
products from India 175
drug registration for
pharmaceutical products 175
harmonization and mutual-
recognition 183–5
non-acceptability of conformity
assessment certificates 176
PSI certificate to be submitted by
Bangladeshi operator 174
sanitary and phyto-sanitary
measures 174
sanitary import permits 175
SARSO, establishment of 176
setting up of accreditation centres
by India 176

Staniland, Paul 57
State Environmental Management
Agency (SEMA) 220
State Law and Order Restoration
Council (SLORC) 73
Stimson Centre 208
strategic trust 60
Subansiri Basin 231
Sukarno 17
Supreme Court 217, 224
Suu Kyi, Aung San 74–5, 92–3
democracy movement by 71–3
Thein Sein engagement with 72
victory in 2015 elections 104
swadeshi (national self-reliance) 22–3
Swaraj, Sushma 127
Syria 62–3

Tai, Bernard 60
tan-dhan-manbhed approach 114
tariff liberalization 154
Tata Airlines 26
Tatmadaw (the Burmese military) 72,
74–5, 79–80, 82, 85n7
Techno-Economic Clearance (TEC)
by CEA 232
Teesta Treaty 178
terrorism 63 (see also Counterterrorism; Islamic State of Iraq and
al-Sham (ISIS))
ASEAN de-politicization of 56
cause securitized 64n2
in India
primary sources 58
types of problems 57
India's views Pakistan as source of 57
partnership between ASEAN and
India to fight 54
state-sponsored 57
Textile (Consumer Protection)
Regulation of 1988 175

Thai Baan 207
Thailand 13, 18, 27–8, 70, 72, 83, 250n2
Thinley, Jigme Yosier 122n6
Tibet 118, 216
  hydropower development in 218, 223
  Manipuri rebels training in 96
  signed demarcation of border 108
Tong, Goh Chok 12, 25–6
trade barriers in India, hodge-podge of reforms 6
trade deficit 133, 153
trade East policy of India
  barriers and challenges in trade enhancement 140–4
  bilateral free trade agreements with eastern neighbours 137–9
  changing political engagement and trade flow pattern 128–32
  engagement with regional trade associations 132–7
  facilitation of eastward trade through development cooperation 140
Transatlantic Trade and Investment Partnership (TTIP) 152, 183
transboundary waters/transboundary water sharing 195, 250
  challenges of 197–201
  development projects 7–8
  harnessing of resources 196
  multilateral river agreements 236
  potential to foster dialogue 204–5
Trans Pacific Partnership (TPP) 150, 152–3, 183, 186
transparency 7–8, 142, 208
transport and transit facilitation protocols between India and Bangladesh

policy implications and concerns 177–82
  recommendations 186–8
Trilateral Highway Project 13, 15, 27, 29, 34n8
Tripura 109–10
Turkemistan–Afghanistan–Pakistan– India pipeline 27
Turkey 251n6

United Liberation Front of Asom (ULFA) 96–7, 110, 112, 122n3
United National Liberation Front (UNLF) 97
United Nations (UN) 58
  condemning Myanmar human rights violations 73
United Nations Economic and Social Commission for Asia-Pacific 21
United Nations Framework Convention on Climate Change (UNFCCC) 218
United States (US) 30, 91, 100, 121
  counterterrorism policy towards Iraq 55
  dominance over Indo-Pacific 69
  military alliances promotion 1
  New Delhi participation in strategic rebalance in Asia 13
  terrorists attack on 9/11 in 54
  Vietnam War, involvement in 1
  war against terrorism 56
United Wa State Army (UWSA) 94–5, 98, 102, 104
U.S. Department of State 216
US–Pakistan military alliance of 1954 1

Vajpayee, Atal Bihari 14, 23, 29, 86n10
  support for Aung San Suu Kyi 74

Varma, Richard 117
Velcan Energy Holdings 232
Verma, Amar Nath 21
Vietnam 3, 13, 24, 30, 72, 83, 250n2
  dispute with China over maritime
    boundaries 30
Vietnam War 1
Villaruel, Jemimah 53
Vision Statement ASEAN–India
  Commemorative Summit 2012
  13
volume-civil engineering perspective
  246

Wangchuck, Ashi Dorji Wangmi
  122n5
Wangchuk, Jigme Singye (King) 112
Westminster-style parliamentary
  democracy 85n2
Win, Ne 73
World Bank 207, 248
  on poverty
    headcount ratio 165n9
    in India, report 158

report on regulatory barriers 24
World Commission on Dams 202
World Economic Forum 35n30
World Organization for Animal
  Health (OIE) 184
World Trade Organization (WTO)
  152
  Aid for Trade Initiative 176
  Doha Round 23
  negotiation on agriculture 159
  trade facilitation agreement 23
World War II 73

Xiaoping, Deng 96

Yangon 71, 77, 81, 85n8
Yarlung Tsangpo River, Tibet 231,
  233–4
Yew, Lee Kuan 12, 18–19, 32, 36n36
Yugoslavia 101

Zedong, Mao 81
zero-sum calculations 23
Zimbabwe 182

Editors and Contributors

Kelly D. Alley is Alma Holladay Professor of Anthropology at Auburn University. She has carried out research in northern India for over twenty-five years, focusing on public culture and environmental issues. Her book, *On the Banks of the Ganga: When Wastewater Meets a Sacred River* (2002), explores Hindu interpretations of the sacred river Ganga in light of current environmental problems. She is currently studying water governance in the Ganges–Brahmaputra–Meghna basin and just produced an interactive website on hydropower across the Himalayas with colleagues and students.

Julio S. Amador III is Deputy Director-General of the Philippine Foreign Service Institute (FSI). He serves as deputy to the FSI Director-General and assists him on technical and academic issues. He provides policy analysis and strategic advice on ASEAN issues, Southeast Asia security and international relations, and foreign policy to several offices in the Department of Foreign Affairs. His research and policy interests are Philippine Foreign and Economic Policy, East Asian Integration, Southeast Asia security and politics, ASEAN, and US–Southeast Asia relations. Mr Amador has published peer-reviewed journal articles, book chapters, and op-eds/commentaries in on-line news media.

Jonah Blank has been Professorial Lecturer at Johns Hopkins School of Advanced International Studies (SAIS) for the past nine years and is a Senior Political Scientist for the RAND Corporation, with a focus on National Security and Intelligence. His geographical area of expertise is South and Southeast Asia. An anthropologist by training, he is author of the books *Mullahs on the Mainframe: Islam & Modernity Among the*

Daudi Bohras and *Arrow of the Blue-Skinned God: Retracing the Ramayana through India*. Dr Blank has written for publications ranging from policy opinion-leaders (*Foreign Affairs*, the *New Yorker*, the *Atlantic*, *Foreign Policy*, *Fortune*) to scholarly journals to mass-circulation newspapers (*Washington Post*, *Boston Globe*, *Christian Science Monitor*, *Dallas Morning News*, *Orlando Sentinel*, *Toronto Star*). He provides foreign policy analysis for radio and television venues including CNN, National Public Radio, CCTV, and the Voice of America.

Bipul Chatterjee is the Executive Director of CUTS International, a non-governmental think-tank on economic policy research, advocacy, networking, and capacity building with its headquarters in Jaipur, India and centers in Chittorgarh, Kolkata, New Delhi, Geneva, Hanoi, Nairobi, Lusaka, and Accra. He holds an MA in Economics from Delhi University and a BSc in Economics from the University of Calcutta. He has published and edited several books and papers on the political economy of trade and development. His current areas of interest are political economy of sub-regional cooperation in eastern South Asia, and linkages between trade and sustainable development.

Rohan D'Souza is Associate Professor at the Graduate School of Asian and African Area Studies, Kyoto University. He is the author of *Drowned and Dammed: Colonial Capitalism and Flood Control in Eastern India* (2006). His interests and research publications cover themes in environmental history, conservation, ecological politics, sustainable development, and modern technology.

Karen Stoll Farrell is Head of the Area Studies Department at Indiana University Libraries, Bloomington, and Librarian for South Asian and Southeast Asian Studies. Her primary research interests are web archives, collection development, and access for international materials, and area studies librarianship.

Sumit Ganguly is Professor of Political Science, holds the Rabindranath Tagore Chair in Indian Cultures and Civilizations, and directs the Center on American and Global Security at Indiana University, Bloomington. Professor Ganguly has previously taught at James Madison College of Michigan State University, Hunter College, and the Graduate Center of the City University of New York and the University of Texas at Austin. His book (with Karen Rasler and William Thompson), *How Rivalries End*, received the triennial J. David Singer Award from the Midwest section of the International Studies Association in 2015. Professor Ganguly serves on the editorial boards of *Asian Security, Current History*, the *Journal of Democracy*, and *Foreign Policy Analysis and International Security*. He also serves as the Associate Editor of *Security Studies*.

Surupa Gupta is Associate Professor of Political Science and International Affairs at the University of Mary Washington. Her research focuses on: Indian foreign economic policy; India's role in global governance in economic issues and the politics of trade liberalization; and agricultural policy reform in India. She is the author of *The Political Economy of Agricultural Policy Reform in India* (with Regina Birner and Neeru Sharma, published by *International Food Policy Research Institute*, 2011). Among her most recent publications are 'Agriculture and its Discontents: Coalitional Politics at the WTO with Special Reference to India's Food Security Interests' (with J.P. Singh in International Negotiations, 2016, forthcoming), 'Modi Bets the Farm' (with Sumit Ganguly in ForeignAffairs.com, 2014). She is a 2015–16 Asia Studies Fellow at the East-West Center in Washington D.C.

Sanjoy Hazarika holds the Dr Saifuddin Kitchlew Chair at Jamia Millia Islamia, New Delhi, where he is also Director, Centre for North East Studies and Policy Research. He has been a member of various academic organizations and official committees, including the Justice Jeevan Reddy Committee to Review AFSPA, the Society of Indian Institute of Advanced Studies, Shimla, and the North East India Studies Programme, Jawaharlal Nehru University. His books include *Rites of Passage, Strangers of the Mist, Writing on the Wall* and *The State Strikes Back: India and the Naga Insurgency, Bhopal: The Lessons of a Tragedy, The Eastern Himalaya: Climate Change, Poverty, and Livelihoods*, and *Hope Floats: The Boat Clinics of the Brahmaputra*. Hazarika has also produced and scripted eight documentaries largely about Northeast India, as well as two television series' about the Brahmaputra River.

Douglas P. Hill joined the Department of Geography, University of Otago, in 2006. His research has focused on four main areas: Rural Development,

Environmental Management and Food Security; Transboundary Water Resources; Ports and Migrant Labour; and Indian Cities and Socio-Spatial Changes associated with the 'new' India. His current research projects include: Geopolitics, Transboundary Water Resources and Civil Society in South Asia; the port sector and labour relations in Bangladesh, India, and Malaysia; and the transformation of urban space in Kolkata.

David J. Karl is President of the Asia Strategy Initiative, an analysis and advisory firm focused on the intersection of politics and economics, and heads its South Asia practice group. He is also co-founder and chief knowledge officer at Geoskope LLC, a market intelligence company focused on key emerging countries. Dr Karl has served as an adjunct professor at the University of Southern California and Occidental College, an elite liberal arts institution in Los Angeles. He comments frequently on politics, economics, and international relations in South Asia on his blog site, 'Chanakya's Notebook'.

Bertil Lintner is a Swedish journalist and author living in Thailand. He has covered Myanmar for more than three decades, mainly for the now defunct *Far Eastern Economic Review* and more recently for *Asia Times Online*, and has written fifteen books about the country and its neighbours, including *Burma in Revolt: Opium and Insurgency Since 1948*, *Aung San Suu Kyi and Burma's Struggle for Democracy*, and *Great Game East: India, China and the Struggle for Asia's Most Volatile Frontier*. His work can be viewed at www.asiapacificms.com.

Rani D. Mullen is Associate Professor of Government at the College of William and Mary, as well as the Director of the Indian Development Cooperation Research (IDCR) at the Centre for Policy Research in New Delhi, where she is also a non-resident Senior Fellow. Her research focuses on democratization and development in South Asia, in India and Afghanistan in particular, as well as foreign policy issues. She is the author of *Decentralization, Local Governance, and Social Wellbeing in India* (Routledge, 2012) and was a Fulbright-Nehru Senior Fellow in New Delhi (2013–14). Her recent publications include 'The New Great Game: A Battle for Access and Influence in the Indo-Pacific' (with Cody Poplin in *Foreign Affairs*, 2015) and several chapters in edited volumes on Indian foreign policy.

Prithviraj Nath is a Policy Analyst with CUTS International. His expertise is in participatory research in trade, sustainability, and energy. His recent and current research includes the political economy of cross-border trade and its impact on regional integration and local economic development, with particular emphasis on eastern South Asia. His other work spans energy governance, renewable energy, and sustainable development issues. Before joining CUTS, he worked with the Department of Municipal Affairs, Government of West Bengal. He completed a master's in Business Management after graduating in Economics from the University of Calcutta, and has published several research papers and articles.